MCSE

repudetion

Core NT Exams

Includes coverage of the TCP/IP Exam

ESSENTIAL REFERENCE

New Riders

Other Books for the Networking Professional

Windows NT TCP/IP
Karanjit Siyan
ISBN 1-56205-887-8

Windows NT DNS
Michael Masterson & Herman
Kneif
ISBN: 1-56205-943-2

Windows NT Registry
Sandra Osborne
ISBN: 1-56205-941-6

Windows NT Performance
Mark Edmead
ISBN: 1-56205-942-4

Windows NT Security
Richard Puckett
ISBN: 1-56205-945-9

Windows NT Administration
Handbook
Eric Svetcov
ISBN: 1-56205-946-7

Internet Information Server
Administration
Kelli Adam, et. al.
ISBN: 0-7357-0022-2

Windows NT Terminal Server and
Citrix MetaFrame
Ted Harwood
ISBN: 1-56205-944-0

Implementing Exchange Server
Doug Hauger, Marywynne Leon,
and William C. Wade III
ISBN: 1-56205-931-9

SQL Server System Administration
Sean Baird, Chris Miller, et. al.
ISBN: 1-56205-955-6

Linux System Administration
James T. Dennis
ISBN: 1-56205-934-3

Linux Security
John Flowers
ISBN: 0-7357-0035-4

Linux GUI Application
Development
Eric Harlow
ISBN: 0-7357-0021-4

Solaris Essential Reference
John Mulligan
ISBN: 0-7357-0023-0

Domino System Administration
Rob Kirkland
ISBN: 1-56205-948-3

Lotus Notes and Domino Essential
Reference
David Hatter and Timothy Bankes
ISBN: 0-73570-007-9

Cisco Router Configuration and
Troubleshooting
Pablo Espinosa, Stephen Tomic,
and Mark Tripod
ISBN: 0-7357-0024-9

Implementing LDAP
Bob Lamothe
ISBN: 1-56205-947-5

MCSE
Core NT Exams
Includes coverage of the TCP/IP Exam

E S S E N T I A L   R E F E R E N C E

New Riders

201 West 103rd Street
Indianapolis, IN 46290

Matthew Shepker

MCSE Essential Reference: Core NT Exams

International Standard Book Number: 0-7357-0006-0

Library of Congress Catalog Card Number: 98-87234

Printed in the United States of America

First Printing: November 1998

00   99   98   4   3   2   1

Trademarks

Warning and Disclaimer

Publisher
David Dwyer

Executive Editor
Laurie Petrycki

Development Editor
Jim Chalex

Managing Editor
Sarah Kearns

Project Editor
Mike La Bonne

Copy Editor
Audra McFarland

Indexer
Chris Wilcox

Technical Editor
Brian Komar
Tim Crothers

Proofreader
Maribeth Echard

Production
Steve Balle-Gifford

Dedication

*As always, I dedicate this book to my dearest wife, Misty Shepker.
Without your patience, understanding, and love, I would
have never been able to complete this book. Thank you.*

About the Author

Matthew Shepker is a computer consultant and trainer for Empower Trainers and Consultants in Overland Park, Kansas. He is a Microsoft Certified Systems Engineer and a Microsoft Certified Trainer, with 11 certifications.

Matthew attended Fort Hays State University in Hays, Kansas, majoring in communications. Since receiving this degree, he has been everything from a bench tech to a systems administrator in a large corporation.

This is Matthew's third book, and his first solo book. The other two titles he co-authored are *Sams Teach Yourself MCSE Systems Administrator for SQL Server in 14 Days*, and New Riders' *MCSE TestPrep SQL Server 6.5 Administration*. He also recently finished writing a portion of *Using SQL Server 7.0*.

Matthew currently lives in Overland Park, Kansas, with his wife, Misty. Other living things in the house include one permanent dog, Sam, and usually a rotating foster dog. Matthew can be reached at `shepker@planetkc.com`.

Contents

Acknowledgments

When you sit down to write a book, it is hard to estimate how many people have helped you out, both in the past and in the present. As I sit back and think about it, several people come to mind.

To get a book from the initial development stage to what you are holding in your hands is a team effort. I thank Laurie Petrycki for her confidence in me. Jim Chalex gets the award for being extremely patient when time was getting short and for helping me produce a top-notch book. I also thank Brian Komar and Tim Crothers for keeping me honest and accurate. I could have never gotten here without you guys.

For my technical skills, I thank Mike Nease who gave me a chance to learn all that I could, and Sharon DiVernieri for the chance to prove that I knew it. These were the people who gave me a start in the world of IS. Without both of these people taking a chance on me, I would have never made it this far this fast.

For my writing skills, I have two teachers I must thank. The first was my high school English teacher, Pat Fellers. Mrs. Fellers made it perfectly clear that you had to be able to write well. The second was a college composition and literature professor named Sharon Wilson. She took up where Mrs. Fellers left off and made me polish my writing skills.

Finally, I thank all of the people who have stood beside me. Mom and Dad, without you, I wouldn't be here. To Aunt Gloria, thanks for teaching me how to take notes and reminding me that life is too short to throw it away. Brian Steck and Jeff Péo, thanks for keeping me sane at work. Becky and Norby, thanks for helping Misty tear me away from the computer. And to my wonderful wife, Misty, I owe all of this to you. Thank you.

Tell Us What You Think!

As the reader of this book, *you* are our most important critic and commentator. We value your opinion and want to know what we're doing right, what we could do better, what areas you'd like to see us publish in, and any other words of wisdom you're willing to pass our way.

As the Executive Editor for the Networking team at Macmillan Computer Publishing, I welcome your comments. You can fax, email, or write me directly to let me know what you did or didn't like about this book—as well as what we can do to make our books stronger.

Please note that I cannot help you with technical problems related to the topic of this book, and that due to the high volume of mail I receive, I might not be able to reply to every message.

When you write, please be sure to include this book's title and author, as well as your name and phone or fax number. I will carefully review your comments and share them with the author and editors who worked on the book.

Fax:	317-581-4663
Email:	certification@mcp.com
Mail:	Laurie Petrycki
	Networking
	Macmillan Computer Publishing
	201 West 103rd Street
	Indianapolis, IN 46290 USA

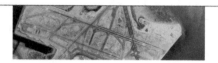

Introduction

This book is simply a reference book. It was created for you to use in concert with any other book that you have already purchased. When you are studying for any of the Microsoft exams, it is not uncommon for you to come across topics that you are either not familiar with or that have not been introduced in the text that you are using. This book will assist you in discovering what those terms are. It is important to understand, however, that I have covered only the most important, *essential* information you will need to know while studying for the core NT exams—not all possible topics.

Out of necessity, this book does not cover only information required for MCSE candidates; it also covers background information required outside of the MCSE arena, as well as covering some information that leans more toward the MCSD track.

Information is covered in this book in a nonlinear format. Topics are covered on a single-topic basis, so there is a significant amount of conceptual overlap throughout the book. To help you learn from this overlap, we have provided extra information by cross-referencing you to other related topics in the book. For instance, if looking up information on NTFS, you would find a cross-reference to *FAT*, the *Master File Table,* and *NTFS Permissions.* Each one of these extra references could, in turn, point you to other related topics.

Features of the Book

When reading through this book, keep in mind the following features and conventions:

- All topics are presented in alphabetical order.
- Listed at the beginning of each topic are the test number, test name, and objective that the topic refers to. If a topic is covered on more than one test (as many are), I list two or sometimes three tests, as necessary.
- At the beginning of the book is an "objective jump table" that contains information about each test objective and which topics are directly related to it, as well as the page number where each topic can be found.
- In Appendix A are several tables, which contain important information that compares similar topics and technologies.
- At the end of each topic are other topics that you might want to reference to gain extra information related to the topic.

The following conventions are used throughout the text:

Conventions	Use
Italic	Text in *italic* denotes that this term can be referenced elsewhere in the book for more information.
Bold	Text in **bold** denotes that this is an option that you can click on, such as a button or a tab.
Monospace	Text that is listed in monospace denotes a file that can be executed.

Objectives for the Core Exams

The objectives for each of the four core NT exams and the TCP/IP Elective covered in this book are listed by exam name and number in this section. These objectives serve as the basis for the questions developed for the exams. Use them to help you see and understand the nature and organization of the material upon which you will be tested. Notice that some objectives have no associated entries in this book. For these objectives, we strongly suggest you consult additional texts for more information.

Networking Essentials (Exam #70-058)

The "Networking Essentials" exam focuses on determining your skill in four major categories of network-related skills. The specific objectives for these topics are described in the following sections.

Standards and Terminology

Objective	Entry	Page
Define common networking terms for LANs and WANs.	*Peer-to-peer*	149
	Client-Server	60
	LAN	45
Compare a file-and-print server with an application server.		
Compare user-level security with access permissions assigned to a shared directory on a server.	*Assigning NTFS permissions*	39
	Network Shares	137
Compare a client/server network with a peer-to-peer network.	*Peer-to-peer*	149
	Client Server	60
	Appendix A	203
Compare the implications of using connection-related communications with connectionless communications.	*TCP/IP*	177
Distinguish whether SLIP or PPP is used as the communications protocol for various situations.	*SLIP*	169
	PPP	151
Define the communication devices that communicate at each level of the OSI model.	*OSI Model*	143
Describe the characteristics and purpose of the media used in IEEE 802.3 and IEEE 802.5 standards.	*IEEE 802.3*	106
	IEEE 802.5	106
	Ethernet	85
	Token Ring	180
Explain the purpose of NDIS and Novell ODI network standards.	*NDIS*	131
	ODI	141

Planning

Objective	Entry	Page
Select the appropriate media for various situations. Media choices include: Coaxial cable, Twisted-pair cable, Fiber-optic cable, Wireless communications. Situational elements include Cost, Distance limitations, Number of nodes.	*Coax*	61
	STP	172
	UTP	190
	Fiber	90
	Wireless	198
	Twisted Pair	181
	Appendix A	203
Select the appropriate topology for various Token Ring and Ethernet networks.	*Token Ring*	180
	Ethernet	85
Select the appropriate network and transport protocols for various Token Ring and Ethernet networks. Protocols include: DLC, AppleTalk, IPX, TCP/IP, NFS, SMB	*Protocols*	154
	TCP/IP	177
	DLC	76
	NWLink IPX/SPX	139
	AppleTalk	35
	NFS	138
Select the appropriate connectivity devices for various Token Ring and Ethernet networks. Connectivity devices include Repeaters, Bridges, Routers, Brouters, Gateways	*Token Ring*	180
	Ethernet	85
	Repeaters	161
	Bridges	52
	Routers	162
	Gateways	95
List the characteristics, requirements, and appropriate situations for WAN connection services. WAN connection services include X.25, ISDN, Frame Relay, ATM.	*X.25*	201
	ISDN	113
	Frame Relay	91
	ATM	40
	SONET	171
	Mesh Topology	126

Implementation

Objective	Entry	Page
Choose an administrative plan to meet specified needs, including performance management, account management, and security.	*Counters*	66
	Performance Monitor	149
Choose a disaster recovery plan.	*RAID*	157
Given the manufacturer's documentation for the network adapter, install, configure, and resolve hardware conflicts for multiple network adapters in a Token Ring or Ethernet network.	*Token Ring*	180
	Ethernet	85
	NIC	137
	IRQ	112
Implement a NetBIOS naming scheme for all computers on a given network.	*NetBIOS*	133
	NetBIOS Naming scheme	133
Select the appropriate hardware and software tools to monitor trends in the network.	*Performance Monitor*	149
	Network Sniffer	147

Troubleshooting

Objective	Entry	Page
Identify common errors associated with components required for communications.		
Diagnose and resolve common connectivity problems with cards, cables, and related hardware.	*NIC*	137
Resolve broadcast storms.	*Broadcast Storm*	53
Identify and resolve network performance problems.	*Bottlenecks*	52

Internetworking with Microsoft TCP/IP on Microsoft Windows NT 4.0 Exam (#70-059)

The "Internetworking with Microsoft TCP/IP on Microsoft Windows NT 4.0" exam (#70-059) covers the four main topic areas represented by the conceptual groupings of the test objectives. This test is referred to in this book as "TCP/IP." The exam objectives are listed by topic area in the following sections.

Planning

Objective	Entry	Page
Given a scenario, identify valid network configurations.		

Installation and Configuration

Objective	Entry	Page
Given a scenario, select the appropriate services to install when using Microsoft TCP/IP on a Microsoft Windows NT Server computer.	*TCP/IP*	177
	Windows NT	194
	DHCP	70
	WINS	196
	HOSTS	101
	LMHOSTS	118
On a Windows NT Server computer, configure Microsoft TCP/IP to support multiple network adapters.	*TCP/IP*	177
Configure scopes by using DHCP Manager.	*DHCP*	70
Install and configure a WINS server: Import LMHOSTS files to WINS, Run WINS on a multihomed computer, Configure WINS replication, Configure static mappings in the WINS database.	*WINS*	196
	LMHOSTS	118
	WINS Replication	197
Configure subnet masks.	*Subnet*	172
	Subnetting	172
	Subnet Masking	173
Configure a Windows NT Server computer to function as an IP router: Install and configure the DHCP Relay.	*RIP*	161
	BOOTP/DHCP Relay Agent	52

Objective	Entry	Page
Install and configure the Microsoft DNS Server service on a Windows NT Server computer: Integrate DNS with other name servers, Connect a DNS server to a DNS root server, Configure DNS server roles.	*DNS* *DNS Manager*	77 79
Configure HOSTS and LMHOSTS files.	*HOSTS files* *LMHOSTS*	101 118
Configure a Windows NT Server computer to support TCP/IP printing.	*LPR* *LPQ* *TCP/IP Printing*	122 121 177
Configure SNMP.	*SNMP*	170

Connectivity

Objective	Entry	Page
Given a scenario, identify which utility to use to connect to a TCP/IP-based UNIX host.	*TCP/IP* *UNIX*	177 187
Configure a RAS server and dial-up networking for use on a TCP/IP network.	*RAS* *TCP/IP*	158 177
Configure and support browsing in a multiple-domain routed network.	*Domain* *Router*	79 162

Monitoring and Optimization

Objective	Entry	Page
Given a scenario, identify which tool to use to monitor TCP/IP traffic.	*TCP/IP* *Network Monitor*	177 136

Troubleshooting

Objective	Entry	Page
Diagnose and resolve IP addressing problems.	*IP Address*	112
Use Microsoft TCP/IP utilities to diagnose IP configuration problems: Identify which Microsoft TCP/IP utility to use to diagnose IP configuration problems.	*IP Address* *TCP/IP*	112 177
Diagnose and resolve name resolution problems.	*WINS* *DNS* *LMHOSTS* *HOSTS*	196 77 118 101

Implementing and Supporting Windows NT Server 4.0 (Exam #70-067)

The "Implementing and Supporting Windows NT Server 4.0" exam (#70-067) focuses on determining your skill in six major categories of implementing and supporting Windows NT Server. You will find this exam listed as "NT Server (Core)" in this book. These categories are outlined in the following sections.

Planning

Objective	Entry	Page
Plan the disk drive configuration for various requirements. Requirements include choosing a file system and choosing a fault-tolerance method.	*Fault Tolerance* *NTFS* *RAID*	89 138 157
Choose a protocol for various situations. Protocols include TCP/IP, NWLink IPX/SPX Compatible Transport, and NetBEUI.	*TCP/IP* *NWLink IPX/SPX* *NetBEUI* *Protocol*	177 139 133 154

Installation and Configuration

Objective	Entry	Page
Install Windows NT Server on Intel-based platforms.	*Installing* *Windows NT*	109
Install Windows NT Server to perform various server roles. Server roles include primary domain controller (PDC), backup domain controller (BDC), and member server.	*PDC* *BDC* *Member Server* *Installing* *Windows NT*	148 46 109 109
Install Windows NT Server by using various methods. Installation methods include Using CD-ROM, over-the-network, Installing Using Network Client Administrator, Performing express versus custom.	*Installing* *Windows NT* *Network Client* *Administrator*	109 31
Configure protocols and protocol bindings. Protocols include TCP/IP, NWLink IPX/SPX Compatible Transport, and NetBEUI.	*TCP/IP* *NWLink IPX/SPX* *NetBEUI*	177 139 133
Configure network adapters. Considerations include changing IRQ, IO base, and memory addresses, as well as configuring multiple adapters.	*Network Adapters* *IRQ*	135 112
Configure Windows NT Server core services. Services include Directory Replicator, License Manager, and other services.	*Directory* *Replication* *License Manager*	73 118

Objective	Entry	Page
Configure peripherals and devices. Peripherals and devices include Communication devices, SCSI devices, Tape device drivers, UPS devices and UPS service, Mouse drivers, display drivers, and keyboard drivers.	*Devices Control Panel*	70
	SCSI Devices	165
	Tape Devices	177
	UPS	188
	Mouse Control Panel	127
	Display Adapters	76
	Keyboard Control Panel	115
Configure hard disks to meet various requirements. Requirements include Allocating disk space capacity, Providing redundancy, Improving performance, Providing security, Formatting.	*Hard Drives*	99
	RAID	157
Configure printers. Tasks include adding and configuring a printer, implementing a printer pool, and setting print priorities.	*Printers*	153
	Print Devices	152
Configure a Windows NT Server computer for various types of client computers. Client computer types include Windows NT Workstation, Windows 95, and MS-DOS-based computers.	*Windows NT*	194
	Windows NT Workstation	196
	Windows 95	194
	DOS	79

Managing Resources

Objective	Entry	Page
Manage user and group accounts. Considerations include Managing Windows NT groups, Managing Windows NT user rights, Administering account policies and Auditing changes to the user account database.	*Local Groups*	120
	Global Groups	96
	Local Users	120
	Global Users	96
	User Manager	189
Create and manage policies and profiles for various situations. Policies and profiles include local user profiles, roaming user profiles, and system policies.	*User Policies*	189
	User Profiles	189
Administer remote servers from various types of client computers. Client computer types include Windows 95 and Windows NT Workstation.	*User Manager*	189
Manage disk resources. Tasks include Copying and moving files between file systems, Creating and sharing resources, Implementing permissions and security, Establishing file auditing.	*Auditing*	41
	Audit Log	41
	File System Auditing	41

Connectivity

Objective	Entry	Page
Configure Windows NT Server for interoperability with NetWare servers by using various tools. Tools include Gateway Service for NetWare and Migration Tool for NetWare.	*Windows NT* *GSNW* *CSNW*	194 95 95
Install and configure Remote Access Service (RAS). Configuration options include Configuring RAS communications, Configuring RAS protocols, Configuring RAS security, Configuring dial-up networking clients.	*RAS*	158

Monitoring and Optimization

Objective	Entry	Page
Monitor performance of various functions by using Performance Monitor. Functions include processors, memory, disks, and networks.	*Performance Monitor* *Counters*	149 66
Identify performance bottlenecks.	*Bottlenecks*	52

Troubleshooting

Objective	Entry	Page
Choose the appropriate course of action to take to resolve installation failures.		
Choose the appropriate course of action to take to resolve boot failures.	*Boot Process, Intel* *Boot Process, Alpha*	49 49
Choose the appropriate course of action to take to resolve configuration errors.		
Choose the appropriate course of action to take to resolve printer problems.	*Printers*	153
Choose the appropriate course of action to take to resolve RAS problems.	*RAS*	158
Choose the appropriate course of action to take to resolve connectivity problems.		

Objective	Entry	Page
Choose the appropriate course of action to take to resolve resource access problems and permission problems.		
Choose the appropriate course of action to take to resolve fault-tolerance failures. Fault-tolerance methods include tape backup, mirroring, stripe set with parity, and disk duplexing.	*Backing Up* *Backup Systems*	43 44

Implementing and Supporting Microsoft Windows NT Server 4.0 in the Enterprise (Exam #70-068)

The "Implementing and Supporting Microsoft Windows NT Server 4.0 in the Enterprise" exam (#70-068) covers six main topic areas, arranged in accordance with the test objectives. This test will be referred to as "NT Server (Enterprise)" in the entries. The exam objectives are listed by topic area in the following sections.

Planning

Objective	Entry	Page
Plan the implementation of a directory services architecture. Considerations include Selecting the appropriate domain model, Supporting a single logon account, and Allowing users to access resources in different domains.	*Domain* *Single Domain Model* *Single Master Domain Model* *Multiple Master Domain Model* *Complete Trust Domain Model*	79 168 168 128 62
Plan the disk drive configuration for various requirements. Requirements include choosing a fault-tolerance method.	*Fault Tolerance*	89
Choose a protocol for various situations. Protocols include TCP/IP, TCP/IP with DHCP and WINS, NWLink IPX/SPX Compatible Transport Protocol, Data Link Control (DLC), and AppleTalk	*TCP/IP* *DHCP* *WINS* *NWLink IPX/SPX* *DLC* *AppleTalk*	177 70 196 139 76 35

Installation and Configuration

Objective	Entry	Page
Install Windows NT Server to perform various server roles. Server roles include primary domain controller, backup domain controller, and member server.	*PDC*	148
	BDC	46
	Member Server	125
Configure protocols and protocol bindings. Protocols include: TCP/IP, TCP/IP with DHCP and WINS, NWLink IPX/SPX Compatible Transport Protocol, DLC, and AppleTalk.	*TCP/IP*	177
	DHCP	70
	NWLink IPX/SPX	139
	DLC	76
	AppleTalk	35
	Protocols	154
Configure Windows NT Server core services. Services include Directory Replicator and Computer Browser.	*Directory Replication*	73
	Browser Service	54
Configure hard disks to meet various requirements. Requirements include providing redundancy improving performance.	*Hard Drives*	99
	Fault Tolerance	89
	RAID	157
Configure printers. Tasks include: Adding and configuring a printer, Implementing a printer pool, and Setting print priorities	*Printers*	153
	Print Devices	152
Configure a Windows NT Server computer for various types of client computers. Client computer types include Windows NT Workstation, Windows 95, and Macintosh.	*Windows NT*	194
	Windows NT Workstation	194
	Windows 95	194
	Macintosh	123

Managing Resources

Objective	Entry	Page
Manage user and group accounts. Considerations include: Managing Windows NT user accounts, Managing Windows NT user rights, Managing Windows NT groups, Administering account policies, and Auditing changes to the user account database	*Global Account*	96
	Local Account	119
	Global Group	96
	Local Group	120
	User Manager	189
	Auditing	41
Create and manage policies and profiles for various situations. Policies and profiles include Local user profiles, Roaming user profiles, and System policies	*User Policies*	189
	User Profiles	189
Administer remote servers from various types of client computers. Client computer types include Windows 95 and Windows NT Workstation.	*User Manager*	189

Manage disk resources. Tasks include
Creating and sharing resources,
Implementing permissions and security,
and Establishing file auditing.

Connectivity

Configure a Windows NT Server for
interoperability with NetWare servers by
using various tools. Tools include
Gateway Services for NetWare
and Migration Tool for NetWare.

Install and configure multiprotocol
routing to serve various functions.
Functions include Internet router,
BOOTP/DHCP Relay Agent, and
IPX router.

Install and configure Internet
information services. Services
include World Wide Web, DNS
and Intranet.

Install and configure Remote Access
Service (RAS). Configuration options
include Configuring RAS
communications, Configuring RAS
protocols, and Configuring RAS security.

Monitoring and Optimization

Establish a baseline for measuring
system performance. Tasks include
creating a database of measurement data.

Monitor performance of various
functions by using Performance
Monitor. Functions include processor,
memory, disk, and network.

Monitor network traffic by using
Network Monitor. Tasks include
collecting, presenting, and filtering data.

Identify performance bottlenecks.

Optimize performance for various
results. Results include Controlling
network traffic and Controlling
server load.

Troubleshooting

Objective	Entry	Page
Choose the appropriate course of action to resolve installation failures.		
Choose the appropriate course of action to resolve boot failures.	Boot Process, Intel	49
	Boot Process, Alpha	49
Choose the appropriate course of action to resolve configuration errors. Tasks include Backing up and restoring the Registry and Editing the Registry.	Backing Up	43
	Registry	158
Choose the appropriate course of action to resolve RAS problems.	RAS	158
Choose the appropriate course of action to resolve connectivity problems.	Assigning NTFS permissions	39
Choose the appropriate course of action to resolve resource access and permission problems.	Assigning NTFS permissions	39
	Network Share	137
Choose the appropriate course of action to resolve fault-tolerance failures. Fault-tolerance methods include Tape backup, Mirroring, and Stripe set with parity.	Fault Tolerance	89
	Backup	43
Perform advanced problem resolution. Tasks include Diagnosing and interpreting a blue screen, Configuring a memory dump, and Using the Event Log service.	Blue Screen	46
	Event Log	85

Implementing and Supporting Microsoft Windows NT Workstation 4.0 (Exam #70-073)

The "Implementing and Supporting Microsoft Windows NT Workstation 4.0" exam (#70-073) covers seven main topic areas. This test is simply referred to as "NT Workstation" in this book. You can review the exam objectives in the following sections.

Planning

Objective	Entry	Page
Create unattended installation files.	Unattended Install	186
	UDF	185
	Answer File	33
Plan strategies for sharing and securing resources.	Network Share	137
Choose the appropriate file systems to use in a given situation. File systems and situations include NTFS, FAT, HPFS, Security, Dual-boot systems.	NTFS	138
	FAT	89
	HPFS	102
	Dual Boot	80

Installation and Configuration

Managing Resources

Connectivity

Objective	Entry	Page
Add and configure the network components of Windows NT Workstation.		
Use various methods to access network resources.	*UNC*	187
	Network Neighborhood	136
Implement Windows NT Workstation as a client in a NetWare environment.	*CSNW*	67
Use various configurations to install Windows NT Workstation as a TCP/IP client.	*TCP/IP*	177
Configure and install dial-up networking in a given situation.	*RAS*	158
Configure Microsoft Peer Web Services in a given situation.	*Peer-Web Server*	149

Running Applications

Objective	Entry	Page
Start applications on Intel and RISC platforms in various operating system environments.	*RISC*	161
Start applications at various priorities.	*Application Priorities*	36

Monitoring and Optimization

Objective	Entry	Page
Monitor system performance by using various tools.	*Performance Monitor*	149
Identify and resolve a given performance problem.		
Optimize system performance in various areas.		

Troubleshooting

Objective	Entry	Page
Choose the appropriate course of action to take when the boot process fails.	*Boot Process, Intel*	49
	Boot Process, Alpha	49
Choose the appropriate course of action to take when a print job fails.		
Choose the appropriate course of action to take when the installation process fails.		
Choose the appropriate course of action to take when an application fails.		

Objective	Entry	Page
Choose the appropriate course of action to take when a user cannot access a resource.	*Assigning NTFS Permissions*	39
Modify the Registry by using the appropriate tool in a given situation.	*Registry*	158
Implement advanced techniques to resolve various problems.	*Interactive Debugging*	109

Certification Requirements

The requirements for certification in each of the seven areas are detailed in the following sections. An asterisk after an exam indicates that the exam is slated for retirement.

How to Become a Microsoft Certified Professional

Passing any Microsoft exam (with the exception of Networking Essentials) is all you need to do to become certified as an MCP.

How to Become a Microsoft Certified Professional+Internet

You must pass the following exams to become an MCP specializing in Internet technology:

Internetworking Microsoft TCP/IP on Microsoft Windows NT 4.0, #70-059

Implementing and Supporting Microsoft Windows NT Server 4.0, #70-067

Implementing and Supporting Microsoft Internet Information Server 3.0 and Microsoft Index Server 1.1, #70-077

OR Implementing and Supporting Microsoft Internet Information Server 4.0, #70-087

How to Become a Microsoft Certified Professional+Site Building

You need to pass two of the following exams in order to be certified as an MCP+Site Building

Designing and Implementing Web Sites with Microsoft FrontPage 98, #70-055

Designing and Implementing Commerce Solutions with Microsoft Site Server 3.0, Commerce Edition, #70-057

Designing and Implementing Web Solutions with Microsoft Visual InterDev 6.0, #70-152

How to Become a Microsoft Certified Systems Engineer

You must pass four operating system exams and two elective exams to become an MCSE. The MCSE certification path is divided into two tracks: the Windows NT 3.51 track and the Windows NT 4.0 track.

The following lists show the core requirements (four operating system exams) for both the Windows NT 3.51 and 4.0 tracks, and the elective courses (two exams) you can take for either track.

The four Windows NT 3.51 Track Core Requirements for MCSE certification are as follows:

Implementing and Supporting Microsoft Windows NT Server 3.51, #70–043★

Implementing and Supporting Microsoft Windows NT Workstation 3.51, #70–042★

Microsoft Windows 3.1, #70–030★

>   OR Microsoft Windows for Workgroups 3.11, #70–048★

>   OR Implementing and Supporting Microsoft Windows 95, #70–064

>   OR Implementing and Supporting Microsoft Windows 98, #70–098

Networking Essentials, #70–058

The four Windows NT 4.0 Track Core Requirements for MCSE certification are as follows:

Implementing and Supporting Microsoft Windows NT Server 4.0, #70–067

Implementing and Supporting Microsoft Windows NT Server 4.0 in the Enterprise, #70–068

Microsoft Windows 3.1, #70–030★

>   OR Microsoft Windows for Workgroups 3.11, #70–048★

>   OR Implementing and Supporting Microsoft Windows 95, #70–064

>   OR Implementing and Supporting Microsoft Windows NT Workstation 4.0, #70–073

>   OR Implementing and Supporting Microsoft Windows 98, #70–098

Networking Essentials, #70–058

For both the Windows NT 3.51 and the 4.0 track, you must pass two of the following elective exams for MCSE certification:

Implementing and Supporting Microsoft SNA Server 3.0, #70–013

>   OR Implementing and Supporting Microsoft SNA Server 4.0, #70–085

Implementing and Supporting Microsoft Systems Management Server 1.0, #70–014★

>   OR Implementing and Supporting Microsoft Systems Management Server 1.2, #70–018

>   OR Implementing and Supporting Microsoft Systems Management Server 2.0, #70–086

Microsoft SQL Server 4.2 Database Implementation, #70–021

>   OR Implementing a Database Design on Microsoft SQL Server 6.5, #70–027

>   OR Implementing a Database Design on Microsoft SQL Server 7.0, #70–029 Microsoft SQL Server 4.2 Database Administration for Microsoft Windows NT, #70–022

>   OR System Administration for Microsoft SQL Server 6.5 (or 6.0), #70–026

>   OR System Administration for Microsoft SQL Server 7.0, #70–028

Microsoft Mail for PC Networks 3.2-Enterprise, #70–037

Internetworking with Microsoft TCP/IP on Microsoft Windows NT (3.5-3.51), #70-053

> *OR* Internetworking with Microsoft TCP/IP on Microsoft Windows NT 4.0, #70-059

Implementing and Supporting Microsoft Exchange Server 4.0, #70-075★

> *OR* Implementing and Supporting Microsoft Exchange Server 5.0, #70-076

> *OR* Implementing and Supporting Microsoft Exchange Server 5.5, #70-081

Implementing and Supporting Microsoft Internet Information Server 3.0 and Microsoft Index Server 1.1, #70-077

> *OR* Implementing and Supporting Microsoft Internet Information Server 4.0, #70-087

Implementing and Supporting Microsoft Proxy Server 1.0, #70-078

> *OR* Implementing and Microsoft Proxy Server 2.0, #70-088

Implementing and Supporting Microsoft Internet Explorer 4.0 by Using the Internet Explorer Resource Kit, #70-079

How to Become a Microsoft Certified Systems Engineer+Internet

You must pass seven operating system exams and two elective exams to become an MCSE specializing in Internet technology.

The seven MCSE+Internet core exams required for certification are as follows:

Networking Essentials, #70-058

Internetworking with Microsoft TCP/IP on Microsoft Windows NT 4.0, #70-059

Implementing and Supporting Microsoft Windows 95, #70-064

> *OR* Implementing and Supporting Microsoft Windows NT Workstation 4.0, #70-073

> *OR* Implementing and Supporting Microsoft Windows 98, #70-098

Implementing and Supporting Microsoft Windows NT Server 4.0, #70-067

Implementing and Supporting Microsoft Windows NT Server 4.0 in the Enterprise, #70-068

Implementing and Supporting Microsoft Internet Information Server 3.0 and Microsoft Index Server 1.1, #70-077

> *OR* Implementing and Supporting Microsoft Internet Information Server 4.0, #70-087

Implementing and Supporting Microsoft Internet Explorer 4.0 by Using the Internet Explorer Resource Kit, #70-079

You must also pass two of the following elective exams for MCSE+Internet certification:

System Administration for Microsoft SQL Server 6.5, #70-026

Implementing a Database Design on Microsoft SQL Server 6.5, #70-027

Implementing and Supporting Web Sites Using Microsoft Site Server 3.0, # 70-056

Implementing and Supporting Microsoft Exchange Server 5.0, #70–076

OR Implementing and Supporting Microsoft Exchange Server 5.5, #70–081

Implementing and Supporting Microsoft Proxy Server 1.0, #70–078

OR Implementing and Supporting Microsoft Proxy Server 2.0, #70–088

Implementing and Supporting Microsoft SNA Server 4.0, #70–085

How to Become a Microsoft Certified Solution Developer

The MCSD certification is undergoing substantial revision. Listed in the following sections are the requirements for the new track (available fourth quarter 1998), as well as the old.

For the new track, you must pass three core exams and one elective exam. The three core exam areas are listed as follows, as well as the elective exams from which you can choose.

Desktop Applications Development (1 required)

Designing and Implementing Desktop Applications with Microsoft Visual C++ 6.0, #70–016

OR Designing and Implementing Desktop Applications with Microsoft Visual Basic 6.0, #70–176

Distributed Applications Development (1 required)

■ Designing and Implementing Distributed Applications with Microsoft Visual C++ 6.0, #70–015

OR   Designing and Implementing Distributed Applications with Microsoft Visual Basic 6.0, #70–175

Solution Architecture (required)

■ Analyzing Requirements and Defining Solution Architectures, #70–100

You must pass one of the following elective exams:

■ Designing and Implementing Distributed Applications with Microsoft Visual C++ 6.0, #70–015

OR Designing and Implementing Desktop Applications with Microsoft Visual C++ 6.0, #70–016

OR Microsoft SQL Server 4.2

Database Implementation, #70–021★

Implementing a Database Design on Microsoft SQL Server 6.5, #70–027

OR Implementing a Database

Design on Microsoft SQL Server 7.0, #70–029

Developing Applications with C++ Using the Microsoft Foundation Class Library, #70-024

■ Implementing OLE in Microsoft Foundation Class Applications, #70-025

Designing and Implementing Web Sites with Microsoft FrontPage 98, #70-055

Designing and Implementing Commerce Solutions with Microsoft Site Server 3.0, Commerce Edition, #70-057

Programming with Microsoft Visual Basic 4.0, #70-065

> *OR* Developing Applications with Microsoft Visual Basic 5.0, #70-165

> *OR*   Designing and

Implementing Distributed Applications with Microsoft Visual Basic 6.0, #70-175

> *OR* Designing and Implementing

Desktop Applications with Microsoft Visual Basic 6.0, #70-176

Microsoft Access for Windows 95 and the Microsoft Access Development Toolkit, #70-069

Designing and Implementing Solutions with Microsoft Office (Code-named Office 9) and Microsoft Visual Basic for Applications, #70-091

Designing and Implementing Web Solutions with Microsoft Visual InterDev 6.0, #70-152

For the old track, you must pass two core technology exams and two elective exams for MCSD certification. The following lists show the required technology exams and elective exams needed to become an MCSD.

You must pass the following two core technology exams to qualify for MCSD certification:

Microsoft Windows Architecture I, #70-160★

Microsoft Windows Architecture II, #70-161★

You must also pass two of the following elective exams to become an MSCD:

Designing and Implementing Distributed Applications with Microsoft Visual C++ 6.0, #70-015

Designing and Implementing Desktop Applications with Microsoft Visual C++ 6.0, #70-016

Microsoft SQL Server 4.2 Database Implementation, #70-021★

> *OR* Implementing a Database Design on Microsoft SQL Server 6.5, #70-027

> *OR* Implementing a Database Design on Microsoft SQL Server 7.0, #70-029

Developing Applications with C++ Using the Microsoft Foundation Class Library, #70-024

■ Implementing OLE in Microsoft Foundation Class Applications, #70-025

Programming with Microsoft Visual Basic 4.0, #70-065

OR Developing Applications with Microsoft Visual Basic 5.0, #70-165

OR Designing and Implementing Distributed Applications with Microsoft Visual Basic 6.0, #70-175

OR Designing and Implementing Desktop Applications with Microsoft Visual Basic 6.0, #70-176

Microsoft Access 2.0 for Windows-Application Development, #70-051

OR Microsoft Access for Windows 95 and the Microsoft Access Development Toolkit, #70-069

Developing Applications with Microsoft Excel 5.0 Using Visual Basic for Applications, #70-052

Programming in Microsoft Visual FoxPro 3.0 for Windows, #70-054

Designing and Implementing Web Sites with Microsoft FrontPage 98, #70-055

Designing and Implementing Commerce Solutions with Microsoft Site Server 3.0, Commerce Edition, #70-057

Designing and Implementing Solutions with Microsoft Office (Code-named Office 9) and Microsoft Visual Basic for Applications, #70-091

Designing and Implementing Web Solutions with Microsoft Visual InterDev 6.0, #70-152

Becoming a Microsoft Certified Trainer

To understand the requirements and process for becoming an MCT, you need to obtain the Microsoft Certified Trainer Guide document from the following WWW site:

http://www.microsoft.com/train_cert/mct/

At this site, you can read the document as Web pages or display and download it as a Word file. The MCT Guide explains the four-step process of becoming an MCT. The general steps for the MCT certification are as follows:

1. Complete and mail a Microsoft Certified Trainer application to Microsoft. You must include proof of your skills for presenting instructional material. The options for doing so are described in the MCT Guide.

2. Obtain and study the Microsoft Trainer Kit for the Microsoft Official Curricula (MOC) courses for which you want to be certified. Microsoft Trainer Kits can be ordered by calling 800-688-0496 in North America. Those of you in other regions should review the MCT Guide for information on how to order a Trainer Kit.

3. Take the Microsoft certification exam for the product about which you want to be certified to teach.

4. Attend the MOC course for the course for which you want to be certified. This is done so you can understand how the course is structured, how labs are completed, and how the course flows.

You should consider the preceding steps a general overview of the MCT certification process. The precise steps that you need to take are described in detail on the Web site mentioned earlier. Do not misinterpret the preceding steps as the exact process you need to undergo.

If you are interested in becoming an MCT, you can receive more information by visiting the Microsoft Certified Training WWW site at **http://www.microsoft.com/train_cert/mct/** or by calling 800-688-0496.

Study Tips

Although people vary in the ways they learn information, some basic principles of learning apply to everyone. You should adopt some study strategies that take advantage of these principles. Learning can be broken into various depths. Recognition (of terms, for example) exemplifies a more surface level of learning; you rely on a prompt of some sort to elicit recall. Comprehension or understanding (of the concepts behind the terms, for instance) represents a deeper level of learning. The ability to analyze a concept and apply your understanding of it in a new way or novel setting represents further depth of learning.

Your learning strategy should enable you to know the material at a level or two deeper than mere recognition, which helps you perform better on an exam. You will know the material so thoroughly that you can easily handle the recognition-level types of questions that are used in multiple-choice testing.

Macro and Micro Study Strategies

One strategy that can lead to this deeper learning includes preparing an outline that covers all the objectives and subobjectives for the particular exam you are working on. You should delve a bit further into the material and include a level or two of detail beyond the stated objectives and subobjectives for the exam. Then flesh out the outline by coming up with a statement of definition or a summary for each point in the outline.

This outline provides two approaches to studying. First, you can study the outline by focusing on the organization of the material. You then can work your way through the points and subpoints of your outline with the goal of learning how they relate to one another. For example, be sure you understand how each of the main objective areas is similar to and different from one another. Then do the same thing with the subobjectives; be sure you know which subobjectives pertain to each objective area and how they relate to one another.

Next, you can work through the outline, focusing on learning the details. Memorize and understand terms and their definitions, facts, rules and strategies to follow, and so on. In this pass through the outline, attempt to learn detail rather than the big picture (the organizational information that you worked on in the first pass through the outline).

Research has shown that attempting to assimilate both types of information at the same time seems to interfere with the overall learning process. Separate your studying into these two approaches, and you will perform better on the exam than if you attempt to study the material in a more conventional manner.

Active Study Strategies

In addition, the process of writing and defining the objectives, subobjectives, terms, facts, and definitions is a more active learning strategy than merely reading material. In human information processing terms, writing forces you to engage in more active encoding of the information. Simply reading over it is more passive processing.

Next, determine whether you can apply the information you have learned by attempting to create examples and scenarios of your own. Think about how or where you could apply the concepts you are learning. Again, write down this information to process the facts and concepts in a more active fashion.

Common Sense Strategies

Finally, you should also follow common sense practices in studying. Study when you are alert, reduce or eliminate distractions, take breaks when you become fatigued, and so on.

Exam Hints and Tips

When you go to the testing site to take the actual exam, be prepared. Arrive early and be ready to present two forms of identification. Expect some wordy questions. Although you typically have 75 to 90 minutes to answer 50 to 70 questions, depending on the exam, you have just over one minute to answer each question. This amount may seem like ample time for each question, but remember that many of the questions are lengthy word problems, which can ramble on for paragraphs and include several exhibits. Your 90 minutes of exam time can be consumed very quickly.

Microsoft has begun to use a new type of exam format called "adaptive testing." You will be glad to know that, in this new format, the questions themselves have not changed. The way they are presented has changed, however. Questions are provided based on their difficulty. They are also scored immediately by the computer. Based on how well you respond to the initial questions, you are then given either more difficult or easier questions, depending on how you are doing. If you continue to get most of the increasingly difficult questions correct, the exam will stop, and you will eventually be told you have passed the exam. If you do not consistently answer questions correctly, eventually the exam will stop, and you will be told that you have failed to pass it. These exams thus have no fixed length; there is no set number of questions.

Why has Microsoft gone to this approach? There are two reasons. One is that this testing approach is more efficient. It is just as valid as traditional exams, but takes significantly less time. The other has to do with exam security.

Estimates are that approximately 85 percent of the candidates taking their first Microsoft exam fail. This result is not so much based on the fact that the candidates have not studied, but rather that they don't know what to expect and are immediately intimidated by the wordiness of some questions and the similarity of the possible answers.

For every exam that Microsoft offers, a particular passing score is required. Although Microsoft does not want to publicize the exact passing score for each test, they are typically in the 70 to 75 percent range.

Things to Watch For

When you take the exam, read very carefully. Make sure that you understand just what the question requires, and take notice of the number of correct choices you need to make. Remember that some questions require that you select a single correct answer; other questions have more than one correct answer. Similar to what appears in Top Score, radio buttons next to the answer choices indicate that the answers are mutually exclusive; there is but one correct answer. On the other hand, check boxes indicate that the answers are not mutually exclusive, and multiple answers are correct.

Again, read the questions fully. With lengthy questions, the last sentence often dramatically changes the scenario. When taking the exam, you are given pencils and two sheets of paper. If you are uncertain of what the question requires, map out the scenario on the paper until you have it clear in your mind. Keep in mind that you must turn in the scrap paper at the end of the exam.

Choosing the Right Answer

Adopt a strategy for evaluating possible answers. Eliminate those answers that are impossible or implausible. Carefully evaluate those that remain. Be careful: Some answers are true statements as they stand on their own but, in the context of the question, might not make sense as correct answers. The answers must match or relate to the question before they can serve as correct choices.

Marking Answers for Return

Remember, you can mark questions on the actual exam and refer back to them later. If you are presented with a wordy question that will take a long time to read and decipher, mark it and return to it after you have completed the rest of the exam. You should also use this approach with questions for which the right answer is not immediately obvious. This trick prevents you from wasting time and running out of time on the exam. This option of marking questions to return to them later may not be available to you in the new adaptive tests.

Changing Answers

As for changing your answers, the rule of thumb here is *don't*! If you read the question carefully and completely, and you felt like you knew the right answer, you probably did. Don't second-guess yourself. If, as you check your answers, one stands out as clearly marked incorrectly, however, of course you should change it in that instance. If you are at all unsure, go with your first impression.

Attaching Notes to Test Questions

At the conclusion of the exam, before the grading takes place, you are given the opportunity to attach a message to any of the questions. If you feel that a question is too ambiguous or tests for knowledge you do not need to possess to work with the product, take this opportunity to state your case. Unheard of is the instance in which Microsoft changes a test score as a result of an attached message; however, it never hurts to try—and it helps to vent your frustration before blowing the proverbial 50-amp fuse.

Good luck!

Certification Series from New Riders Publishing

New Riders is committed to providing you with the best study materials available. What follows in this section is a description of the various book series that New Riders offers the candidate for Microsoft certification.

New Riders MCSE and MCSD Training Guides

The *Training Guides* serve as the comprehensive solution for your test preparation needs. They are written by MCSEs, MCSDs, and MCTs who have instructed thousands of candidates. These guides provide thorough coverage of the exams, organized around the specific objectives that Microsoft establishes for each exam. The Training Guides include abundant learning aids, including objective explanations, study strategies, review questions, exam questions, case studies, step-by-step tutorials, and exercises. They also include New Riders Top Score software for the particular exam that the book covers. These books also serve as excellent reference books. All *MCSE* and *MCSD Training Guides* are approved by Microsoft.

New Riders MCSE and MCSD TestPreps

These workbooks provide the perfect supplement to other training materials. They contain hundreds of questions and two complete practice exams that enable you to ascertain your level of knowledge and build your confidence level. Organized around the exam objectives, they supply feedback to you on your answer to each question. The question answers don't just provide the correct answer; they include detailed explanations as to why it is correct.

New Riders MCSE and MCSD Fast Tracks

Fast Tracks are for those candidates who already have a solid background in networking technology and who want an efficient test preparation tool. These books provide just the information necessary to pass the exam. Organized around the exam objectives, these books focus on the concepts, facts, and tasks that you must master to pass the exams. They include numerous tables, lists, and other summary elements providing you with quick and easy access to the essential exam information. If you already have the technical knowledge but need key exam information, these books will work for you.

New Riders MCSE Essential Reference

Essential Reference (ER) books are intended for use in combination with any of the aforementioned books. ERs provide additional information about individual topics that you may have questions about. They are not written to be study materials on their own; rather, as the name implies, they should be used to learn and recall the most *essential* information you will need to study for your exam.

Other users that may find this book useful are consultants that are trying to communicate project plans to non-technical client contacts. These contacts often have many questions that are not easily answered. To assist these contacts, it may be useful to supply them with a copy of an ER to help them answer questions.

For more information on these and other study materials, please visit your local bookstore or the Macmillan Computer Publishing Web site at **www.mcp.com**.

100BASE-X

70-058 Networking Essentials   *Select appropriate media for various situations*

100BASE-X utilizes the *star* topology (much like *10BASE-T*) while providing data transmission rates of up to 100 megabits. 100BASE-X is sometimes also known as "Fast Ethernet." It is compatible with 10BASE-T, enabling both 100BASE-X and 10BASE-T to be utilized on the same network. Currently, three supported cabling specifications are provided by 100BASE-X, as shown in Table 1.

Table 1 **Supported Cabling Types**

Specification	Cable Type
100BASE-FX	Two-strand fiber-optic cable
100BASE-T4	Four pairs of Category 3, 4, or 5 *UTP*
100BASE-TX	Two pairs of Category 5 UTP or *STP*

100VG–AnyLAN

70-058 Networking Essentials   *Select appropriate media for various situations*

100VG-AnyLAN is a relatively new technology that is outlined in the *IEEE 802.12* standard. This technology provides 100-megabit access to the network by using an access method known as demand priority. In a demand priority network, all computers are connected in a *star topology*. Unlike regular *Ethernet*, computers in a 100VG-AnyLAN network cannot communicate unless the *hub* gives them permission to. The hubs manage the network by performing round-robin searches for requests to transmit. All transmissions go through the hub; there are no broadcasts on this network.

For more information, see the following sections:

- *Ethernet.* This is a standard that utilizes CSMA/CD to reduce collisions on the network.

- *Hub.* This is a piece of networking hardware that is used to connect computers to the network.

10BASE2

70-058 Networking Essentials   *Select appropriate media for various situations*

10BASE2 is a relatively simplistic cabling topology that utilizes *Thinnet cable*, which is a type of *coaxial cable*. 10BASE2 uses *BNC connectors* to connect directly to the network segment, and both ends of the segment must be terminated. 10BASE2 networks commonly use network cards that have transceivers built into them.

The biggest advantage of using 10BASE2 is that it is a relatively inexpensive way to network a small area. The biggest disadvantages of using 10BASE2 are that its transmission speed is slower than most of the other cabling types and that it can be run over only a short distance. Table 2 outlines some of the restrictions for using 10BASE2.

Table 2   **10BASE2 Restrictions**

Restriction Type	Limit/Description
Minimum distance between nodes	0.5 meter (1.5 feet)
Maximum segment length	185 meters (607 feet)
Maximum network length	925 meters (3,035 feet)
Maximum nodes per network segment	30 (includes both client computers and repeaters)
Other	Each end of the network segment must have a 50-ohm terminator attached. One of the terminated ends must be grounded.
Other	A 10BASE2 network can contain no more than 5 network segments, connected with no more than 4 network segments, of which no more than 3 contain clients.

The 5–4–3 Rule

When working with some cabling technologies, the easiest way to remember the number of segments and nodes is to memorize the 5-4-3 Rule. The 5 in the 5-4-3 Rule reminds you that you can have no more than 5 network segments in a single network. The 4 tells you that you can have no more than four repeaters in a network. The 3 indicates that no more than three segments can contain clients.

10BASE5

70-058 Networking Essentials   *Select appropriate media for various situations*

The 10BASE5 cabling topology is primarily used to overcome the restrictions of *10BASE2*. 10BASE5 cabling utilizes an external transceiver to connect to the network card. The transceiver attaches directly to the *Thicknet* cable, and an Attachment Universal Interface (AUI) cable, or drop cable, runs between the transceiver and the network card. Each network segment must be terminated at both ends, and one of the terminated ends must be grounded. As with 10BASE2, the 5-4-3 Rule applies.

The primary advantage of working with 10BASE5 cabling is that it can be used to overcome some of the restrictions of 10BASE2 cabling. The primary disadvantage is that 10BASE5 cabling is expensive to run and is slower than newer cabling technologies such as *10BASE-T*. Table 3 outlines the restrictions for 10BASE5.

Table 3   **10BASE5 Restrictions**

Restriction Type	Limit/Description
Minimum distance between nodes	2.5 meters (8 feet)
Maximum segment length	500 meters (1,640 feet)
Maximum network length	2,500 meters (8,200 feet)
Maximum nodes per network segment	100 (includes both client computers and repeaters)
Other	Each end of the network segment must have a 50-ohm terminator attached, and one of the terminated ends must be grounded.
Other	The drop cables can be as short as needed, but cannot exceed 50 meters (164 feet).

10BASE-F

70-058 Networking Essentials   *Select appropriate media for various situations*

10BASE-F is the cabling specification for *Ethernet* over *fiber-optic cable*. 10BASE-F is not commonly run to desktop machines; rather, it's used as a backbone between other network segments.

The primary advantages of using 10BASE-F cabling are the potential length of the cabling runs (up to 4,000 meters or 12,800 feet) and the elimination of any possible electromagnetic interference (*EMI*). The main disadvantage of using 10BASE-F is that it is very expensive to run.

10BASE-T

70-058 Networking Essentials   *Select appropriate media for various situations*

10BASE-T is the most popular implementation of *Ethernet*. 10BASE-T utilizes unshielded twisted-pair (UTP) cabling and is wired in a *star* topology. 10BASE-T is based on the 802.3 standard (*IEEE 802.3*) and can support data rates of up to 10 megabits per second. 10BASE-T uses the star topology where all nodes are wired to a central hub. When the hub receives a signal, it repeats it out to all nodes. Each node competes for transmission access to the hub. Individual 10BASE-T segments can be connected by using *Thicknet*, *fiber-optic cable,* or other UTP backbone segments. 10BASE-T allows you to build a network one segment at a time, expanding your network as your needs grow.

The primary advantage of using 10BASE-T is that it is a relatively inexpensive way to set up a network. The biggest disadvantage of using 10BASE-T is that is susceptible to electromagnetic interference (EMI). Table 4 outlines the restrictions for using 10BASE-T.

Table 4 **10BASE-T Restrictions**

Restriction Type	Limit/Description
Minimum distance between nodes	2.5 meters (8 feet)
Maximum segment length	100 meters (328 feet)
Maximum nodes per network segment	1,024 (includes both client computers and repeaters)
Other	The cabling should be Category 3, 4, or 5 UTP.

10BROAD36

70-058 Networking Essentials   *Select appropriate media for various situations*

10BROAD36 is an older cabling specification that calls for heavy-duty 75-ohm coaxial cable wired in a *bus* topology. Each network segment must be terminated at both ends, and one of the terminated ends must be grounded. Table 5 outlines the restrictions for using 10BROAD36.

Table 5 **10BROAD36 Restrictions**

Restriction Type	Limit/Description
Minimum distance between nodes	2.5 meters (8 feet)
Maximum segment length	1,800 meters (5,760 feet)
Maximum network length	3,600 meters (11,520 feet)
Maximum nodes per network segment	100 (includes both client computers and repeaters)
Other	Each end of the network segment must have a 75-ohm terminator attached, and one of the terminated ends must be grounded.

1BASE5

70-058   Networking Essentials   *Select appropriate media for various situations*

1BASE5 is a relatively unused cabling specification that utilizes *UTP* cabling in a *star* topology. 1BASE5 supports a data rate of 1 megabit per second.

The primary advantage of using 1BASE5 is that it is extremely inexpensive to set up. The major disadvantage, and the primary reason that it is unused today, is that it has a very low data rate. Table 6 outlines the restrictions for using 1BASE5.

Table 6   **1BASE5 Restrictions**

Restriction Type	Description
Minimum distance between nodes	2.5 meters (8 feet)
Maximum segment length	250 meters (800 feet)
Maximum network length	500 meters (1,600 feet)
Maximum nodes per network segment	1,024 (includes both client computers and repeaters)

Access Control Entry

See *ACE.*

Access Control List

See *ACL.*

accounts domain

See *trusted domain.*

ACE

70-067   NT Server (Core)   *Managing Disk Resources*

An ACE (Access Control Entry) is a single entry in an *Access Control List*, or *ACL*. An ACE contains the *Security ID*, or *SID*, for a user or group of users and a set of access rights to the object associated with the ACL. The rights in the ACE can allow access, deny access, or allow access with auditing. Following is a list of the actual rights that can be assigned in an ACE:

- **Read.** Allows the specified users to read from and copy a file.
- **Write.** Allows the specified user to write to a file.
- **Delete.** Specifies that the user can delete the file.
- **No Access.** Specifies that the user explicitly has no rights to access the file.
- **Permissions.** Specifies that the user can assign permissions to the file.
- **Ownership.** Indicates that the user has ownership of the file.

For more information, see the *file system auditing* section, which allows you to track who accesses a file at any point in time.

ACL

70-067   NT Server (Core)   *Managing Disk Resources*

The ACL is the list of permissions attached to a file or directory. Each ACL is made up of a group of *Access Control Entries*, or *ACEs*, that determines the access for specific users or groups of users. The owner of the file or directory can change the ACL to allow or prevent access to it.

Security is implemented in an ACL in a way that is designed to speed up the access checking process. Users and groups that have No Access ACE entries are located at the top of the ACL so the system can quickly evaluate that they do not have access. The rights for an individual user are based on the combination of all the ACEs in the ACL: The most restrictive permission wins out.

ActiveX

General information pertaining to all tests

ActiveX is the name of the technology Microsoft has created to allow developers to create encapsulated easy-to-use content for their applications. ActiveX replaces the older OLE, or Object Linking and Embedding, technology and follows the COM specification model.

Add/Remove Programs Control Panel

70-067   NT Server (Core)   *Installation and Configuration*
70-073   NT Workstation   *Running Applications*

The Add/Remove Programs Control Panel is used to install and uninstall applications on a *Windows NT* system. The Control Panel is divided into three separate areas: **installing a new application** and **removing an existing application** (on one tab) and the **Windows NT Setup section** (on another tab).

To install a new application by using the Add/Remove Programs Control Panel, place the installation media (CD-ROM or floppy disk) into the drive and click the Install button. This starts a *wizard* that will walk you through starting the installation process. This process will work only for applications that come with built-in setup programs.

The **Remove Programs** area of the Add/Remove Programs Control Panel lists applications that were installed with a Windows-compliant 32-bit installation program. To remove a program, choose the name of the program from the list box and click the **Add/Remove...** button. This starts up the uninstall program that will uninstall the original program. In some cases, removing the application may require that you have the original installation media available.

The **Windows NT Setup** portion of the Add/Remove Programs Control Panel is used to install and uninstall Windows NT components. To add or remove a component, check or uncheck the box next to it. Some listings, such as the Accessories area have subcategories that can be accessed by highlighting the category and then clicking on the **Details...** button.

Address Resolution Protocol

See *ARP.*

administrative wizards

70-067   NT Server (Core)   *Managing Resources*

Administrative wizards are small applications that Microsoft has included with *Windows NT* to assist administrators in such day-to-day administrative tasks as creating users and groups, allocating and sharing resources, and setting up printers. These applications provide a straightforward way of performing these tasks with little or no training or knowledge.

administrator
70-067   NT Server (Core)   *General Information*

The administrator is the person who is responsible for setting up and managing all servers and all user accounts in a *domain*. This person is usually in charge of all things that happen to the computers at a specific location.

The administrator, by way of membership in the *Administrators group*, has permission to perform all tasks in a domain; therefore, care should be taken that no one but the designated administrator knows the password. The administrator is also a member of the Domain Admins global group that is added to all Administrators local groups on all servers and workstations. As a security measure, you should consider renaming the Administrator account.

Administrators group
70-067   NT Server (Core)   *Managing Resources*

The Administrators local group enables you to add users to a computer and allow them to perform the same tasks as the administrator login. There are two different administrator groups on most *Windows NT* computers: the Administrators group and the Domain Admins group.

The Administrators group contains people who can administer the local computer. The Administrators group on a *domain controller* contains all people who can administer any domain controller in the *domain*. These people can add new users to the local computer, add new hardware, and install applications, for example.

Care should be taken when assigning people to either the Administrators group or the Domain Admins group. Of these two groups, the Domain Admins group is the more dangerous group because whenever a *Windows NT Workstation* or a member server joins the domain, the Domain Admins group is added to that system's local Administrators group. These people can perform actions that can be detrimental to the operation of the servers if they have not received proper training. It is also imperative that these people recognize that their passwords must be difficult to guess.

ADSL
70-058   Networking Essentials   *WAN Transmission Technologies*

ADSL, or Asymmetric Digital Subscriber Line, is a technology that uses standard phone lines. An ADSL circuit is much faster than a regular phone connection, but the wires coming into the subscriber's premises are the same wires used for regular phone service. This technology is frequently used as a replacement for *ISDN*. For more information, see the following section:

■ *ISDN*. This is a technology that was developed to provide high-speed data transfer.

Advanced RISC Computing
See *ARC*.

alerts
70-067   NT Server (Core)   *Monitoring and Optimization*

An alert is set within *Performance Monitor* to allow you to monitor a specific *counter* and perform some action when a predefined threshold has been reached. This useful tool can be used when monitoring a system for specific problems, such as processor or memory utilization. The following list outlines the procedure for setting up and working with alerts in Performance Monitor:

1. From the **Start** menu, select **Programs, Administrative Tools, Performance Monitor**.

2. From the **View** menu, choose **Alert**. This opens the Alert dialog box shown in Figure A.1.

3. To add a new alert, click on the plus sign (**+**) on the toolbar. This opens the Add to Alert dialog box (see Figure A.2).

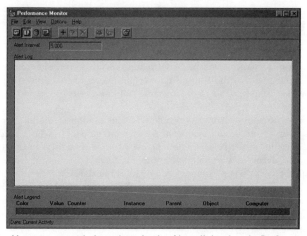

Figure A.1 You can set and view alerts in the Alert dialog box in Performance Monitor.

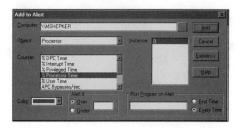

Figure A.2 The Add to Alert dialog box is used to specify which counters are to be monitored.

4. In the **Object** drop-down box, choose the object you will be monitoring. For example, choose **System**.

5. In the **Counter** box, choose the specific counter that you want to monitor, such as **% Total Processor Time**.

6. In the **Alert If** box, choose whether you want the system to alert you if the chosen counter goes above or below a certain value. For example, indicate that you want to be alerted if % Total Processor Time goes above 95.

7. In the **Run Program on Alert** list, you can specify an external program, such as paging software or email, that is to be activated when the threshold is reached.

8. When you have correctly chosen what to monitor and what actions to take to alert the administrator, click on the **Add** button to add and activate the alert.

answer file

70-073	NT Workstation	*Installation and Configuration*
70-067	NT Server (Core)	*Installation and Configuration*

An answer file is used along with a *uniqueness database file*, or *UDF*, and the *sysdiff* utility to complete an *unattended install*. The answer file allows the *administrator* the freedom of not having to sit at a particular computer replying to the specific prompts that the installation routine asks for.

Creating an Answer File

The answer file is a standard text file that can be edited by using any text editor. There are two ways to create an unattended answer file. First, you can use the sample unattended answer file called UNATTEND.TXT on the *Windows NT* Workstation CD. The other option for creating an answer file is to use the Windows NT Setup Manager application included in the Windows NT Workstation Resource Kit. This application is a graphical utility that will write the answer file for you.

Parts of the Answer File

The information in the answer file is divided into several different sections. The actual section headings do not change; only the parameter values under the section headings do. Table A.1 outlines the sections of the answer file.

Table A.1

Section Heading	Description	In UDF	In Answer File
[Unattended]	This section is used during the text mode portion of the setup program. The type of installation, the file system, and the path are specified in this section.		✔
[OEMBootFiles]	This section is used to specify any OEM boot files that are required for the hardware.		✔
[MassStorageDrivers]	This section specifies which mass storage drivers will be installed during the text mode portion of the		✔

continues

Table A.1 **Continued**

Section Heading	Description	In UDF	In Answer File
	installation. If this section is missing, setup will attempt to detect the drivers.		
[DisplayDrivers]	This section determines which display drivers will be loaded during the text mode portion of the installation. If this section is missing, setup will attempt to detect the drivers.	✔	✔
[KeyboardDrivers]	This section specifies which keyboard driver will be loaded during setup.		✔
[PointingDeviceDrivers]	This section specifies which mouse drivers will be loaded during the text mode portion of the setup process.		✔
[OEM_Ads]	This section is used to modify the default user interface displayed during the GUI portion of the setup program. Modifications can include the banner, background bitmap, and logo.	✔	✔
[GUIUnattended]	This section is used to specify the settings for the GUI portion of the setup, including the time zone, computer role, and administrative password.	✔	✔
[UserData]	This section is used to specify such user information as user name, organization name, computer name, and product name.	✔	✔
[LicenseFilePrintData]	This section is used during the installation of Windows NT Server only. It is used to specify the preferred licensing option.	✔	✔
[Network]	This section is used to specify network settings including the network adapter, services, and protocols to be installed. The section specifies the domain or workgroup to join and the account and password information that is required to create a computer account in the domain. If this section is not present in either the answer file or the UDF, networking will not be installed.	✔	✔

A

Section Heading	Description	In UDF	In Answer File
[Modem]	This section is used to specify the type of modem, if any, that will be installed on the computer.	✔	✔
[Display]	This section is used to specify the display settings, including color depth, screen resolution, and refresh rate. All of these settings must be supported by the display adapter.	✔	✔
[DetectMassStorage]	This section is used to specify which storage devices the setup application should recognize, even if they are not currently installed in the computer.	✔	

API

70-067	NT Server (Core)	*General Information*
70-073	NT Workstation	*General Information*

An API, or *Application Programming Interface*, is a set of routines that developers can use to carry out precreated system functions. These functions, often low-level system functions, make it easier for developers to develop streamlined applications.

AppleTalk

70-058	Networking Essentials	*Select appropriate network and transport protocols*
70-067	NT Server (Core)	*Configure protocols and protocol bindings*

AppleTalk is a suite of *protocols* that was originally designed to support Apple Macintosh's proprietary LocalTalk cabling system. This protocol is required to install Services for Macintosh. Table A.2 lists the protocols included in the AppleTalk suite.

Table A.2 **AppleTalk Protocols**

Protocol	Description
Datagram Delivery Protocol (DDP)	DDP is a network layer protocol that provides connectionless service between two sockets (a socket is a term for a service address). DDP is a routable protocol.
Routing Table Maintenance Protocol (RTMP)	RTMP performs network routing and maintenance of the routing tables.
AppleTalk Transaction Protocol (ATP)	ATP is a connectionless Transport layer protocol that provides reliable service by using a set of acknowledgments and retransmissions. Each packet includes a sequence number that allows for message reassembly and retransmission of lost packets. Only lost or damaged packets are retransmitted.
AppleTalk File Protocol (AFP)	AFP is a connection-based protocol that translates local file service requests into requests for network file services. AFP provides a method for file system security and verifies and encrypts user names and passwords.

A

For more information, see the section on *Services for Macintosh*, which is a service that can be installed in conjunction with AppleTalk to enable *Windows NT* to serve Macintosh clients.

Application layer

See *OSI Model*.

application log

70-067   NT Server (Core)   *Installation and Configuration*

The application log is used to log events that occur in native *Windows NT* applications. The application log contains the same sort of information as that logged in the system log. Occasionally, messages that look like they should appear in the security log, such as one person accessing another person's email box in a Microsoft Exchange environment, also appear here.

For more information, see the following sections:

■ *Event Viewer.* The application used to view the application log.

■ *system log.* A type of log viewable with the Event Viewer.

■ *security log.* Another type of log viewable with the Event Viewer.

application priorities

70-067   NT Server (Core)   *Monitoring and Optimization*
70-073   Windows NT Workstation   *Starting applications at different priorities*

Windows NT uses a system of preemptive multitasking in which the operating system determines which application needs to access the CPU. It does this by assigning a priority level to each *process*, or thread. The base priority level is eight. During processing, the operating system adjusts the priorities to give each application access to the processor. The process that has the highest priority level is then executed next. The system uses three factors when determining how to adjust the priority of a process:

■ The priority of the process that is currently running in the foreground is boosted to ensure that the response time for the current application is maximized.

■ The priority of any thread that has gone into a voluntary wait state is automatically boosted. The longer the thread has been waiting, the higher the thread will be boosted.

■ Lower-priority threads are randomly boosted by the operating system. This ensures that higher-priority applications do not monopolize resources that lower-priority applications need. It also ensures that the lower-priority applications will be run.

Windows NT uses 32 priority levels numbered zero through 31. Levels 0 through 15 are used for dynamic applications (ones that can be written to the Windows NT pagefile). These priority levels are commonly used for user applications. Levels 16 through 31 are considered real-time priorities. (Applications running at real-time cannot be written to the Windows NT pagefile.) These priorities are used for the executive services and the Windows NT kernel.

Starting Applications at Different Priorities

Windows NT allows users to start applications at priorities higher than the normal priority of 8. To start an application with a higher priority, the user specifies the priority level at the command line. Table A.3 provides the syntax for the appropriate commands.

Table A.3   **Priority Levels**

Base Priority	Switch	Command Syntax
4	/LOW	start /low command.exe
8	/NORMAL	start /normal command.exe
13	/HIGH	start /high command.exe
24	/REALTIME	start /realtime command.exe

Changing Application Priority

It is possible to change the base priority of an application after it's started. Changing the priority at runtime allows the user to modify the apparent speed at which the application is running. Care should be taken to ensure that the priority is not set too high because the application could, in essence, take over the CPU and prevent other applications from running. The Windows NT Task Manager is used to change the priority of the application. Right-click on the process, choose the **Set Priority** option, and then choose a priority, as shown in Figure A.3.

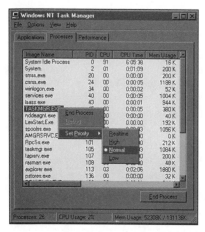

Figure A.3   The Windows NT Task Manager can be used to change the priority of an application after it has been started.

Application Programming Interface

See *API*.

ARC

70-067   NT Server (Core)   *Installation and Configuration*

ARC (Advanced RISC Computing) naming conventions are standards used to identify the location of a file on a device such as a *hard drive* or floppy drive. ARC-based path names are outlined in the section on the *BOOT.INI* file. For more information, see the following sections:

- *BOOT.INI*. This is the file that utilizes ARC naming conventions to start Windows NT.

- *Boot process, Intel*. This section outlines the process that Intel computers use when booting Windows NT.

■ *Boot process, Alpha.* This section outlines the process that Alpha computers use when booting Windows NT.

ARP

A

ARP, the *Address Resolution Protocol*, is one of the maintenance protocols that is a part of the *TCP/IP* protocol suite. In order for two hosts to communicate on a TCP/IP network, each host must be able to determine the other's *IP address* when given the physical, or *MAC*, address for the machine.

If the sending host does not have the destination computer's MAC address in its ARP cache, it broadcasts a packet called an ARP request packet to all computers on the local network segment. If the destination IP address is not on the local segment, the computer requests the MAC address for the gateway. The ARP request packet contains the IP address of the destination host, the IP address of the source host, and the MAC address of the source host. All hosts on the network detect the ARP request packet, and the host with the IP address matching the destination IP address in the packet replies to the sender with its MAC address. The IP address combinations of both hosts are then stored in each computer's ARP cache for future use.

When Microsoft TCP/IP is installed on a *Windows NT* computer, a utility for working with the ARP cache is installed as well. That utility can be used to view the ARP cache, delete entries from the ARP cache, and add new entries to the ARP cache. The syntax of the ARP commands is outlined here.

To view the ARP cache:

```
ARP -a [inet_addr] [-N if_addr]
```

To delete entries from the ARP cache:

```
ARP -d inet_addr [if_addr]
```

To add entries to the ARP cache:

```
ARP -s inet_addr eth_addr [if_addr]
```

The ARP commands take the following options:

Option	Description
-a	Displays current ARP entries by interrogating the current protocol data. If an address is specified, only the IP and physical addresses for the specified computer are displayed. If more than one network interface uses ARP, entries for each ARP table are displayed.
-g	Same as -a.
inet_addr	Specifies an Internet address.
-N if_addr	Displays the ARP entries for the network interface specified by if_addr.
-d	Deletes the host specified by the Internet address.
-s	Adds the host and associates the Internet address inet_addr with the Physical address eth_addr. The physical address is given as 6 hexadecimal bytes separated by hyphens. The entry is permanent.
eth_addr	Specifies a physical, or MAC, address.
if_addr	If this is provided, it specifies the Internet address of the interface whose address translation table should be modified. If this is not provided, the first applicable interface will be used.

For more information, see the following sections:

- *IP address.* This is the address assigned to all computers on a TCP/IP network.
- *MAC address.* This is the physical address of the network adapter.

assigning NTFS permissions

70-067   NT Server (Core)   *Managing Resources*

Windows NT allows you to assign *NTFS permissions* to resources on the server. These permissions can be assigned to the file or directory by clicking on the file or directory in Windows NT Explorer and choosing the **Properties** option from the **File** menu. The permissions are assigned by using the **Permissions** button located on the **Security** tab of the file's properties sheet. The permissions that you can assign are listed in the section on the *ACL*.

For more information, see the following sections:

- *ACE.*
- *ACL.*

Asymmetric Digital Subscriber Line

See *ADSL.*

Asynchronous Transfer Mode

See *ATM.*

AT command

General information pertaining to all tests

The AT command, sometimes called the *command scheduler,* is a very useful utility that allows administrators to schedule processes to run on specific dates and at specific times. The AT command relies on the schedule service; therefore, the service must be running in order to execute the command.

Scheduling a Command

The default way to schedule commands is with the AT command, `at.exe`, which is installed with *Windows NT.* Although other interfaces are available, the `at.exe` command is the default. (One of the other interfaces is known as WinAT, which is a graphical interface to the AT command and is included with the Windows NT Resource Kit.) The syntax for scheduling a command using the AT command is

```
at [\\computername] time [/interactive] ¦ [/every:date[,...] ¦
/next:date[,...]] "command"
```

with the following options:

Option	Description
\\computername	Specifies that the command is to be scheduled on a remote computer. If this option is omitted, the command will be scheduled on the local computer.
time	Specifies the time that the command will run.

continues

continued

Option	Description
/interactive	Allows the job to interact with the desktop of the user currently logged in to the computer.
/every:date	Indicates that the job will run on the specified days. If the date is omitted, the current day is assumed.
/next:date	Indicates that the job will run on the following date. If the data is omitted, the current day of the month is assumed.
command	Indicates the name of the command or batch file being scheduled to run.

For example, to schedule a batch file called ARCHIVE.BAT to run at 1:00 a.m. every Monday through Friday, the command would be this:

```
at 1:00am /every:M,T,W,Th,F archive.bat
```

Note that you can specify a computer name when running the command. Doing so allows you to schedule commands on any Windows NT computer that has the schedule service running. Some of the most common uses of the AT command are to run the NTBACKUP.EXE utility and the net time /set command.

Viewing Scheduled Commands

To check which commands are scheduled to run on a computer, type **at.exe** at the command prompt. The results will look something like the following:

```
Status ID Day       Time      Command Line
------------------------------------------------------------------
3 Each M T W Th F  1:00 AM   archive.bat
```

Every command scheduled is assigned an ID, which is listed in the first column. This ID number can be used to cancel or delete the command.

Deleting Scheduled Commands

To delete a scheduled command and stop it from running on the computer, use the command at.exe with the /delete option:

```
at.exe 3 /delete
```

In this example, the command with ID 3 is removed from the system.

at.exe

See *AT command.*

ATM

70-058 Networking Essentials   *WAN Connection Services*

ATM, or Asynchronous Transfer Mode, is a relatively new high-speed switching technology that allows extremely high-speed data rates. Some ATM systems can operate at speeds of up to 622Mbps; however, a typical speed is 155Mbps.

The biggest difference between ATM and other switching technologies is that ATM is based on a fixed-length 53-byte cell. Other switching technologies allow for variable-length frames. Because the ATM switches always know what the length of the cell will be, they can operate at highly efficient speeds.

ATM utilizes 53-byte cells as a unit of transmission. Each cell has a 5-byte header and 48 bytes of data. The 5-byte cell header allows ATM to mark time-critical cells, such as those containing voice or video data, for delivery before data that can be delayed slightly. This process is called asynchronous delivery.

auditing

70-067   NT Server (Core)   *Managing Resources*

Auditing is the process of tracking user activities by choosing which activities you want to track in a *Windows NT* network. The auditing level is configured in *User Manager for Domains*, and the results of the audit are displayed in the security log of the *Event Viewer*. The categories for audit events are listed here:

- **Logon and Logoff.** These events indicate a single successful or unsuccessful logon or logoff. Included in the description is an indication of what type of logon was requested or performed.

- **File and Object Access.** These events describe both successful and unsuccessful accesses to protected objects. These objects (files, directories, and printers) must be specifically set up to allow auditing to take place.

- **Use of User Rights.** These events describe both successful and unsuccessful attempts to exercise user rights. This includes all user rights assigned in User Manager for Domains except logon and logoff.

- **User and Group Management.** The events in this category outline changes to the security account database. These changes include creation of user accounts or changes in group membership.

- **Security Policy Changes.** These events show high-level changes in security policy. These changes include the assignment of privileges or changes in the audit policy.

- **Restart, Shutdown, and System.** If enabled, this logs any attempts to shut down or restart the system. This also includes any events that affect system security or the security log.

- **Process Tracking.** The events in this category provide detailed-subject tracking information, such as program activation.

For more information, see the following sections:

- *File system auditing.* This topic outlines the use of file system auditing.

- *Event Viewer.* This application is used to view the security log.

A

b-node

70-059 TCP/IP   *Windows Internet Name Service*

B-node name resolution does not use the *WINS* server during name resolution. B-node resolution relies on name broadcasts to resolve and register *NetBIOS* names on a network. This type of name resolution is useful in environments that do not have a WINS server. On larger networks, it is not advisable to use this form of name resolution because it can produce a large amount of network traffic due to the excessive broadcasts. Another limitation of b-node name resolution is that the broadcasts do not cross over *routers*, so names are known only on the local network segment.

For more information, see the following sections:

- *WINS* (a way to automatically map NetBIOS names to IP addresses)
- *M-node*
- *P-node*
- *H-node*

backing up

70-067 NT Server (Core)   *Recovering from fault tolerance failures*

All *administrators* should realize the importance of backing up the data on their servers. This process can mean the difference between having a server down for a few minutes to an hour and having a server down for several hours, if not days. Backing up should not be done only for data security purposes, it should also be done for job security reasons.

Windows NT ships with an application that allows you to back up and restore data from your Windows NT servers. This application is called NT Backup. NT Backup is part of the Administrative Tools group and can be accessed by choosing **Start**, **Programs**, **Administrative Tools**, **Backup**. The Backup application, shown in Figure B.1, will open, initialize the file system, and then search for any tape drives installed on your system. If you do not have a tape drive installed in the machine, NT Backup will not let you perform a backup.

To perform a backup, click on the drives you want to back up, and then choose the individual files you are going to back up (see Figure B.2). After you have selected the files to back up, click on the **Backup** button to start the backup process.

After the backup process is complete, you should store the tapes in a location other than where your servers are. This ensures that there will always be a copy of your data available, even if your servers suffer catastrophic damage such as fire or flood. If the tapes are stored in the same room as your servers and a fire breaks out, you have lost both the original and the backup copies of your data.

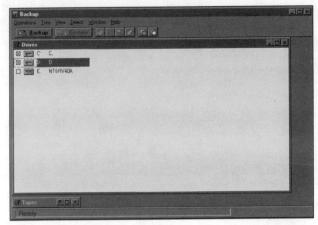

Figure B.1   Windows NT provides an application that allows you to back up the data on your machines.

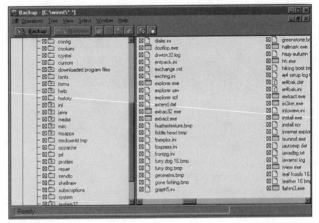

Figure B.2   The NT Backup application allows you to select individual files and directories to back up.

backup devices

70-067   NT Server (Core)   *General Information*

A backup device is usually a tape drive or other form of media used to make an archival copy of data on a server in preparation for the event of data corruption or media failure.

backup domain controller

See *BDC.*

bandwidth

70-058   Networking Essentials   *Standards and Terminology*

Bandwidth defines the total amount of data you can transmit over a network at any one point. Normally, bandwidth is measured in megabits per second, or 10Mbps. A megabit is one million bits, which equal about 50 pages of text.

baseband

70-058   Networking Essentials   *Standards and Terminology*

Baseband describes how bandwidth is allocated on the transmission media. Baseband is the most common mode of operation for *LANs*. Baseband transmission uses the entire capacity of network media for one single communications channel. This type of signaling is primarily used for digital signaling.

For more information, see the section titled *broadband*, which is another type of signaling used on some networks.

B

baseline

70-068   NT Server (Enterprise)   *Monitoring and Optimization*

When monitoring a server for performance issues, you must first establish a baseline. A baseline is standard by which to compare all other measurements during monitoring. Without an accurate baseline, it is difficult to tell what type of performance—good or bad—you are getting. A baseline is also useful when predicting the maximum number of users a server can accommodate. If you know how the server reacts with one user, you can use that information to estimate how it will run with 100.

The baseline for your servers will indicate how the system as a whole reacts. The information you collect can then be used to monitor system usage later. To set up a baseline, you use *Performance Monitor*. Performance Monitor allows you to choose individual objects and counters that are important. When creating the initial baseline, remember that you will always monitor the same counters you monitor the first time. Some of the most common counters to choose are:

- Cache
- Logical Disk
- Memory
- Network Adapter
- Physical Disk
- Process
- Processor
- Server
- System

After you have set up the counters, configured an interval time for data collection, and started the log file, let it run until you have collected enough data to compare future logs to. Depending on your system, this could take as little as an hour or as long as a few days. The best plan for collecting a baseline is to perform regular data collection during weekdays between 8:00 a.m. and 10:00 a.m. Over time, this will assist you in finding the average usage pattern.

For more information, see the following sections:

- *Performance Monitor*. This is the application that is used to monitor and gather data on the server.
- *Counter*. This is an individual piece of information that is gathered by Performance Monitor.

BDC

70-067   NT Server (Core)   *Installation and Configuration*

A BDC, or backup domain controller, is a server that assists the *PDC*, or primary domain controller, in maintaining copies of the directory database. The directory database is a listing of all users and computers in a *domain*. The BDC runs the *netlogon service* and can validate users logging on to the domain. A domain can have multiple BDCs.

In the event that the PDC fails, a BDC can be promoted to be the PDC using Server Manager. However, any changes that were made to the directory database while the PDC was down that were not replicated out to the BDC will be lost. If you need to bring the PDC down for any reason, it is a good idea to first promote a BDC to become the PDC using Server Manager. This ensures that the *SAM* database is synchronized before the BDC becomes the PDC.

B

beaconing

70-058   Networking Essentials   *Standards and Terminology*

Beaconing is a process used on *token-ring* networks to help diagnose and repair errors in the ring. The first computer turned on in a token-ring network becomes what is known as the active monitor station. The active monitor must announce itself on the network as the active monitor and request that the next active downstream computer announce its next active downstream neighbor. The active monitor sends this request out to the network every seven seconds. In this way, every computer on the network remains aware of its next active neighbors, both upstream and downstream.

When all computers on the network are aware of their neighbors, the beaconing process continues. If any of the computers does not respond to one of the seven-second announcements, it notifies the rest of the computers on the network. The rest of the computers on the network take the information from the problem announcement and attempt to correct the problem. This problem correction is known as autoreconfiguration.

For more information, see the following sections:

■ *Token-ring network*. This is a type of network that passes tokens to eliminate collisions.

■ *Token*. This is a special type of packet used to allow access to the network.

BIOS

General information pertaining to all tests

BIOS is a chip on most hardware devices (such as *network cards*, *video cards*, and *SCSI* adapters) that is used to store configuration information about the hardware. BIOS stands for Basic Input/Output System. This chip is also used to manage data flow between the *operating system* and attached devices such as the *hard drive*, video card, keyboard, mouse, and *printer*.

blue screen

70-068   NT Server (Enterprise)   *Troubleshooting*

The blue screen is often one of the most frustrating errors that you will have to deal with. The blue screen, sometimes called a stop screen or blue screen of death, occurs when the *operating system* encounters something that it cannot handle by using internal error processing. The operating system stops abruptly, leaving you with a great deal of hexadecimal information on a blue-colored screen.

There are several ways to deal with blue screen errors. Many people simply reboot the machine and see whether it happens again. If it doesn't, they don't worry about it. If it does, they reinstall the operating system. This is often a drastic step that is unnecessary. Most of the time, you will be able to discern from information provided to you on the blue screen what the cause of the error was; and if you can't, a call placed to Microsoft Technical Support may help.

The blue screen provides five sections of information:

- **Port Status Indicators.** This information tells you the status of the serial port on the server. This information will be available to you only if debugging is enabled.

- **BugCheck Information.** This section provides you with the actual error code and any extra information that the developer included in the error handling routine. It is possible that you might get only one line of this information. If that is the case, the error affected the error handling routine.

- **Driver Information.** This section lists all *drivers* loaded in memory at the time the blue screen occurred. This information tells you the name of the driver, the date of the driver, and the memory location where it was loaded.

- **Kernel Build Number and Stack Dump.** This section provides the build number of the *kernel* and a dump of the last few instructions that were executed prior to the dump.

- **Debug Port Information.** This contains information about the port in use for debugging.

Of all the information listed in a blue screen, the most important is the BugCheck information. If you do not have time to troubleshoot the error to the fullest extent and must try to get the server back online, copy down the information listed in the BugCheck. You can then use that information to call Microsoft and attempt to get it fixed. The following is an example of the BugCheck section:

```
*** STOP:   0X0000000A
(0X00000000, 0X0000001A, 0X00000000, 0XFC873D6C)
IRQL_NOT_LESS_OR_EQUAL *** Address fc87d6c has base at fc870000 -
i8042prt.sys
CPUID:GenuineIntel 5.1.5 irql:1f  SYSVER 0Xf0000421
```

BNC connectors

70-058 Networking Essentials   *Standards and Terminology*

A BNC, or British Naval Connector, is a piece of hardware used to connect *Thinnet coax* segments into network adapter cards. With these types of connectors, the cables are locked together by inserting one connector into another and twisting them 90 degrees.

boot files

70-067 NT Server (Core)   *Troubleshooting boot failures*

Five files are used in the boot process. Four of these files are used during the Intel boot process (see also *boot process, Intel*), and two are used during the Alpha boot process (see also *boot process, Alpha*). Table B.1 lists and describes each of the boot files.

Table B.1   **Windows NT Boot Files**

File Name	Function	Intel/Alpha
NTLDR	NTLDR is a read-only system stored in the root directory of the active, or system, partition. This file is responsible for loading and executing all the other files.	Intel
BOOT.INI	The BOOT.INI file contains the menu from which you can choose the options to boot Windows NT with and allows you to boot to other operating systems if they are present on the system.	Intel
NTBOOTDD.SYS	NTBOOTDD.SYS contains a non-BIOS-enabled SCSI controller that hosts the hard drives that contain the system or boot partition.	Intel
NTDETECT.COM	NTDETECT.COM builds a list of all hardware detected on the machine. This list is then returned to the NTLDR.	Intel
NTOSKRNL.EXE	The NTOSKRNL.EXE is the actual kernel of the operating system.	Alpha
OSLOADER.EXE	The OSLOADER.EXE file takes the place of the NTLDR file on Alpha-based systems. This file retrieves the hardware configuration for the system from the firmware.	Alpha

For more information, see the following sections:

■ *Boot process, Alpha*. Describes the boot process of Alpha-based computers running Windows NT.

■ *Boot process, Intel*. Describes the boot process of Intel-based computers running Windows NT.

■ *BOOT.INI*. Contains the menu from which you can choose the options to start Windows NT with.

boot partition

70-067   NT Server (Core)   *Managing Resources*

The boot partition of a *Windows NT* computer contains all the *operating system* and support files on an Intel-based system. This is often confused with the *system partition*. The system partition contains the files required to boot the system. The boot partition is specified when you tell the setup application where to *install Windows NT*.

For more information, see the following sections:

■ *System partition*. This partition contains the files required to boot Windows NT.

■ *Boot Process, Intel*. This section describes the boot process for an Intel-based machine running Windows NT.

boot process, Alpha

70-067   NT Server (Core)   *Troubleshooting boot failures*

The Alpha boot process is much simpler than the Intel boot process (see also *boot process, Intel*). All information about the computer's hardware is stored in the computer's firmware, or nonvolatile RAM. Because of this, the boot process does not have to rely on NTDETECT.COM to identify all the hardware on the machine. The boot process of an Alpha-based machine follows the steps described here:

1. When the power is turned on, the machine looks to the system partition for the OSLOADER.EXE file. The OSLOADER.EXE file interrogates the firmware for hardware configuration information and for the list of valid operating systems installed on the machine.

2. The OSLOADER.EXE file loads the NTOSKRNL.EXE. At this point, the screen clears, and then the OS Loader information appears at the top of the screen.

3. The OSLOADER.EXE file loads the Hardware Abstraction Layer, or *HAL*. This file is used to mask exceptions and interrupts from the *kernel*.

4. The OSLOADER.EXE then loads the SYSTEM. This is the HKEY_LOCAL_MACHINE\SYSTEM hive in the *Registry*.

5. Control is passed from OSLOADER.EXE to NTOSKRNL.EXE, the boot process concludes, and the operating system continues to load.

B

boot process, Intel

70-067   NT Server (Core)   *Troubleshooting boot failures*

The boot process of an Intel-based system is much more complicated than that of an Alpha-based system because Intel-based systems do not keep track of their hardware configuration in the same way that Alpha systems do. The boot process for an Intel-based system follows the steps outlined here:

1. When the power is turned on, the system looks to the root of the active partition, known as the *system partition*, for the *NTLDR* file. This file is responsible for loading and activating the rest of the operating system.

2. NTLDR switches the processor to the flat 32-bit memory model that is required for Windows NT to address 4GB of RAM.

3. NTLDR loads the minifile system drivers. These files contain enough instructions to allow Windows NT to access the system and boot partitions of the hard drives. After the operating system is loaded, more complete drivers are loaded.

4. NTLDR displays the boot menu, which is loaded from the *BOOT.INI* file. If Windows NT is selected as the operating system, the process continues as listed. If any other operating system is chosen, NTLDR loads the BOOTSECT.DOS file and passes control to it.

5. Next, NTLDR activates the NTDETECT.COM application to perform a hardware inventory. NTDETECT.COM builds a list of all hardware installed on the machine and passes it back to NTLDR.

6. NTLDR then loads the NTOSKRNL.EXE file. This is the actual kernel of the operating system. At this point, the screen clears, and the OS Loader information is displayed at the top. This file is located in the %SYSTEMROOT%\System32 directory.

7. The NTLDR file then loads the *Hardware Abstraction Layer*, or *HAL*. This file is used to mask exceptions and interrupts from the kernel.

8. Next, NTLDR loads the SYSTEM. This is the HKEY_LOCAL_MACHINE\SYSTEM hive in the *Registry*. This file is located in the %SYSTEMROOT%\System32\Config directory.

9. The NTLDR file then loads any boot-time device drivers that are required to start the operating system. These drivers are not initialized until the load phase.

10. Finally, NTLDR passes control to NTOSKRNL.EXE. Along with control, it passes the hardware list that was created in step 5 so the kernel can continue loading drivers.

B

BOOT.INI

70-067   NT Server (Core)   *Troubleshooting boot failures*

The BOOT.INI file controls the boot loader menu displayed during the Intel boot process (see also *boot process, Intel*). BOOT.INI is divided two sections. The first is the [boot loader] section that specifies the default operating system to load. The second section is the [operating systems] section that references every operating system installed on the machine. All paths to the operating systems are listed in *Advanced RISC Computing*, or *ARC*, style paths.

ARC

Advanced RISC Computing style paths are used instead of MS-DOS–style paths in the BOOT.INI because not all computers support the MS-DOS format. An ARC pathname will always consist of the following parameters:

Parameter	Description
scsi(x) or multi(x)	Identifies which hardware adapter to use. This parameter is almost always multi, unless you have a SCSI controller that does not have the BIOS turned on.
disk(y)	Identifies the SCSI bus number. This is always set to 0 for multi systems.
rdisk(z)	Identifies the physical disk number. This is ignored for SCSI drives.
partition(a)	This is the logical partition number of the drive.

The first three parameters are zero-based options. This means that the first physical disk is rdisk(0) and the second physical disk is rdisk(1). The partition parameter is a one-based number. This means that the first partition on the first disk would be rdisk(0)partition(1). When you set up an ARC-compliant path, all parts of the path must be included, even the ones that are ignored.

[boot loader]

The [boot loader] section of the BOOT.INI specifies the default operating system that will load and the amount of time it will wait for the user to make a decision about which operating system to load. By default, the [boot loader] section looks something like this:

```
[boot loader]
timeout=30
default=multi(0)disk(0)rdisk(0)partition(1)\WINNT
```

The first line of the section specifies the timeout value, in seconds, that the NTLDR will wait for the user to make a decision. If you want the operating system to load immediately without waiting for the user, specify a 0 for the timeout value. If you specify a -1, the computer will wait indefinitely for the user to decide which operating system to start.

The second line is the ARC-compliant path to the default operating system. If the default does not match any of the entries listed in the [operating systems] section, the default will appear as Windows NT (default) in the list of possible operating systems.

[operating systems]

The [operating systems] section of the BOOT.INI specifies entries for every other operating system on the computer. One of the entries in this list should match the default= entry in the [boot loader] section. A typical [operating systems] section looks something like this:

```
[operating systems]
multi(0)disk(0)rdisk(0)partition(1)\WINNT="Windows NT Workstation Version
4.00"
multi(0)disk(0)rdisk(0)partition(1)\WINNT="Windows NT Workstation Version
4.00 [VGA mode]" /basevideo /sos
```

Note that there are two entries in the [operating systems] section for Windows NT Workstation. They are essentially the same entry except that the second one has some switches that control the way in which Windows NT starts.

BOOT.INI Switches

You can add several switches to the [operating systems] section of the BOOT.INI file to control the way in which Windows NT starts. For the most part, these switches are used during the troubleshooting process. Table B.2 outlines the switches.

Table B.2   **Common BOOT.INI Switches**

Switch	Description
/BASEVIDEO	This switch forces Windows NT to start using the standard VGA driver. This is useful if you install a new video driver and Windows NT will not start properly. This will allow you to start Windows NT and choose a different video driver.
/BAUDRATE=n	The switch allows you to specify the baud rate that will be used in the debugging process. If you do not specify a value, Windows NT will default to 9,600 baud for a modem and 19,200 baud for a null modem. This switch also forces the /DEBUG switch to be activated.
/CRASHDEBUG	This switch causes the debugger information to be loaded during startup, but it does not activate the debugger until a kernel error occurs. You should use this mode if you are debugging randomly occurring errors.
/DEBUG	This switch causes the debugger information to be loaded and allows it to be activated by a debugging computer. The mode should be used when you are troubleshooting easily reproducible errors.
/DEBUGPORT=comx	This switch allows you to specify which COM port will be used for debugging. This switch will also force the /DEBUG switch to be activated.
/MAXMEM:n	This switch allows you to specify the amount of memory Windows NT can use. This is useful when attempting to troubleshoot memory errors. It is important to note that /MAXMEM:16 means that Windows NT will use 16MB, not 16KB, of RAM.
/NODEBUG	This switch specifies that no debugging information is being used.
/NOSERIALMICE= [COMx ¦ COMx,y,z]	This switch disables Windows NT from checking for serial mice on specific COM ports. This is useful when you have hardware other than a serial mouse hooked up to a COM port. One specific time that this is particularly useful is when you have a UPS hooked up to the computer. The serial mouse detection routine can shut down the UPS.
/SOS	This option is used when troubleshooting startup errors that deal with missing device drivers. This forces Windows NT to list each individual driver as it is loaded.

B

For more information, see the following sections:

- *Boot process, Intel.*
- *Boot process, Alpha.*

BOOTP/DHCP Relay Agent

70-059 TCP/IP   *Dynamic Host Configuration Protocol*

The BOOTP/DHCP Relay Agent is responsible for routing DHCP broadcasts from DHCP servers and clients across IP *routers*. This allows administrators to set up one DHCP server that will function for several *subnets*. The relay agent can be installed on any Windows NT Server computer. This service requires the use of a BOOTP-compliant router.

For more information, see the following sections:

- *Installing Network Services.* This section goes through the steps required to install network services.
- *DHCP.* This server can be used to dynamically configure IP addresses.

bottlenecks

70-068 NT Server (Enterprise)   *Monitoring and Optimization*

When monitoring a server for performance issues, it is common to find that one resource is not performing at the same level as the rest of the components in the machine. As a result, this one resource slows the overall performance of the machine. The offending resource is known as a bottleneck.

A bottleneck is a single resource that restricts workflow and performance on a server. More than one resource can cause different bottlenecks, but frequently only one bottleneck will be apparent at a time. For example, suppose your server is showing a high level of disk access. To alleviate this, you add another drive controller and implement disk striping. After adding this extra hardware, you notice that there is still a great deal of disk access but that paging accounts for more than 80 percent of all disk access. This points to the need for more memory. You add more memory to the server, and it performs as expected.

For more information, see the section entitled *Performance Monitor*. The Performance Monitor application is used to monitor system performance.

bridges

70-058 Networking Essentials   *Connectivity Devices*

A bridge is a piece of networking hardware that can be used to both reduce the amount of overall network traffic and extend the total size of a network. Bridges operate on the MAC sublayer of the Data Link layer of the *OSI Model*. A bridge selectively forwards packets to another section of a LAN based on the destination address of the packet.

The process for communicating over a bridged network is described in the following steps. In this example, a bridge connects LANX and LANY, as you can see in Figure B.3.

1. The bridge receives every packet sent on both LANX and LANY.

2. The bridge builds a table containing information about which computer addresses reside on each LAN by examining each packet.

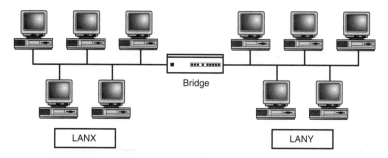

Figure B.3   In this example, a bridge lies between LANX and LANY.

3. Packets sent from computers on LANX that are addressed to computers on LANX are ignored, as are packets sent and addressed to computers on LANY. These packets are automatically delivered.

4. Packets that are sent across the bridge between the LANs, such as from LANX to LANY, are automatically retransmitted to the appropriate LAN.

This process helps reduce the overall amount of network traffic by reducing the number of packets being sent from one side to the other. The only time packets from one side of the LAN are transmitted to the other side is when it is specifically addressed to go there.

broadband

70-058 Networking Essentials   *Standards and Terminology*

Broadband signaling is a type of signaling that is not frequently used in data networks. Broadband signaling divides the total amount of *bandwidth* of the networking media into multiple channels. Each channel can carry different information. Although not frequently used in data networks, this type of signaling is commonly used in cable TV. Multiple signals travel over a single cable, and the TV tuner is used to separate the different signals.

For more information, see the entry entitled *baseband*, which describes another type of signaling that can be used on some networks.

broadcast storm

70-058 Networking Essentials   *Troubleshooting broadcast storms*

A broadcast storm is a flood of broadcast packets that can completely fill up a network, often forcing network utilization to nearly 100 percent. In a worst-case scenario, a broadcast storm can keep computers from even connecting to the network.

A broadcast storm is usually caused by a malfunctioning *network interface card*, but can sometimes be caused by a computer trying to connect to a resource that is unavailable. When trying to isolate the source of a broadcast storm, you are sometimes able to use a network monitoring utility or a *packet sniffer* to determine the source of the packets and remove that computer from the network. If a packet sniffer is not able to discern the source of the broadcast storm, your only option is to methodically remove computers from the network until the broadcast storm ends.

For more information, see the following sections:

■ *Network Interface Card.* Used to attach a computer to a network.

■ *Packet sniffer.* A piece of hardware that is used to track down problems on a network.

brouters
70-058 Networking Essentials   Connectivity Devices

A brouter is a piece of hardware that acts as both a *router* and a *bridge* on a network. A brouter will first attempt to deliver a packet based on network layer information. If this is not possible, the brouter switches to physical, or *MAC*, layer addressing to deliver the packet.

browse list
70-067 NT Server (Core)   *General Information*

The browse list is a listing of all *domains*, servers, and computers on which File and Print Services are installed that are available on the network. This list is maintained by the *master browser.* The list is updated every time a computer logs in to the domain. The master browser makes an announcement every 12 minutes on every *protocol* on the computer. If you have three protocols installed on the computer, for example, the master browser will make three messages every 12 minutes.

browser elections
70-067 NT Server (Core)   *Installation and Configuration*

A browser election occurs whenever the *master browser* on the network fails. This can occur if a client computer or one of the backup browsers fails to receive the browse list from the master browser. An election will also occur every time a *PDC* or *BDC* is rebooted because they usually win the elections. Every backup browser and potential browser ranks itself according to specific criteria, and the computer with the highest ranking wins. Some of the criteria used during the browser elections include the following:

■ **Operating system**. Each computer's operating system is taken into account. The relative rankings are, from highest to lowest: *Windows NT* Server, *Windows NT Workstation*, and *Windows 95*.

■ **Version**. The version of the operating systems, including service packs, is figured into the ranking. Windows NT 4.0 has a higher value than Windows NT 3.51. Windows NT 4.0 with Service Pack 3 has a higher value than Windows NT 4.0 with Service Pack 2.

■ **Current server role**. The role of the server within the domain is taken into account. The PDC has the highest value, followed by the BDC and member servers, respectively.

■ **Current browser role**. The browser role is also taken into consideration. A backup browser has a higher value than a potential browser does.

The computer that wins the election replaces the existing master browser and continues in that role until the next browser election.

For more information, see the section entitled *master browser*, which describes the computer that maintains the master copy of the browse list.

bus

70-058   Networking Essentials   *Network Topologies and Architecture*

The bus topology, shown in Figure B.4, is one in which all devices on the network—including workstations, servers, and printers—are connected to a common cable. This cable is the transmission medium for all signals on the network. Each node on the network is connected to the network by way of a T-conector. Each end of the network cable must be terminated to prevent a signal from bouncing off an unterminated end. The most common implementation of the bus topology is in *10BASE5* and *10BASE2* networks.

B

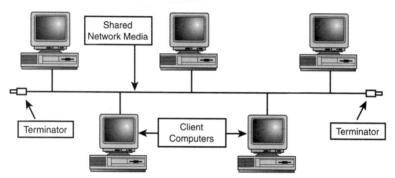

Figure B.4   A bus network is one in which all workstations are connected to a common cable.

For more information, see the following sections:

■ *Coax* (the type of cabling that is used in bus networks)

■ *Star*

■ *Mesh topology*

C2 security

70-067 NT Server (Core)   *General Information*

C2 is a security level that has been outlined by the National Computer Security Center, or NCSC. The NCSC is a United States government agency that evaluates software for security purposes. The standards the government uses when evaluating software are outlined in the Department of Defense Trusted Computer System Evaluation Criteria, commonly referred to as the "Orange Book."

Windows NT has been evaluated at the level of C2. Some of the requirements of C2 security are outlined here:

- Users must be identified by a unique login id and password before being allowed access to the system.

- User activity must be able to be tracked using the login id the user provides.

- The *administrator* must be able to *audit* security-related events, and the log of events must be available only to authorized users.

- The owner of a resource must be able to control who accesses the resource.

- The *operating system* must protect system resources so they cannot be used by other processes. For example, after a process has released memory, another process should not be able to read any data that is left in memory.

- After a file has been deleted, no user or system process can access the file.

- The system must be able to protect itself from outside tampering.

cascaded star

70-058 Networking Essentials   *Network Topologies*

The cascaded star is a network topology that consists of several *star* topologies. The computers on the network are all hooked into child hubs. The child hubs are then attached to a single parent hub, as shown in Figure C.1. The parent hub is sometimes replaced by a switch to allow for faster throughput.

For more information, see the following sections:

- *Star topology.* This is a simpler version of the cascaded star topology.

- *Twisted-pair.* This is the type of cabling that is most commonly found in a cascaded star topology.

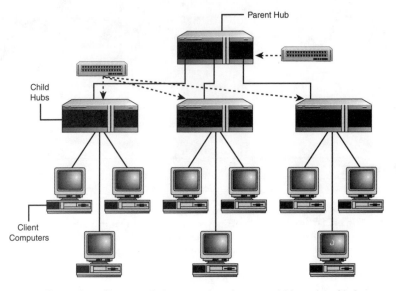

Figure C.1   The cascaded star topology is a nested hierarchy of hubs.

Cat 1

See *Category 1 UTP.*

Cat 2

See *Category 2 UTP.*

Cat 3

See *Category 3 UTP.*

Cat 4

See *Category 4 UTP.*

Cat 5

See *Category 5 UTP.*

Category 1 UTP

70-058 Networking Essentials   *Connecting Network Components*

Category 1 unshielded twisted-pair (UTP) cabling, also known as CAT 1, refers to the traditional cabling that can carry voice traffic but not data. This was the primary type of cable that was installed as phone wire prior to 1983.

Category 2 UTP

70-058 Networking Essentials   *Connecting Network Components*

Category 2 unshielded twisted-pair (UTP) cabling, also known as CAT 2, is UTP cabling that is certified to carry data transmissions of up to 4Mbps. This type of cable consists of four twisted pairs of wire.

Category 3 UTP

70-058 Networking Essentials   *Connecting Network Components*

Category 3 unshielded twisted-pair (UTP), also known as CAT 3, is UTP cabling that is certified to carry data at speeds of up to 10 Mbps. This was the primary type of cable installed in the early days of 10BASET networks. It consists of four twisted pairs of wire with three twists per foot.

Category 4 UTP

70-058 Networking Essentials   *Connecting Network Components*

Category 4 unshielded twisted-pair (UTP), also known as CAT 4, is UTP cabling that is certified to handle data transmissions of up to 16Mbps. This cabling is sometimes used in token-ring installations. It consists of four twisted pairs with four twists per foot.

Category 5 UTP

70-058 Networking Essentials   *Connecting Network Components*

Category 5 unshielded twisted-pair (UTP), also known as CAT 5, is UTP cabling that is certified to handle data transmissions of up to 100Mbps. This is the de facto standard for *10BASET* installations. It consists of four twisted pairs of wire.

CGI

70-067 NT Server (Core)   *General Information*

CGI, or Common Gateway Interface, is a technology that was developed by the National Center for Supercomputing Applications. CGI allows developers to create applications that run on the Web server to provide functionality such as email, hit counters, and database lookup. These applications are commonly written in PERL, although sometimes they are written in C or C++.

client access license

70-067 NT Server (Core)   *Managing Resources*

A client access license, or CAL, is what is purchased from a software vendor to allow users to connect to a specific BackOffice component. For example, when you purchase a basic *Windows NT* Server package, you get the Windows NT Server *operating system* and a certain number of client access licenses. These licenses allow users to access the server. It doesn't matter which operating system is running on the client that is accessing the server. There must be one license for every user accessing the server. These client access licenses are purchased in addition to the price of the client operating system. Windows NT uses two types of client access licenses: per-server and per-seat.

Per-Server Licensing

In a per-server licensing setup, all client access licenses are assigned to a server. If you have a single server with 30 clients, you will need to purchase 30 client access licenses. With per-server licensing, if you add a second server, you will need to purchase another 30 licenses. Every server that a client accesses requires an access license. If you are not sure which licensing mode you need to use, choose per-server licensing. If you originally choose per-server licensing, you can make a one-way, one-time migration from per-server to per-seat licensing.

Per-Seat Licensing

In a per-seat licensing setup, all client access licenses are assigned to individual clients. When you purchase client access licenses, you assign them to clients. A client can access any number of servers by using a single client access license.

For more information, see the following sections:

- *Licensing Control Panel.* This Control Panel allows you to view and change licensing information on Windows NT Server.

- *License Manager.* This application allows you to view license information for all servers in a domain.

C

Client Services for NetWare

70-073   NT Workstation   *Installation and Configuration*

Client Services for NetWare, or CSNW, is a service that can be installed on *Windows NT Workstations* to enable the computers to log in to and interact with *NetWare* servers. With this service, you can access file and print resources on a NetWare server. You can also run some NetWare-aware applications and NetWare utilities from a *Windows NT* computer. This service is installed through the *Network Control Panel.* In addition, if the *NWLink IPX/SPX* protocol stack is not present when the service is installed, it is also installed with CSNW.

For more information, see the following sections:

- *Gateway Services for NetWare.* This service allows other Windows NT computers to connect to a NetWare resource without logging in to the *NetWare* server.

- *NWLink IPX/SPX.* This is a NetWare protocol that must be present for CSNW to work.

client-server

70-067   NT Server (Core)   *General*

Client-server computing is simply a term for the use of servers providing information and resources for client machines to access. Server computers are typically high-powered computers that are specifically designed for network throughput. Client computers are usually not as powerful as servers and are used to access information and services provided on the servers. This type of computer is primarily used to relieve the client from having to perform all the processing on the data that is sent to it from the server. In client-server terms, any computer that offers resources to another computer can be considered a server, and any machine that uses a server can be considered a client.

CMOS

General information pertaining to all tests

The CMOS, or Complementary Metal Oxide Semiconductor, is a chip used to store configuration information about the devices attached to the computer. This chip is attached to a battery so that the information is kept available even when the computer is turned off.

For more information, see the section entitled *BIOS*, which describes a chip that contains configuration information for devices.

coax

70-058 Networking Essentials   *Networking Media*

Coax, or coaxial cable, was the first type of cable used in early networking. In older installations of *Ethernet*, it is not uncommon to still see coax wiring. Coax consists of two conducting elements sharing the same axis.

Table C.1 describes the four main parts of a coaxial cable.

Table C.1   **The Four Main Parts of Coax**

Element	Description
Inner conductor	The inner conductor is usually made of solid copper wire, although some types have a stranded core.
Insulation Layer	The insulation layer lies between the inner and the outer conductor, keeping the two portions evenly spaced.
Outer Conductor	The outer conductor, sometimes called a braid or shield, is a braided conductive layer that serves as a ground and protects the inner layer from electromagnetic interference (EMI). This layer can also consist of a foil shield.
Jacket	The jacket is an outer layer of plastic that serves to insulate and pro-tect the outer conductor from damage.

For more information related to coax, see the following sections:

- *Fiber-optic cable.* This is another type of cable, which supports much faster transfer rates than coax.

- *Twisted-pair.* This is a type of cable that has replaced coax as the standard for Ethernet installations.

- Appendix A, which contains a cable comparison chart to study from.

collisions

70-058 Networking Essentials   *Standards and Terminology*

A collision is a network event that occurs when more than one computer on the network attempts to transmit data at the same time. The mixed signals interfere with one other and destroy any data that is being sent. Most networks use some sort of access method to reduce or eliminate collisions.

For more information, see the following sections:

- *CSMA/CA.*
- *CSMA/CD.*

Common Gateway Interface

See *CGI.*

Complete Trust Domain Model

70-068 NT Server (Enterprise)   *Planning*

The Complete Trust Domain Model enables every *domain* to control its own users and resources while allowing any domain to assign permissions in its domain to users in another domain. The Complete Trust Domain Model is difficult to administer. The administrator in each domain is in control of its own resources. You have to be able to trust the administrator of remote domains that they will put the correct users into global groups, which you will use to assign to local groups, thus allowing access to your resources.

The Complete Trust Domain Model is implemented by creating *two-way trusts* between all domains in the model (see Figure C.2). This creates a large number of trusts that have to be created and administered.

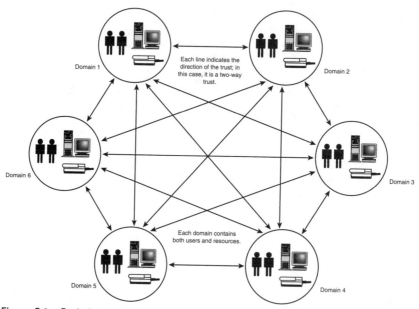

Figure C.2   Each domain must establish a two-way trust with every other domain in the model.

To determine the number of trusts that must be created, you use the formula $N \times (N-1)$, where N is the total number of domains in the model. For example, if you are setting up a Complete Trust Domain Model involving six domains, the formula would be this:

$6 \times (6-1) = 30$

You would have to establish 30 trusts to make this scenario work.

For more information regarding the Complete Trust Domain Model, see the following sections:

- *Trust relationship.* This is a setting that allows the users from one domain to access the resources in another domain.

- *Single Master Domain Model.* This is a domain model that has only one master, or accounts, domain.

- *Multiple Master Domain Model.* This is a domain model that has more than one master, or accounts, domain.

- *Single Domain Model.* This is a domain model that consists of only one domain.

Compressed Serial Line Internet Protocol

See *CSLIP.*

computer browser service

70-067 NT Server (Core)   *Installation and Configuration*

The computer browser service is a service that maintains an up-to-date list of computers on the network that have server services enabled and provides this list to other computers upon request. This optimizes network browsing because only the computers that are functioning as browsers maintain the server lists. Other clients on the networks do not have to keep track of this information. This is the list of computers that is displayed in Network Neighborhood, in the Select Domain and Select Computer boxes in Use Manager, and in the server manager.

For more information, see the following sections:

- *Master browser.* This is the computer that keeps the master copy of the browse list.

- *Browse list.* This is a list of the computers on the network that have File and Print Services turned on.

- *Browser election.* This is the process by which a master browser is chosen.

concentrator

See *hub.*

Console Control Panel

70-067 NT Server (Core)   *Installation and Configuration*

The Console Control Panel controls how the console, or command prompt, looks. The Control Panel is divided into four tabs, as outlined in Table C.2.

Table C.2 **Parts of the Console Control Panel**

Tab	Functionality
Options	The Options tab allows you to configure the size of the cursor, the number of typed commands stored in memory for recall, whether the console starts in a window or full screen, and options determining the way you can cut and paste from the window.
Font	The Font tab allows you to choose the type and size of the font displayed in the console window. This tab also contains options that allow you to determine the starting size of the screen if you are not working in full-screen mode.
Layout	The Layout tab allows you to configure the number of lines displayed on the screen, as well as the startup position of the screen. The Layout tab also contains an option with which you can configure the size of the screen buffer. This

continues

Table C.2   **Continued**

Tab	Functionality
	option offers a scroll bar to allow you to go back and view old messages in the current console window.
Color	The Color tab allows you to choose both the background color and the text color for the console window, as well as for any pop-up boxes that occur within the window.

Changes made in the Console Control Panel affect only those windows created after you make the changes.

contention

70-058 Networking Essentials   *Standards and Terminology*

Contention is the competition on a network between computers trying to put data on the networking media. Contention helps to reduce *collisions* on the network, which destroy data.

For more information, see the following sections:

- *CSMA/CD.* This is an access method used by Ethernet.

- *Ethernet.* This is the networking standard that uses contention.

Control Panels

70-067 NT Server (Core)   *Installation and Configuration*

The Control Panels are applications that allow you to edit settings dealing with specific portions of the operating system. Several Control Panels are installed with *Windows NT.* User applications can also install Control Panels. Some of the more common Control Panels are listed in Table C.3.

Table C.3   **Common Windows NT Control Panels**

Control Panel	Description
Accessibility Options	Provides options that make it easier for users with physical difficulties to use the computer.
Add/Remove Programs	Installs and creates shortcuts to user applications and installs Windows NT options. This Control Panel is also used to remove applications that have been installed on the computer.
Console	Configures options for the Windows NT console, or command prompt.
Date/Time	Configures the date, time, and time zone information.
Devices	Used to stop and start installed *device drivers.*
Display	Configures display settings, including *video card* and monitor, color schemes, wallpapers, and screen resolution.
Fonts	Adds, removes, and displays fonts.
Internet	Enables the user to change settings dealing with Internet Explorer, including general information such as the start page, dial-up settings, and security settings.
Keyboard	Changes keyboard settings such as key repeat, cursor blink rate, and language.
Mail and Fax	Enables the user to view, edit, change, and delete Microsoft Messaging Profiles.
Microsoft Mail Postoffice	Configures the path to a Microsoft Mail postoffice. This Control Panel is available only when Microsoft Mail is installed on the computer.

Control Panel	Description
Modems	Installs new modems and changes existing *modem* properties.
Mouse	Changes mouse settings such as the mouse driver and mouse cursors.
MS Licensing	Configures the licensing mode and licensing options for the Microsoft software installed on the computer.
Multimedia	Changes multimedia settings, including the preferred playback devices, video configuration, MIDI configuration, CD-ROM, and device settings. This Control Panel is also used to install sound card drivers and audio and video CODECs.
Network	Configures network settings including adapters, *protocols*, and services.
ODBC	Contains options for changing, viewing, and editing data source connections and drivers based on the applications you are using.
PC Card (PCMCIA)	Enables *PCMCIA* sockets and configures PC cards.
Ports	Configures serial port communications settings.
Printers	Enables the user to add, configure, and remove *printers* from the system.
Regional Settings	Changes the appearance of the time, date, numbers, and currency.
SCSI Adapters	Contains options for adding and removing *SCSI* adapters, as well as for viewing their properties.
Server	Displays and manages the local server properties. From this Control Panel, you can view open files, view connected users, configure file and *directory replication*, and set up which computers receive administrative alerts.
Services	Enables the user to stop, start, and configure services on the local computer.
Sounds	Changes system and program sounds.
System	Enables the user to view system information and make changes to environment settings. Options for the virtual memory settings and the crash recovery options are set here. Local account profiles can also be modified and deleted from this Control Panel.
Tape Devices	Contains options for detecting, installing, and configuring tape drives.
Telephony	Configures telephony devices and dialing properties.
UPS	Configures uninterruptible power supplies.

convert utility

70-067   NT Server (Core)   *Choosing a file system*

The convert utility is used to convert a *FAT* file system to an *NTFS* file system without losing any of the files on the partition. In order to run the convert utility, you must have administrative rights to the local machine. When the utility is run, it must be able to gain exclusive access to the drive. If you are attempting to convert a drive in which the utility cannot gain complete access, the drive will simply be marked for conversion, and the next time you restart the computer, the conversion will take place. This is a one-time command and cannot be reversed. The syntax of the command is as follows:

```
convert.exe drive: /FS:NTFS [/V]
```

The convert command uses the following options:

Option	Description
drive:	Represents the drive you want to convert. This is a required option.
/FS:NTFS	Specifies that you want to convert the file system to NTFS. This is a required option.
/V	Specifies that you want the convert utility to run in verbose mode.

For more information regarding the convert utility, see the following sections:

- *NTFS.* This is the preferred file system for Windows NT.
- *FAT.* This is another type of file system that is compatible with other versions of Windows.

convert.exe

See *convert utility.*

copy files on an NTFS partition

70-067   NT Server (Core)   *Managing Resources*

When you copy files between NTFS partitions, note that a new instance of the file is created in the destination directory. This new instance of the file will inherit the security and compression attributes of the new directory. For example, if the administrator copies a file from a directory that User1 has no permissions on into a directory that User1 does have permissions on, User1 *will* be able to access the file. Also, if you copy a file from a directory that is compressed into a directory that is not compressed, the file will not be compressed in the destination directory.

When you copy a file from one directory to another on an NTFS partition, all security and compression attributes are retained.

counters

70-067   NT Server (Core)   *Monitoring and Optimization*
70-068   NT Server Enterprise   *Monitoring and Optimization*

When using *Performance Monitor* to monitor system performance, you are actually monitoring specific objects of the operating system. These objects are broken down into individual items, or counters. The counters are loaded into Performance Monitor, and then system performance is monitored through them. Similar counters are grouped together under objects.

For more information, see the *Performance Monitor* section. Performance Monitor is the utility that uses counters to display information about Windows NT servers.

CSLIP

70-058   Networking Essentials   *Networking Standards*

CSLIP, or Compressed Serial Line Internet Protocol, is a compressed version of *SLIP.* This version provides higher throughput by compressing all data that is passed between the server and the client. This dial-up protocol is not supported by *Windows NT* as a server; Windows NT uses *PPP,* or Point-to-Point Protocol. Windows NT can act as a CSLIP client.

For more information related to CSLIP, see the following sections:

- *SLIP.* This is the protocol that CSLIP is based on.
- *PPP.* This is the protocol that has replaced SLIP and CSLIP.
- *RAS.* This service can be installed on a Windows NT Server to provide remote access.

CSMA/CA

70-058 Networking Essentials   *Standards and Terminology*

CSMA/CA, or Carrier Sense Multiple Access with Collision Avoidance, is a way to control access to the networking media. In CSMA/CA, all computers on the network listen for data to be transmitted. When the cable is quiet, any computer on the network can transmit data. Because only one computer can transmit at a time, the computer that intends to place data on the wire sends out a packet telling all other computers on the network that it is about to send data. All other computers on the network then wait for the data to be sent. This type of access control drastically reduces the number of collisions on the network, but reduces overall system performance because every computer has to listen to what every other computer is doing. This type of access control is used in *AppleTalk* networks.

For more information, see the following sections:

- *CSMA/CD.* This is another type of access control.
- *AppleTalk.* This is the type of network that uses CSMA/CA.

C

CSMA/CD

70-058 Networking Essentials   *Standards and Terminology*

CSMA/CD, or Carrier Sense Multiple Access with Collision Detection, is a way to control access to the networking media and to keep multiple computers from communicating at the same time. In CSMA/CD, all computers on the network listen to the traffic on the network. When no other computer is communicating on the network, any computer can attempt to place data on the wire. When two computers try to communicate at the same time, a *collision* occurs. At that time, both computers stop transmitting. The computers then wait a random amount of time before retransmitting their data. The most common implementation of CSMA/CD is *Ethernet.*

For more information, see the following sections:

- *CSMA/CA.* This is another type of access control.
- *Ethernet.* This is a type of network that uses CSMA/CD.

CSNW

See *Client Services for NetWare.*

D

Data Link control

See *OSI Model.*

Data Link layer

See *OSI Model.*

Date/Time Control Panel

70-067 NT Server (Core)   *Installation and Configuration*

The Date/Time Control Panel is used to adjust the time, date, and time zone in which your computer is currently located. This Control Panel offers two tabs: Date & Time and Time Zone.

On the Date & Time tab, you can adjust the day, month, year, hour, and minute. The time you put in here is synchronized with the computer's onboard clock and calendar. On the Time Zone tab, you can select the time zone the computer currently resides in. This number is based on Greenwich Mean Time, or GMT.

For more information, see the following sections:

■ *Control Panels.* This section contains a list of all of the Control Panels normally installed on a *Windows NT* machine.

■ *Net command.* The NETTIME command can be used to set the system time.

device driver

General information pertaining to all tests

A device driver is software that enables a specific piece of hardware to communicate with the *operating system.* Although a device is installed on a system, it will not be able to communicate with the system until the driver has been installed. With *Windows NT,* every driver that is listed in the Hardware Compatibility List, or *HCL,* is shipped with Windows NT or in a Service Pack. In some cases, the driver is included with the hardware when it is purchased. Device drivers are installed via the *Control Panel* that corresponds to the device being installed. For example, to install a sound card driver, you would use the *Multimedia Devices Control Panel.*

For more information, see the following sections:

■ *Control Panels.* This section contains a list of Windows NT Control Panels.

■ *HCL.* This is a list of all hardware that has been approved for use with Windows NT.

Devices Control Panel

70-067   NT Server (Core)   *Installation and Configuration*

The Devices Control Panel is used to start, stop, and adjust the startup of parameters for device drivers on the computer. The Status column of the *Control Panel* indicates whether the driver is started. When configuring a device driver, you can choose from five options that control how the driver starts:

■ **Boot.** Drivers that are essential to the operation of the system are marked as "boot'" and are started every time the computer starts. These drivers start during the boot process.

■ **System.** Drivers marked as "system" start every time the system starts, after the boot devices start. This option is used for devices that are essential to system operation.

■ **Automatic.** These drivers start when the system starts, after the boot and system devices start. Devices marked as "automatic" are not critical for basic system operation.

■ **Manual.** Devices marked as "manual" must be started by a user or a dependent device.

■ **Disabled.** Devices marked as "disabled" cannot be started by users, although the system can still start disabled devices.

For more information, see the section titled *device drivers*. Device drivers are small applications written to interact with the system to enable access to hardware.

DHCP

70-067   NT Server (Core)   *Installation and Configuration*
70-059   TCP/IP   *Dynamic Host Configuration Protocol*

DHCP (the Dynamic Host Configuration Protocol) allows you to set up a network without having to manually configure and reconfigure all *TCP/IP* parameters. Using DHCP greatly reduces the overhead of administering a TCP/IP network. When properly set up, DHCP allows *administrators* to greatly reduce the number of errors that can occur on a TCP/IP network. The administrator simply sets up a range of *IP addresses* that the clients are allowed to use (called a DHCP scope) and then activates it. When a DHCP client computer is turned on, it asks a DHCP server to assign, or lease it, an IP address.

Benefits of DHCP

DHCP offers network administrators several benefits in addition to centralized administration. Those benefits are listed here.

■ DHCP eliminates clerical errors associated with manually setting up every workstation in a network with a hard-coded IP address.

■ A single DHCP server will not lease the same address to multiple clients on the network. This eliminates duplicate IP address errors.

■ The systems administrator can reconfigure the IP scheme of the entire network from a central location using the DHCP Manager. The administrator can also verify the address of any DHCP client on the network by using this utility.

- The administrator can control which IP addresses are issued to clients on a network by specifying which addresses are available in the scope.

- The DHCP server can also be configured to set options such as the *default gateway*, *WINS* server address, and *DNS* server address on client computers.

- IP addresses are leased to clients only for a limited amount of time. If the client does not renew its lease before the lease expires, the server reclaims the address and can issue it to another computer on the network.

- If a DHCP client is moved from one DHCP-enabled network to another, the DHCP server on the new network can reconfigure the client with the proper TCP/IP information.

How DHCP Works

A DHCP client uses a specific process to request an IP address from a DHCP server. The client computer is responsible for initiating the process and for asking for lease renewal. The following list outlines the process a client uses to request an address from a DHCP server:

1. When a DHCP client computer initializes its DHCP stack, it sends a broadcast called a DHCPDiscover packet to all computers on the network. This packet is what the client uses to request an IP address from any available DHCP servers.

2. When the server receives the DHCPDiscover packet, the server checks its database of possible IP addresses to find an available address. It then broadcasts an available IP address from its pool out to the network in the form of a DHCPOffer packet. If a network has multiple DHCP servers, it is possible for the client to receive more than one offer. Typically, the client accepts only the first offer it receives. The client is able to identify its DHCPOffer packet because the *MAC Address* of the requesting client is included in the DHCPOffer packet. If the client does not request the IP address that is included in the DHCPOffer, the server pulls back the offered IP address.

3. After the client receives the DHCPOffer packet, it sends a broadcast packet requesting the offered IP address. This packet is called a DHCPRequest, and it includes the IP address of the DHCP server from which it has accepted the DHCPOffer packet.

4. When the server receives the DHCPRequest packet, it rechecks the database for availability. If everything is in order, the server marks the address in its database as used and sends a broadcast packet containing the clientís MAC address, which is called a DHCPAck. The DHCPAck packet will contain any options that have been configured in the scope from which the IP address was leased. If, for any reason, the server cannot fill the request, it broadcasts a packet to the network denying the request. This denial packet is called a DHCPNack. If the request is denied, TCP/IP will be disabled on the client computer.

When the administrator sets up a DHCP scope, he or she specifies the lease duration. When 50 percent of the time allocated for the lease duration has passed, the client must send a DHCPRequest packet to the original DHCP server re-requesting the IP address that it has been assigned. If the server does not respond to the request, the client will wait until 87.5 percent of the time has passed, and then it will attempt to contact any DHCP server on the network to request an IP address. If 100 percent of the lease duration passes without the client renewing the lease or receiving a new one, the client will discontinue using the IP address and will have to begin the request process all over again.

For more information, see the following sections:

- *DHCP Relay Agent.* The server component that is responsible for transmitting DHCP requests and responses across routers.

- *DHCP Manager.* A tool that is used to configure DHCP scopes.
- *IP address.* An individual address that is assigned to every computer on a TCP/IP network.

DHCP Manager

| 70-067 | NT Server (Core) | *Installation and Configuration* |
| 70-059 | TCP/IP | *Dynamic Host Configuration Protocol* |

The DHCP Manager is an administrative utility that is installed when *DHCP* is installed on a server. This utility allows the administrator to add, modify, and delete available IP ranges, administer IP reservations, and view current leases.

For more information, see the following sections:

- *DHCP Relay Agent.* This is the server component that is responsible for transmitting DHCP requests and responses across routers.
- *DHCP.* This is a server component that can be used to dynamically assign IP addresses to clients.
- *IP address.* This is an individual address that is assigned to every computer on a TCP/IP network.

Dial-Up Networking

| 70-067 | NT Server (Core) | *Connectivity* |
| 70-073 | NT Workstation | *Connectivity* |

Dial-Up Networking is a feature of *Windows NT* that allows users to connect to a Windows NT server by using standard telephone lines and a modem. Connections are made to the server by using *PPP, SLIP,* or *PPTP.* Dial-Up Networking allows you to expand your network to any location that has access to telephone lines.

Dial-Up Networking is used for two major purposes. The first is to access an Internet service provider. The second is to access a remote Windows NT computer or domain. If you are setting up Dial-Up Networking to access an Internet service provider, it is important that you know you do not have to be dialing in to a Windows NT computer. As long as PPP or SLIP is supported, you will be able to access the computer.

Dialup Monitor Control Panel

| 70-067 | NT Server (Core) | *Installation and Configuration* |

The Dialup Monitor Control Panel is used to view statistics on devices installed on the computer that are set up for remote access. You can access the Dialup Monitor Control Panel by choosing **Start**, **Settings**, **Control Panel**. This opens the *Control Panel* window. Select **Dialup Monitor** to open the Dial-Up Networking Monitor.

The Dial-Up Networking Monitor offers three tabs. The first tab (**Status**) contains information about the device specified in the Device drop-down box. This information includes the current baud rate of the connection, the amount of time since the connection was established, and general statistics about the connection itself.

The **Summary** tab lists all the devices on the machine and the status of each. This list indicates which user is logged into which device and how long he or she has been logged in.

The **Preferences** tab allows you to set various options for all dial-up connections. This allows you to configure the computer to play a sound when a connection is made, when a connection is broken, when data is sent or received, and when line errors occur.

It is not recommended that you set the computer to play a sound when data is sent or received. If you do, the computer will constantly make sounds while you are logged on. The other option allows you to configure status lights for the *modem*. This displays an icon on the taskbar that flashes when data is sent or received.

digital volt meter
70-058 Networking Essentials · *Troubleshooting Equipment*

A digital volt meter is a piece of equipment that allows you to measure voltage or resistance across a connection. This tool is useful when trying to find a break or a short in a network cable.

Direct Memory Access

D

See *DMA.*

directory replication
70-067 NT Server (Core) *Installation and Configuration*

Directory replication is a service available on *Windows NT* that simplifies the task of moving updated copies of files from one location to another. The most common use of directory replication is to copy logon scripts from one *domain controller* to the other domain controllers in the network. Other uses would include distributing *user policies*, phone lists, help files, and any other important files. The originating computer in this scenario is called the export server, and the computer that receives the updates is the import server. Any Windows NT Server can be configured to act as both an export and an import server. *Windows NT Workstations* can be configured to act only as an import server.

Directory replication is carried out by the Directory Replicator service. This service must be running on any server that will be participating in replication. In order for computers to replicate data, the Directory Replicator service on all the computers must log into the domain using the same account. You can create an account using User Manager for Domains and assign it to the Administrators group on the computer.

Parameters used to control directory replication are found in the following *Registry* key:

```
HKEY_LOCAL_MACHINE\System\CurrentControlSet\Services\Replicator\Parameters
```

Most Registry key entries can be controlled by using Server Manager; however, two important ones cannot. The first is the Interval value. This value specifies the amount of time the export server waits before checking for changes to the files. This value ranges from 1 to 60 minutes, and the default is 5 minutes. The second entry not controlled via Server Manager is the GuardTime entry. This value specifies the amount of time the export server will wait until the contents of a directory are stable before replicating contents to the import servers. For example, if this value is set to 10, there can be no activity in the directory for 10 minutes before the contents are synced. The value for this can range from 0 to one-half of the Interval value.

By default, the directory on the export server that contains the files and directories to be replicated is `%Systemroot%\system32\repl\export`. When setting up replication, you must create a directory for each set of files that will be sent to the import server. The default directory that contains the replicated files and directories is `%Systemroot%\system32\repl\import`. Any directory that is created on the export server and is configured for export will be created on the import server before the files are copied. It is important to note that an export server can also be an import server.

The process of directory replication follows the format outlined here:

1. The export server monitors the export directory for changes. When changes occur, the export server notifies the import server that changes have occurred.

2. The import computer replies to the export server.

3. The import server reads the export directory on the export server and copies any files that have been updated or added since the last time replication occurred.

DirectX

General information pertaining to all tests

DirectX is a high-performance *API* that hides characteristics of the operating system and hardware from the application. This technology was designed to provide real-time response to the user interface, and it is commonly used by game developers. DirectX was designed for *Windows 95* but has been ported to *Windows NT* with some changes in implementation. For example, in Windows NT, applications do not communicate directly with the hardware; rather, they communicate directly with the *GDI*. Windows NT also supports DirectDraw, DirectSound, and DirectPlay.

Disk Administrator

70-067   NT Server (Core)   *Installation and Configuration*

The Disk Administrator is an application that is used to view information on and change configuration of hard disk drives in a computer. To use the Disk Administrator application, you must be logged in as a member of the Administrators local group. Disk Administrator has different implementations in *Windows NT* Server and *Windows NT Workstation*.

To start the Disk Administrator application, click **Start**, **Programs**, **Administrative Tools**, **Disk Administrator**. The first time you run the Disk Administrator, a specific message appears, indicating that a 32-bit identifier has not been written to the disk. This is a normal message, and you should click the **Yes** button.

After you select the **Yes** button, the application starts (see Figure D.1). This window outlines all the *hard drives* and the partitions they contain.

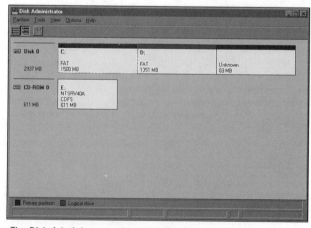

Figure D.1   The Disk Administrator shows all the drives installed in the computer, along with their partitions.

From within the Disk Administrator, you can partition hard drives, format hard drives, and assign drive letters as described in the following list. You can also set up *fault tolerance* on your hard drives.

- **Partitioning hard drives.** To partition a hard drive, choose any unpartitioned section on a hard drive and choose the **Create** option from the **Partition** menu. This opens a dialog box that allows you to specify the size of the partition.

- **Formatting hard drives.** To format a hard drive, choose any partitioned section of a hard drive and select the **Format** option from the **Tools** menu. This opens a dialog box that will allow you to specify the file system.

- **Assigning drive letters.** To assign a drive letter, choose any partitioned section of a hard drive and select the **Assign Drive Letter** option from the **Tools** menu.

D

disk duplexing

70-067   NT Server (Core)   *Installation and Configuration*

Disk duplexing, also known as RAID 1, is the process of duplicating all writes made to a single logical drive to two separate *hard drives* connected to different disk controllers. (This is very similar to *disk mirroring*.) Information is written to both drives in a duplexed set at the same time. All drives and partitions in a *Windows NT* Server can be duplexed, including the boot and system partitions. The biggest drawback to using RAID 1 is that it has the highest cost, per megabyte, of all the available fault-tolerance methods. This is because only 50 percent of the total available disk space can be used.

For more information, see the following sections:

- *RAID.* This is a fault tolerance scheme that is used to ensure that data remains available in the event of hard drive failure.

- *Disk Administrator.* This is the application that is used to configure disk mirroring.

- *Disk mirroring.* This is the process of disk duplexing using the same disk controller.

disk mirroring

70-067   NT Server (Core)   *Installation and Configuration*

Disk mirroring, also known as RAID 1, is the process of duplicating all writes made to a single logical drive to two separate *hard drives* connected to the same disk controller. Information is written to both drives in a mirror set at the same time. All drives and partitions in a *Windows NT* Server can be mirrored, including the *boot partition* and *system partition.* The biggest drawback to using RAID 1 is that it has the highest cost, per megabyte, of all available fault-tolerance methods. This is because only 50 percent of the total available disk space can be used.

For more information, see the following sections:

- *RAID.* This is a fault-tolerance scheme that is used to ensure that data remains available in the event of hard drive failure.

- *Disk Administrator.* This is the application that is used to configure disk mirroring.

- *Disk duplexing.* This is the process of disk mirroring using two different disk controllers.

disk striping

70-067   NT Server (Core)   *Installation and Configuration*

Disk striping, or RAID 0, is a process used to speed up disk operations. Even though this process is defined as RAID, it offers no fault tolerance. Disk striping divides the data into 64KB blocks and writes the data across different physical drives. A minimum of two *hard drives* is required, but you can have a maximum of 32 drives. The set of drives that you set up is known as a stripe set. The biggest limitation of using stripe sets is that neither the *system partition* nor the *boot partition* can be included in a stripe set.

For more information, see the following sections:

- *RAID*. This is a fault-tolerance scheme used to ensure that data remains available in the event of hard drive failure.

- *Disk Administrator*. This is the application used to configure disk mirroring.

display adapters

70-067   NT Server (Core)   *Installation and Configuration*

The display adapter is the hardware portion of the computer that writes information to the monitor of the computer. Display adapter drivers can be modified through the *Display Control Panel*.

Display Control Panel

70-067   NT Server (Core)   *Installation and Configuration*

The Display Control Panel is used to modify settings dealing with how the desktop looks. These settings include the system colors, desktop wallpaper, and screen resolution. To access the Display Control Panel, choose **Start**, **Settings**, **Control Panel**. This opens the *Control Panels* window, where you can choose the **Display Control Panel**.

The Display Control Panel offers four main tabs, but other tabs are added during the installation of other applications. The four main tabs are **Background**, **Screen Saver**, **Appearance**, and **Settings**.

The options on the **Background** tab control the picture that is displayed on your desktop. You can choose any of the default backgrounds installed with *Windows NT*, or you can choose any bitmap image on the system.

The options on the **Screen Saver** tab allow you to choose which screen saver you want to be displayed after a specified amount of time. You can also specify the amount of time that that the computer should wait before activating the screen saver and whether the screen saver is password protected. If you choose to password-protect your screen saver, it will be protected with the password you use to log in to Windows NT.

The options on the **Appearance** tab enable you to specify the colors in which all windows will be displayed. Either you can specify a color scheme that already exists in Windows NT, or you can create your own scheme by choosing different items and then selecting the colors you want them to be.

The **Settings** tab contains options with which you can choose the screen resolution, the number of colors displayed, and the refresh rate. From this section, you can also change the display adapter by clicking on the **Display Adapter** button.

DLC protocol

70-058   Networking Essentials   *Transport Protocols*

The DLC protocol is a session layer protocol used in Windows NT to provide access to Hewlett-Packard JetDirect print servers. It can also be used to provide connectivity to mainframe computers.

DLL

General information pertaining to all tests

A DLL, or dynamic link library, is a specific executable routine or set of routines that are stored separately from regular executable programs. This allows these routines to be called from multiple applications and to be loaded into memory only when needed.

DMA

General information pertaining to all tests

DMA, or Direct Memory Access, is a specific address in memory that applications can write to in order to access peripheral devices without having to involve the computer's processor.

D

DNS

70-059   TCP/IP   *Domain Name Service*

DNS, or Domain Name Service, is the most common method of resolving host names into addresses on a *TCP/IP* network. DNS is used on the Internet for name resolution and will replace *WINS* in Windows NT 5.0.

DNS is a hierarchical database, much like a directory structure. This means that the server will resolve the most general portion of the name first, followed by the next-specific, followed by the most-specific. DNS has several top-level *domains*, which are represented by the most general portion of the name. Those top-level domains are controlled by the Internet Network Information Center, also known as the *InterNIC*. Table D.1 outlines the top-level domains.

Table D.1   **Top Level Domains**

Name	Organization Type
arpa	Reverse DNS servers
com	Commercial organizations and businesses
edu	Educational institutions
gov	Nonmilitary government institutions
mil	Military organizations
net	Internet backbones and Internet service providers
org	Not-for-profit organizations
xx	Two-letter country code

When referring to a computer on the Internet, you use the *fully qualified domain name*, or FQDN, of the computer you are trying to reach. This name is usually comprised of a top-level domain identifier (as listed in Table D.1), a domain name, and a host name, which are separated by periods. Take, for example, the FQDN www.mcp.com. When you refer to www.mcp.com, you are referring to one specific computer on the Internet, but each portion of the name from right to left is more specific in designating the computer.

How DNS Works

When a client computer attempts to contact an IP host by name, it must first get the actual address of the host. It does so by querying a name server. During this process, the client computer is referred to as the "resolver."

When querying the name server, the resolver can use three types of queries: a recursive query, an iterative query, or an inverse query. When responding to a request, the name server will send one of three items: a success message containing the *IP address*, a pointer to another name server, or a failure message.

A recursive query is the most common type of query. This type of query forces the name server to return either the address requested by the client or a failure message. If the name server does not have the address of the host that is requested by the resolver, it must communicate with other DNS servers to attempt to find the name. When the name server receives the host address, it returns that address to the client.

An iterative query is one in which the queried name server is expected to respond with whatever information it has in its local files or from names that it has cached from recursive queries. If it does not have the information the client requests, it returns either a referral to another DNS server or a host name not found error. This process is something like detective work. For example, suppose a client computer requests the address www.123xyz.com. The client sends an iterative query to DNS Server 1. If DNS Serer 1 does not have the address, it tells the client that it doesn't have it but suggests that the client check the .com root server. The client then sends an iterative query to the .com root server asking for www.123xyz.com. The server might respond by telling the client that it does not have the address to www.123xyz.com but giving it the address of the 123xyz.com DNS server. The client can then request the address from the 123xyz.com server. This type of request is typically used by a DNS server to resolve a name for a client that requested information with a recursive query.

The last type of request is an inverse request. In this case, the client computer asks for the host name that corresponds to a specific IP address. To keep the DNS server from having to search the entire database to find the correct name, a special domain name is created. This domain name is called in-addr.arpa. In this structure, nodes are named after IP addresses and then associated with names.

Record Types

Each computer in the DNS database is assigned a record type that indicates what type of host it is. Frequently, these record types simply say that a certain name is associated with a certain IP address. In other instances, the record type specifies that a specific host performs a specific job. Some of the more frequently used record types are outlined in Table D.2.

Table D.2   **Frequently Used DNS Record Types**

Record Type	Description
SOA	The SOA record is the "Start of Authority" record for the domain. This specifies where the primary DNS server for a domain resides. This record also describes the Time to Live for DNS records.
NS	A "Name Server" record specifies the location of other name servers that maintain a copy of the zone information.
A	An "Address" record is a host record. A host record is the actual IP address of a specified host name. Most records in the database are host records.
CNAME other	A "Canonical Name" record is an alias record. These records outline names by which a specific host can be called. For example, a host with the name mailserver.123xyz.com may be aliased to email.123xyz.com.
MX	A "Mail Exchange" record specifies the name of the host that handles all the email in the domain. If a domain has multiple mail servers, each mail server can be assigned a preference number, with the first server having the lowest number.
PTR	A "Pointer" record maps an IP address to a host name in a DNS reverse lookup zone.

For more information, see the following sections:

■ *NSLOOKUP.* This is a command line utility used to view DNS information.

■ *DNS Manager.* This utility is used to administer a Windows NT Server on which the DNS service is installed.

DNS Manager

70-059 TCP/IP   *Domain Name Service*

The DNS Manager is used to add and modify DNS zones on Microsoft's *DNS* server. The application allows you to add the full range of record types to the DNS databases and eliminates the need to manually edit the files. This application is also used to create primary and secondary zones on your Windows NT DNS server.

domain

70-067 NT Server (Core)   *Installation and Configuration*

A domain is a logical grouping of users and computers for administrative reasons. These computers all share a common security accounts database and can all be administered as a group. Any user that has an account in the domain can log in to any computer in the domain.

For more information, see the following sections:

■ *PDC.* This is the first computer installed in a *Windows NT* domain, and it contains the master copy of the security accounts database.

■ *BDC.* This is a computer used to provide backup to the PDC.

domain controller

70-067 NT Server (Core)   *Installation and Configuration*

In a Windows NT *domain,* a domain controller is a computer set up to authenticate user logins and maintain a copy of the security policy and accounts database for the domain. Only *Windows NT* Servers can act as domain controllers.

For more information, see the following sections:

■ *PDC.* This is the first computer installed in a Windows NT domain, and it contains the master copy of the security accounts database.

■ *BDC.* This is a computer used to provide backup to the PDC.

Domain Name Service

See *DNS.*

DOS

General information pertaining to all tests

DOS is an older 16-bit text-based operating system that was used before the release of Windows 95. DOS stands for "disk operating system."

D

Dr. Watson

70-067 NT Server (Core)	*Troubleshooting*
70-068 NT Server Enterprise	*Troubleshooting*

Dr. Watson is an application used by *Windows NT* to detect and diagnose application errors. It logs the information for use by technical support people. When a program error occurs, Dr. Watson automatically starts logging information about the system, running tasks, function information, and a stack dump. This information can then be sent to technical support to assist in diagnosing the error.

drive partition

70-067 NT Server (Core)	*Installation and Configuration*

A drive partition is a section of a *hard drive* that can be formatted, assigned a drive letter, and accessed. A hard drive can contain no more than four partitions. Each partition can be formatted with a different file system. There are two type of partitions: primary and extended.

- **Primary partition.** A primary partition is one that cannot be subpartitioned into smaller drives. A drive can have up to four primary partitions.

- **Extended partition.** An extended partition is one that can be partitioned into smaller logical drives. You can have only one extended partition per hard drive, and a primary partition does not have to be present to create extended partitions. If a drive has an extended partition, only three primary partitions can be created on the drive.

For more information, see the section titled *Disk Administrator*, which describes the tool used to partition hard drives.

dual boot

70-073 NT Workstation	*Installation and Implementation*

A dual-boot system is one that can boot more than one operating system. For example, a system could have both *Windows 95* and *Windows NT* installed. When the system is first started, a menu appears asking which operating system to start.

For more information, see the following sections:

- *BOOT.INI.* This file is used to determine which operating system is started.

- *Boot process, Intel.* This is the process that Intel-based computers use to boot.

Dump Check utility

70-068 NT Server Enterprise	*Troubleshooting*

The Dump Check utility is used to verify that a memory dump file is created successfully and correctly. This utility checks and displays basic information about the file itself and then verifies all the memory addresses in the file. If it finds any errors in the file, it displays them.

The Dump Check utility is a command-line application. The syntax of the command is

```
dumpchk [-?][-p][-v][-q] CrashDumpFile
```

with the following options:

Option	Description
-?	Displays the help file
-p	Prints the header information only; does not check the file

-v   Specifies verbose checking mode

-q   Performs a quick test

Dump Exam utility

70-068 NT Server Enterprise   *Troubleshooting*

The Dump Exam utility examines a memory dump file, extracts information from it, and writes it to a text file. You can then use this text file to try to determine the reason for the STOP error that created the memory dump file. The Dump Exam utility is a command-line application that requires three files to run:

- DUMPEXAM.EXE.

- IMAGEHLP.DLL.

- KDEXT*XXX*.DLL. This file is platform-specific, and the last three characters indicate the platform. For example, the file for an Intel-based system would be called kdextx86.dll.

The syntax of command for the Dump Exam utility is

```
dumpexam.exe [-?][-p][-v] -f filename -y path
```

with the following options:

Option	Action
-?	Displays the command syntax
-p	Prints the header only
-v	Specifies verbose mode
-f filename	Specifies the output filename and path
-y path	Sets the symbol search path

Dynamic Host Configuration Protocol

See *DHCP.*

dynamic link library

See *DLL.*

E

electromagnetic interference

See *EMI*.

E

Emergency Repair Disk

See *ERD*.

EMI

70-058   Networking Essentials   *Standards and Terminology*

EMI, or electromagnetic interference, is some sort of outside electrical interference that interrupts and distorts the signal that is being sent on the network cable. This can occur when network cables are run too close to items that are considered to be electrically noisy. Examples of electrically noisy items would include fluorescent lights and electrical motors. *UTP* cabling is one of the most susceptible forms of network media that can be affected by EMI.

encapsulation

70-058   Networking Essentials   *Standards and Terminology*

Encapsulation is the process of placing information of one type into a container of another type. For example, when using *PPP*, network data that is being sent is encapsulated into PPP for transmission over serial lines. When the data reaches the destination, it is decapsulated, and the original network packet is released on the destination network. This also is what allows the PPP protocol to work with the other *protocols* that it supports. All traffic that is being sent is encapsulated in a PPP packet and, when it arrives at the final destination, is removed from the PPP packet.

encryption

General information pertaining to all tests

Encryption is the process of scrambling data for transmission over network media. Encryption requires that both the sending party and the receiving party have the key that is used to unscramble the data. Encryption algorithms are often extremely complicated mathematical formulas.

ERD

70-067   NT Server (Core)   *Troubleshooting*

An ERD, or Emergency Repair Disk, is a disk that is first created during the installation process and that contains compressed versions of the computer's *Registry*, a list of files installed on the computer, and copies of the *VDM* versions of the AUTOEXEC.BAT and CONFIG.SYS files. These files are also stored in the <winnt_root>\repair directory on the computer. The ERD can also be created after the installation process is complete. An ERD is used in extreme circumstances when a *Windows NT* computer has crashed. You should not always rely on the files in the repair directory being available to you. For example, if you do not have a current ERD and the drive where the repair directory resides crashes, you have no way to recover. After you have created an ERD, you should label it well and put it in a safe place. Never assume that end users will keep this disk safe. Another important thing to remember is that you need to periodically update the ERD, especially before you make such changes to the computer as installing new hardware or software.

RDISK.EXE

The RDISK utility is used to create and update both the ERD and the repair directory. To start RDISK.EXE, click on the **Start** button, choose **Run,** and type **RDISK**. This starts the RDISK utility, shown in Figure E.1. This utility allows you to choose two options, **Update** or **Repair**.

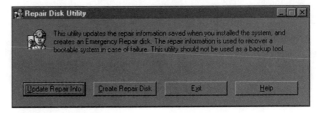

Figure E.1   The RDISK utility allows you to update the information in the repair directory and to create a new emergency repair disk.

Update Repair Info

As backward as it seems, the first part of the utility that you need to run is the Update Repair Info. This option updates the information in the repair directory. After you run this, you will be prompted to update or create an ERD. You should always update the repair directory before creating the ERD to ensure that the disk will be created with the most updated information.

Create Repair Disk

If you are certain that the information in the repair directory is current, you can choose to create an ERD without first updating the repair information. You do not have to format the disk before starting the Create Repair Disk process; RDISK will format the disk for you. If the quantity of information on the disk grows too large for one disk, RDISK will prompt you to insert another.

The biggest issue with using RDISK to create an ERD is that it will not update any of the *Registry* information on the disk or in the repair directory. This is especially troublesome because user account information is not updated. In order to update account information, you must run the RDISK utility with the /S switch, which backs up the *SAM* and security hives of the Registry. /S is an undocumented switch that can take a long time to run if you have a large number of accounts. During the recovery process, *Windows NT* will use this to rebuild the accounts database.

Ethernet

70-058   Networking Essentials   *Standards and Terminology*

Ethernet is one of the most widely implemented network topologies, which was originally developed jointly by Digital, Intel, and Xerox. This standard went on to be the basis
of *IEEE 802.3*, which is the basis of most networks. In most cases, Ethernet networks
use bus physical topologies, although some use a *star* physical topology and a *bus* logical
topology. Ethernet networks run at either 10 or 100 megabits per second and are best
suited for light-to-medium traffic networks.

Ethernet utilizes a mechanism known as *CSMA/CD*, or Carrier Sense Multiple
Access with Collision Detection, to reduce collisions on the network. A *collision* occurs
when two computers attempt to communicate on the network at the same time, and
their packets interfere with each other. With CSMA/CD, all computers listen to the network before they transmit data. If there is traffic on the network, the computer waits
until the network has quieted down before it transmits. While the computer is transmitting, it continues to listen on the network. If the computer detects another signal on the
network that interferes with its own, it stops transmitting and waits a random amount of
time before attempting to transmit again.

For more information regarding Ethernet, see the following sections:

■ *100BASE-X*

■ *10BASE2* ✓

■ *10BASE5* ✓

■ *10BASE-F*

■ *10BASE-T* ✓

■ *10BROAD36*

■ *100VG-AnyLAN*

■ *CSMA-CD.* A mechanism for controlling access to the network.

■ *Bus.* A topology in which all devices are connected on a common shared cable.

■ *Star topology.* A topology in which all devices are connected to a central *hub.*

event log

70-067   NT Server (Core)   *Troubleshooting*

The event log is a *service* that runs on Windows NT to capture and log information
about system, application, and security events. The information in these logs is extremely
important during the troubleshooting process. This information is read by using the *Event
Viewer.*

For more information regarding event logs, see the following sections:

■ *System log.* Gathers information about Windows NT itself.

■ *Application log.* Gathers information about Windows NT–compatible applications
running on the computer.

■ *Audit log.* Gathers information about successful and failed audits.

Event Viewer

70-067 NT Server (Core)   *Troubleshooting*

The Event Viewer, shown in Figure E.2, is used to view log information gathered by the *event log service*. The Event Viewer is usually the first application you should check when you begin to troubleshoot a server. You start this application by clicking **Start**, **Programs**, **Administrative Tools**, **Event Viewer**. The Event Viewer application offers three sections of information: the *System log*, the *Security log,* and the *Application log*.

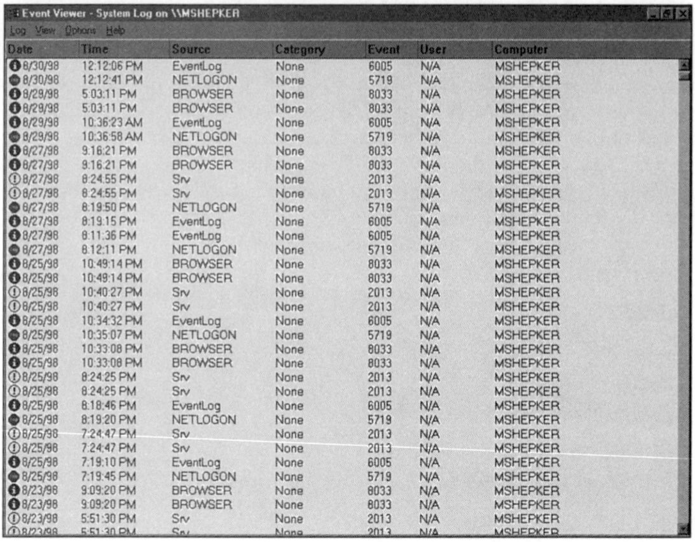

Figure E.2   The Event Viewer enables you to view log information gathered by the event log service.

Exchange Server

General information pertaining to all tests

Exchange Server is Microsoft's messaging and collaboration BackOffice product for messaging and collaboration. Exchange can be installed only on a Windows NT Server computer. This product offers the following features:

- **Email.** Exchange supports the transfer of information by using email. This functionality includes the ability to transfer, deliver, and route messages, as well as maintain your own personal address book. This service also allows you to attach files that are to be transmitted with the email.

- **Scheduling.** Exchange supports the ability that enables users to manage time, organize tasks, and coordinate meetings with other users.

- **Group information sharing.** Exchange supports the ability that enables users to post information to an electronic bulletin board, track customer information, share contact and phone lists, and access information from shared databases. This functionality is implemented by using public folders.

- **Programmability.** Exchange supports the ability that enables users to create custom applications that allow the tracking of business processes, vacation requests, and maintenance requests.

Executive Services

70-067   NT Server (Core)   *Installation and Configuration*

The *Windows NT* Executive Services consist of several services available to all components of the *operating system.* This layer of the executive is called the System Services. Each service is managed by one of the following separate portions of the executive:

- I/O Manager
- Object Manager
- Security Reference Monitor
- Process Manager
- Local Procedure Call facility
- Virtual Memory Manager
- Window Manager
- Graphics Device Interface
- Graphics device drivers

E

FAT

FAT is a type of file system based on a file allocation table. This table maintains and tracks the status of segments of drive space that are used for file storage. This form of file system is useful when you are working with other operating systems. FAT is compatible with MS-DOS, *Windows 95*, *Windows for Workgroups*, and *OS/2*.

When you're planning how you are going to set up a *Windows NT* system, consider using FAT on drive partitions that are going to be smaller than 500 megabytes because a large amount of overhead is required to use *NTFS* on smaller partitions.

For more information, see the following sections:

- *FAT32*. This is another implementation of FAT that supports larger partition sizes.

- *NTFS*. This is another type of file system that is recommended for use with Windows NT.

- Appendix A, which includes a comparison table of FAT, FAT32, and NTFS.

FAT32

General information pertaining to all tests

FAT32 is a new implementation of the *FAT* system. This implementation was first shipped with *Windows 95* OSR2 and was shipped as part of Windows 98. This file system was created to extend the amount of space that could be used on a single partition. FAT32 makes better use of disk space because it uses smaller cluster sizes. FAT32 is not compatible with current versions of *Windows NT*; however, it will be supported when Service Pack 4 is released.

fault tolerance

Fault tolerance ensures that data will remain available in the event of hardware failure. Fault tolerance is implemented in *Windows NT* by using *RAID* to protect data that is being written to the *hard drives*. Fault tolerance can be set up using the *Disk Administrator* application. Windows NT's software fault tolerance supports only RAID 1 and RAID 5.

For more information, see the following sections:

- *RAID*. This is a fault-tolerance scheme that is used to ensure that data remains available in the event of hard drive failure.

- *Disk Administrator*. This is the application that is used to implement fault tolerance.

FDDI

70-058 Networking Essentials   *WAN Transmission Technologies*

FDDI, or Fiber Distributed Data Interface, is a specification that allows for 100Mbps data transfer rates over a token passing *fiber* ring. FDDI supports up to 500 computers, but FDDI rings are limited to 100 kilometers.

Although FDDI utilizes a *token-passing* scheme to communicate, there is a big difference in practice. When a computer in an FDDI network receives the token, it can transmit as many frames of data as it can in a specific amount of time before the token is released.

FDDI operates on what is known as a dual-ring topology. The two rings provide redundancy as a safety precaution in case one of the rings goes down. The main ring is known as the primary ring, and the backup ring is known as the secondary ring. Data flows in opposite directions around these rings.

For more information, see the following section:

■ *Fiber-optic cable.* This is the type of transmission medium used in FDDI.

F

fiber

See *fiber-optic cable.*

Fiber Distributed Data Interface

See *FDDI.*

fiber-optic cable

70-058 Networking Essentials   *Networking Media*

Fiber-optic cable is an excellent cable for data transmission. This type of cable supports very long runs, allows for extremely high bandwidth, and is not susceptible to electromagnetic interference. The biggest disadvantages to using fiber-optic cable are that it is extremely expensive and difficult to install.

The structure of fiber-optic cable, as shown in Figure F.1, is different than that of any other form of transmission media because it lacks a conductor (in the traditional sense). Instead of using a metallic wire that conducts electrical pulses, fiber-optic cable transmits signals in the form of light pulses down a highly refined glass or plastic strand called a fiber. A glass core will support longer cabling distances, but plastic cores are easier to work with. Surrounding the fiber core is a coating that is known as "cladding." Cladding reflects stray signals back into the fiber to reduce signal loss. Finally, a plastic jacket covers and protects the fiber. Some forms of fiber-optic cable have a layer of gel between the cladding and the jacket. This type of cable is known as loose cable. Another form of cable, known as tight cable, has a layer of wire braid between the cladding and the jacket. As mentioned previously, fiber-optic cable does not transmit electrical signals. Instead, the data is converted into light pulses by some sort of device, such as a laser or light-emitting diode (LED). After the light pulses are transmitted over the fiber, the light is converted back into data on the other end.

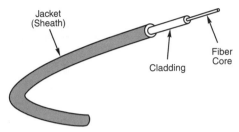

Figure F.1   Fiber-optic cable is used to transmit data signals over long distances.

File Transfer Protocol

See *FTP*.

File Transfer Protocol service

See *FTP service*.

firewall

70-058   Networking Essentials   *General Information*

A firewall is a computer or *router* commonly used to protect a private network from unauthorized access via the Internet. The firewall handles requests from the client computers on the private network and passes packets back and forth between the two networks.

Fonts Control Panel

70-067   NT Server (Core)   *Installation and Configuration*

The Fonts Control Panel enables you to add, remove, and display fonts that are on your system. This *Control Panel* looks very similar to a regular Explorer window. To display any of the fonts listed in the windows, simple double-click it to access a window displaying all the characters in the font at different sizes. To remove a font, click it and press the **Delete** key. This deletes the font and removes all references to it from the system. To install a font, open the **File** menu and select **Install New Font....** In the dialog box that appears, find the file on your *hard drive*, install the font, and copy it to the Fonts folder.

FQDN

See *fully qualified domain name*.

frame relay

70-058   Networking Essentials   *WAN Technologies*

Frame relay is a high-speed packet-switching technology that evolved from *X.25*. This type of technology is frequently used to connect remote branches of a company. It requires a frame-capable router to route data from the server to the client.

Frame relay creates permanent virtual circuits, supplying permanent connections for WANs. Frame relay typically supports transfer speeds ranging from 56Kbps to 1.544Mbps. When a customer purchases frame relay service, he or she typically purchases an amount of bandwidth. This amount of bandwidth is known as a "committed information rate," or CIR, which is the amount of bandwidth that the customer is always able to access. Sometimes the carrier allows the customer to use more bandwidth when he needs it. This is known as "bursting to another bandwidth."

For more information regarding frame relay, see the section on *X.25*, which is the protocol that frame relay evolved from.

frame types

70-058 Networking Essentials   *Standards and Terminology*

A frame is a single piece of information transmitted on a network. Two basic frames types are used in most networks: *Ethernet* frames and token-ring frames.

Ethernet Frames

An Ethernet frame is a package of data being transmitted as a logical unit. A frame can be anywhere from 64 to 1,518 bytes long. The frame itself uses 18 bytes of this space, leaving the remaining bytes for data. Every frame has the same basic configuration, as outlined in Table F.1.

Table F.1   **Parts of an Ethernet Frame**

Field	Contents
Preamble	The preamble marks the start of the frame.
Destination	This is the physical address of the computer that is to receive the frame.
Source	This is the physical address of the computer that sent the frame.
Type	This marks the type of protocol being used.
Data	This is the data being sent.
Cyclic Redundancy Check (CRC)	This is an error-checking field used to check the frame to ensure that it arrived intact.

Token-Ring Frames

Like Ethernet frames, all token-ring frames also have the same basic layout. The frame can be anywhere from 512 to 4,096 bytes long. A token-ring frame has a many more parts than an Ethernet frame. The parts of the token-ring frame are outlined in Table F.2.

Table F.2   **Parts of a Token-Ring Frame**

Field	Contents
Start Delimiter	This field indicates the start of the frame.
Access Control	This field indicates the frame priority and tells all other systems whether it is a token or a standard frame.
Frame Control	This field contains the MAC address of the end station.
Destination Address	This contains the physical address of the computer that is to receive the frame.
Source Address	This contains the physical address of the computer that sent the frame.
Data	This is the data being sent.
Frame Check Sequence	This is the error-checking information.
End Delimiter	This indicates the end of the frame.
Frame Status	This tells the sending computer whether the frame was recognized or copied or the destination address was not available.

FTP

70-059 TCP/IP   *Connectivity Utilities*

FTP (File Transfer Protocol) is a service used to transfer files between local and remote computers. This protocol is especially useful for transferring files from one environment, such as *UNIX*, to another, such as *Windows NT*. FTP supports bidirectional transfer of both ASCII and binary files. A text-based FTP client is installed when you install *TCP/IP* on a client machine. Commands are transferred to the FTP server by using TCP port 20, and information is transferred by using TCP port 21.

For more information regarding FTP, see the section entitled *FTP service*, which describes the service that enables Windows NT to act as an FTP server.

FTP service

70-059 TCP/IP   *Connectivity Utilities*

The FTP service is the service that enables Windows NT to act as an FTP server. An FTP server allows a client computer to connect, request files, and transfer new files to the server. The FTP service is installed when you install Internet Information Server (*IIS*).

For more information, see the following sections:

- *FTP.* This explains how FTP works.

- *IIS.* This describes the Internet Information Server and how it interacts with Windows NT.

fully qualified domain name

70-059 TCP/IP   *Host Name Resolution*

A fully qualified domain name, or *FQDN*, is the format in which *TCP/IP* host names are designated. An FQDN is usually made up of three parts: a host name, a *domain* name, and a top-level domain designator, all of which are separated by periods.

For example, consider the address www.mcp.com. In this address, www is the host name, mcp is the domain name, and com is the top-level domain designator. When a user browses the Internet, the FQDN is passed to a *DNS* server, which returns the *IP address* of the computer.

F

G

Gateway Services for NetWare

Gateway Services for NetWare, or GSNW, is a service that is available only on *Windows NT* Servers that allow client computers to connect to resources available on *Novell NetWare* servers. Clients that are not running a NetWare client can access the resources as if they are accessing Windows NT resources.

A computer running GSNW is a useful solution when you need to provide occasional access to resources on a NetWare server. GSNW is not designed to provide a high-volume solution for a busy network. All clients that access the NetWare resources do so over a single network connection. Consequently, performance decreases as network activity increases.

GSNW is a network service installed through the Network Control Panel. In addition, the *NWLink IPX/SPX* protocol must be installed on the server in order for GSNW to work. Before you can use GSNW, you must create a group called NTGATEWAY, create a user account on the NetWare servers, and assign the user account to the NTGATEWAY group. This account will be used by the Windows NT Server. It is important to note that the most restrictive rights that are assigned to the share are used.

gateway

A gateway is—in its simplest form—a link to another network. A gateway can take different forms depending on the network. On a *TCP/IP* network, this is referred to as a *default gateway*. Another type of gateway is *Gateway Services for NetWare*. In all references, a gateway is a computer or other piece of hardware that connects different types of networks and routes information between them. Some gateways also translate the communications protocols from one network to those of another.

For example, in the case of a default gateway on a TCP/IP network, there is no translation of communications *protocols*. Rather, when the client computer detects that the destination computer does not reside on the local network, it sends the packets to the default gateway. The default gateway then sends the packets to the destination network. For more information regarding gateways, see the following sections:

- *Gateway Services for NetWare*. This service is used to translate requests from Windows NT machines to Novell computers.

- *Default gateway*. This is a portion of the TCP/IP protocol that routes packets from one network to another.

GDI

70-067   NT Server (Core)   *Installation and Configuration*

The GDI, or *Graphical Display Interface*, is a portion of the Windows NT *Executive Services* that displays graphics on the monitor and the *printer*. The GDI provides a standard set of functions that allows applications to communicate with the hardware without knowing anything about the actual devices. This enables developers to create code that is independent of the capabilities of the hardware. Instead of communicating with the drivers themselves, the applications communicate with the GDI, and the GDI communicates with the hardware through the device drivers. Depending on the capabilities of the device driver, the GDI might change the messages that it sends.

For example, suppose an application calls for a square to be drawn on the screen. The GDI receives the request and sends it on to the *video driver*. With one video adapter, the GDI may need to send only a single command, through the video driver, that calls for it to draw a square. However, another video adapter may require the GDI to tell it, again through the video adapter, to draw each individual pixel in the square. The reason this is important is that it does not require different programming on the part of the application developer. The developer simply tells the GDI that it needs a square, and the GDI takes care of the rest.

For more information regarding GDI, see the following sections:

- *Video adapter.* This is a piece of hardware that allows the computer to communicate with the monitor.

- *Video driver.* This is a piece of software that enables Windows NT to communicate with the video adapter.

global accounts

70-067   NT Server (Core)   *Managing Resources*

Windows NT offers two types of user accounts: global and *local accounts*. A normal *user account* is commonly a global account. This type of account crosses over into other *domains* when a *trust* is created (which allows a user to have only one account in one domain that allows access to any other domain that trusts the domain where his or her account is located).

For more information regarding global accounts, see the following sections:

- *Local accounts.* A local account is a special type of account used to provide access to users in untrusted domains.

- *Local groups.* Used to assign permissions to users.

- *Global groups.* Used to group users into manageable groups.

global groups

70-067   NT Server (Core)   *Managing Resources*

As is true of user accounts, two types of groups are available on a *Windows NT* system: global and *local groups*. A global group is a collection of users that can cross *domains* in a trust relationship. Global groups cannot be created on *Windows NT* Server member servers of *Windows NT Workstation*. They can be created and maintained only in the account databases that are stored on primary and backup domain controllers (*PDC/BDC*). These groups are used only to group users together. To assign permissions, you should assign the global groups to local groups and then assign permissions to the local groups.

It is important to note that local groups cannot be placed into global groups, and global groups cannot be placed into other global groups.

Gopher service
70-067   NT Server (Core)   *Installation and Configuration*

Installed with *Internet Information Server* version 3.0 and earlier, Gopher is a service that is used to search and retrieve files from Gopher servers. With the release of *IIS* 4.0, the Gopher service is not supported. If it is present on a machine when IIS 4.0 is installed, it is removed from the server.

This utility was designed to overcome most of the limitations of the *FTP service*. Compared to the FTP service, the Gopher server's interface is easier to use, and one Gopher server can link to other Gopher servers for access to other files and to create custom menus. Gopher is the precursor of the World Wide Web.

For more information regarding Gopher, see the following sections:

- *FTP service.* This service enables a user to transfer files from one machine type to another across the Internet.

- *Web services.* Web services enable clients to connect to a server and receive Web pages.

graphics device drivers
70-067   NT Server (Core)   *Installation and Configuration*

Graphics device drivers are *DLLs* that contain functions that allow the *GDI* to communicate with output devices including monitors, *printers*, and fax machines. *Video drivers* and printer drivers are the most common types of graphics device drivers.

Graphical Display Interface
See *GDI.*

Graphical User Interface
See *GUI.*

ground loop
70-058   Networking Essentials

Ground loops can occur when network cables are connected between two buildings, and the ground potentials between the two buildings differ. When differences exist, the current flows through the grounding conductor of the cable. When current flows through the ground conductor of a cable, a ground loop occurs. Ground loops can result in electrical instability and various other anomalies. One way to help eliminate ground loops is to use *fiber-optic cable* to connect the buildings.

GUI

70-067   NT Server (Core)   *Installation and Configuration*

A GUI (*Graphical User Interface*) is a display format in which buttons, graphics, and icons represent specific application functions. In order to run one of these functions, the user clicks on the button or icon with the mouse. The biggest advantage of using a GUI interface to an application as opposed to command-line execution is that GUI interfaces are more intuitive and easier to use. *Windows NT* and *Windows 95* are examples of GUI-based operating systems.

G

h-node

70-059 TCP/IP   *Windows Internet Name Service*

H-node name resolution is a *NetBIOS* over *TCP/IP* implementation that uses a name
service provider (such as a *WINS* server) first, and then if the service provider is unavailable, broadcasts for name resolution. When registering hostnames on the network,
H-node clients attempt to contact the WINS server first, and then if the WINS server
is unavailable, resort to broadcasts.

For more information regarding H-node, see the following sections:

- *B-node*
- *M-node*
- *P-node*
- *NetBIOS name resolution.* The process by which *Windows NT* computers resolve
  host names.

HAL

70-067 NT Server (Core)   *Installation and Configuration*

The HAL, or *Hardware Abstraction Layer*, is a library of hardware manipulation routines
that lies at the lowest level of the Windows NT Executive. This layer hides the characteristics of different hardware platforms from the *operating system*, enabling the operating system to run on different platforms with different processors. In essence, the HAL makes
all processor architectures and platforms look identical to the operating system.

All components of the operating system and user applications manipulate the hardware through the HAL; no application can access hardware directly. One version of the
HAL is installed when *Windows NT* is first set up and can be upgraded if you make
major changes to the hardware, such as installing a second processor.

Hard Drive

70-067 NT Server (Core)   *Installation and Configuration*

A hard drive is a permanent storage area for data and applications. Inside the hard drive
are individual platters covered on both sides with a special magnetic material. The drives
work by writing small magnetic charges onto the surface of the disk platter. This form
of permanent storage holds *Windows NT* and all other applications installed on the
computer.

For more information regarding the hard drive, see the following sections:

- *System partition*. Partition that contains all the hardware-specific files required to start Windows NT.

- *Boot partition*. Partition that contains all the operating system files.

- *BOOT.INI*. File that contains a list of all operating systems installed on the computer and how they should be started.

Hardware Abstraction Layer
See *HAL*.

Hardware Compatibility List
See *HCL*.

HCL

70-067   NT Server (Core)   *Installation and Configuration*

The HCL, or *Hardware Compatibility List*, is a list of all hardware that has been tested and certified as working with *Windows NT*. Before you install new hardware in a server or gather specifications for a new server, it is imperative that you check the HCL to verify that the components you are planning to use have been tested. The list includes all models that are supported and specifies any special criteria, such as a particular driver, that are required.

If you are unsure what hardware is installed in your computer, you can use the *NT Hardware Qualifier* tool to determine what hardware is in the computer. The list is frequently updated and is available from the following sources:

- *Web site:* http://www.microsoft.com/ntserver/

- *Microsoft's FTP server:* ftp://microsoft.com/bussys/winnt/winnt_docs/hcl

host name resolution

70-059   TCP/IP   *Host Name Resolution*

Host name resolution is the process of taking host names and converting them to *IP addresses* that can be used to route packets over the Internet. There are six basic ways that *Windows NT* uses the following methods in the order provided to resolve host names:

- **Check for a local host name.** The first step is that Windows NT checks to see if the queried host name belongs to the local host. If it does, then the IP address of the local computer is used.

- **Check the *HOSTS* file.** If the queried name does not belong to the local host, the computer then checks to see if the host name is in the HOSTS file on the local computer.

- **Check the *DNS* server.** If the queried name is not in the HOSTS file, then the computer contacts the DNS server to attempt to resolve the host name.

- **Check the *WINS* server.** The computer can communicate with the WINS server to check to see if the queried name resides in the WINS database. This option will work only for local host names.

- **Use local broadcasts.** If the queried name does not reside in the WINS server database, the client can resort to using local broadcasts to attempt to resolve the name.

- **Check the *LMHOSTS* file.** The computer can also attempt to resolve the host name from the LMHOSTS file.

HOSTS files

70-059   TCP/IP   *Name Resolution*

A HOSTS file is a standard ASCII text file used to statically map *IP addresses* to host names on a local computer. This file is stored in the %systemroot%\system32\drivers\etc directory. When *TCP/IP* is installed, a sample file, called HOSTS.SAM, is created. You should use that file as a template when creating a HOSTS file for use on your network.

When attempting to locate a computer's address by using the HOSTS file, the local computer reads the HOSTS file from top to bottom, stopping when it finds a match. This causes duplicate names to be ignored. Therefore, you should place frequently used names toward the top of the list to speed up resolution.

The following is an example of a HOSTS file:

```
# Copyright (c) 1993-1995 Microsoft Corp.
#
# This is a sample HOSTS file used by Microsoft TCP/IP for Windows NT.
#
# This file contains the mappings of IP addresses to host names. Each
# entry should be kept on an individual line. The IP address should
# be placed in the first column followed by the corresponding host name.
# The IP address and the host name should be separated by at least one
# space.
#
# Additionally, comments (such as these) may be inserted on individual
# lines or following the machine name denoted by a '#' symbol.
#
# For example:
#
#   102.54.94.97   rhino.acme.com    # source server
#   38.25.63.10    x.acme.com      # x client host

127.0.0.1      localhost
172.16.0.1     pdc-admin
172.16.0.2     fileserver
172.16.0.3     mailserver mail email
172.16.0.100   client1 James
172.16.0.101   client2 Dan
172.16.0.102   client3 Brian
172.16.0.103   client4 Wayne
172.16.0.104   client5 Jeff
```

You should be aware of several conventions when looking at a HOSTS file. The first is that the pound sign (#) designates a comment. This means that anything following the # sign on a given line is ignored. In addition, the second section of the file contains the actual mappings. The format for this portion is as follows:

```
IP Address <TAB> Name1 [Name2] [Name3]
```

As you can see, you can map more than one name to the same IP address. You do this by placing the different entries on the same line separated with spaces.

For more information regarding the HOSTS file, see the following sections:

- *Host name resolution process.* This is the process by which Windows NT computers try to resolve host names.

- *DNS.* This is a service that can be used to resolve TCP/IP host names dynamically.

HPFS

70-067   NT Server (Core)   *Installation and Configuration*

HPFS, short for High-Performance File System, is a file system that was designed for *OS/2* version 1.2 and later operating systems. In previous versions of *Windows NT*, you were able to access HPFS partitions. In Windows NT 4.0, this support was removed. If you are upgrading a Windows NT 3.51 computer to Windows NT 4.0, you must first use the *convert utility* to convert the partition type to *NTFS*. If you do not perform the conversion before you upgrade, you will have to format the partition after the upgrade, and you will lose all the data on the partition.

For more information regarding HPFS, see the following sections:

- *NTFS*. Windows NT's native file system type.

- *FAT*. File system that's compatible with Windows NT and other Microsoft products.

HTML

General information pertaining to all tests

HTML is a simple language used to create hypertext documents that are portable from one platform to another. These files are ASCII text files, which contain codes that indicate formatting of the text.

HTTP

70-059   TCP/IP   *General Information*
70-067   NT Server (Core)   *Installing and Configuring Windows NT*

HTTP, or *Hypertext Transfer Protocol*, is the underlying protocol that Web browsers and servers use to communicate with one another. This protocol is stateless, which means that it does not maintain a persistent connection to the Web server. The client computer requests a page and the server sends it. The connection is then terminated and is not reinstated until the client requests another page.

For more information pertaining to HTTP, see the following sections:

- *Web browser*. The client that is used to access Web pages using the HTTP protocol.

- *IIS*. The Web server that is integrated into Windows NT server.

hub

70-058   Networking Essentials   *Networking Hardware*

A hub is a connectivity device that is used to create a common connection between a group of computers. Hubs are commonly used in networks that are configured by using a *star topology*. Hubs take packets that are transmitted from one computer and transmit them on to all other computers that are connected to the hub. Hubs are also known as multistation repeaters, concentrators, MAUs, and MSAUs.
For more information, see the following sections:

- *Repeater*. This is a piece of hardware that takes packets from one network segment and transmits them on to another.

- *Star topology*. This is a network topology in which all computers are connected to a central hub.

Hypertext Markup Language

See *HTML*.

Hypertext Transfer Protocol

See *HTTP*.

H

IBM cabling system

70-058   Networking Essentials   *Connecting Network Components*

The IBM cabling system is a system developed in 1984 to define cable types, cable connectors, face plates, and distribution panels. The grades of IBM cabling are outlined in Table I.1.

Table I.1   **Grades of IBM Cabling**

IBM Type	Description
Type 1	This type consists of two shielded twisted pairs. Used for connecting computers and *MAUs*.
Type 2	This is a voice and data shielded cable that consists of two twisted pairs of wire for data with an outer braided shield and then four twisted pairs of wire for voice.
Type 3	This consists of four unshielded twisted pairs (*UTP*) of wire and is used to transmit voice.
Type 4	Not yet defined.
Type 5	This is two multimode optical fibers.
Type 6	This is two twisted pairs with a dual foil and braided shield; it is used for data patch cables.
Type 7	Not yet defined.
Type 8	This is two shielded twisted pairs (*STP*) of wire contained in a flat jacket for use under carpets.
Type 9	This is two shielded twisted pairs contained in a fire-safe jacket. This is similar to plenum cable.

ICMP

70-059   TCP/IP   *Overview of the TCP/IP Suite*

ICMP (Internet Control Messaging Protocol) is a datagram-based *protocol* responsible for reporting errors and informational messages. The functionality of this protocol can be broken down into two categories.

The first responsibility is to report errors such as `destination unreachable` and timeout errors. These errors are reported to whatever application sent the *packet* in the first place, and it is expected to handle the error.

The second includes message querying. The most frequently used application that utilizes ICMP is *PING*. PING, or *Packet Internet Groper*, is used to test and verify the existence of a specified *IP address* and to determine whether the local computer can connect to it. This utility sends an ECHO request to the remote computer. If the computer exists, it sends an ECHO reply to the originating computer. The originating computer then displays the existence of the IP address and the amount of time it took to reach it.

IEEE 802.2

70-058   Networking Essentials   *Networking Standards*

The IEEE 802.2 standard defines the logical link control (LLC) sublayer of the *Data Link layer* in the *OSI model*. The LLC layer appends a header to the packet that identifies the upper-level protocols associated with it. This header information also contains information about the applications associated with it.

For more information on IEEE 802.2, refer to the section *OSI Model*, which outlines all the layers of the OSI Model and describes how they work together.

IEEE 802.3

70-058   Networking Essentials   *Networking Standards*

The IEEE 802.3 is the standard derived from a network developed jointly by Digital, Intel, and Xerox. This type of network relies on a *bus topology* and uses Carrier Sense Multiple Access with Collision Detection (*CSMA/CD*) to reduce *collisions* and help regulate network traffic. This networking standard is also known as *Ethernet*.

For more information on IEEE 802.3, see the following sections:

- *CSMA/CD*. This is a type of access method.

- *Collision*. This occurs when two computers on the network transmit at the same time.

- *Bus*. This is the network topology that was originally designated in the IEEE 802.3 standard.

- *Ethernet*. This is what the IEEE 802.3 standard is commonly known as.

IEEE 802.4

70-058   Networking Essentials   *Networking Standards*

IEEE 802.4 is a networking standard that utilizes a *bus* topology and uses a token mechanism to control access. This standard has not gained much popularity over the years.

IEEE 802.5

70-058   Networking Essentials   *Networking Standards*

The IEEE 802.5 standard is based on the IBM Token Ring network with data rates of 1, 4, and 16 megabits. This standard utilizes a ring topology and token mechanism to control access to the media.

For more information on IEEE 802.5, see the following sections:

- *Token-ring*. The token ring standard is a token passing method.

- *Token*. A token is a special packet used to eliminate contention on the network.

IEEE 802.6

70-058   Networking Essentials   *Networking Standards*

The IEEE 802.6 standard describes a Metropolitan Area Network, or *MAN*, standard called Distributed Queue Dual Bus. This standard is based on using two pairs of *fiber-optic cable* for *fault tolerance*. The traffic on each pair is unidirectional, and both synchronous and asynchronous modes are supported. This standard is suited to video, audio, and voice transmissions.

For more information on IEEE 802.6, see the following sections:

- *MAN.* The MAN standard is what is outlined in the IEEE 802.6 standard.

- *Fiber-optic cable.* Fiber-optic cable is a type of network transmission media.

IEEE 802.9

70-058   Networking Essentials   *Networking Standards*

The IEEE 802.9 standard provides a 10-megabit asynchronous channel along with 96 64-kilobit channels that can be dedicated to individual data streams (providing a total of 16 megabits of bandwidth). This standard is known as Isochronous Ethernet (*IsoNet*).

For more information regarding IEEE 802.9, see the section entitled *IsoNet*.

IEEE 802.11

70-058   Networking Essentials   *Networking Standards*

The IEEE 802.11 standard is currently in development for wireless LANs. This standard utilizes *CSMA/CD* to avoid *contention* on the network.

IEEE 802.12

70-058   Networking Essentials   *Networking Standards*

The IEEE 802.12 standard, also known as *100VG-AnyLAN*, is a 100-megabit standard proposed by AT&T, IBM, and Hewlett-Packard. This standard is based on the star topology and reduces network *contention* by forcing the computer that needs to talk on the network to signal the *hub* and request permission. No device can communicate on the network without first receiving permission from the hub. This standard can operate in both Ethernet and token-ring environments, as it supports both *frame types*.

For more information on IEEE 802.12, see the following sections:

- *100VG-AnyLAN.* This is the standard that is outlined in the IEEE 802.9 standard.

- *Star topology.* A topology in which all computers are connected to a central hub.

- *Ethernet.* This is a standard that is outlined in the IEEE 802.3 standard.

- *Token-ring.* The token ring standard is a token passing method.

in-addr.arpa

70-059   TCP/IP   *Resolving Host Names*

The in-addr.arpa zone (commonly known as a reverse lookup zone) is used to perform resolution of *IP addresses* into host names. These files are named according to the class of the network, except the octets are in reverse order. Table I.2 contains examples of zones for class A, B, and C networks.

Table I.2 **Zones for Class A, B, and C Networks**

Network ID	Zone
38.X.X.X	38.in-addr.arpa
129.105.X.X	105.129.in-addr.arpa
208.198.247.X	247.198.208.in-addr.arpa

For more information, see the following sections:

- *DNS.* This is the service that is designed to aid in resolving host names.
- *HOSTS files.* This is a file that can be used to statically map host names to IP addresses.

index server

70-067   Windows NT Server (Core)   *Installation and Configuration*

Index server is an add-on to IIS that allows the user to take advantage of context indexing and to search from client Web browsers. Index server can analyze the content of both formatted documents, such as Word documents and Excel spreadsheets, and *HTML* documents. A client builds a query by using a Web browser. The query is then sent to the query engine, which searches the database of documents and returns the results to the client computer as a Web page.

installing network protocols

General information pertaining to all tests

Network *protocols* are installed using the *Network Control Panel.* These protocols include *TCP/IP*, *NetBEUI*, and *NWLink IPX/SPX.* The following steps outline the procedure for installing a network protocol:

1. Click on **Start**, **Settings**, **Control Panel**. This opens a window containing all the Control Panels. Double-click the **Network** Control Panel.
2. From the Network Control Panel, choose the **Protocols** tab to display all protocols installed on the computer.
3. To add a new protocol, click the **Add...** button. This opens a dialog box showing all protocols available to be installed.
4. Choose the protocol you want to add and click **OK**. The system starts copying files. You might need to insert the *Windows NT* CD-ROM to install some protocols.
5. After the protocol has been installed, you must rerun the most recent service pack to ensure that all components are the most recent. When you finish doing that, restart the computer.

installing network services

General information pertaining to all tests

Network services are installed through the *Network Control Panel.* These services include *DHCP*, *DNS*, and *WINS.* The following steps outline the procedure for installing a network service:

1. Click **Start**, **Settings**, **Control Panel**. This opens a window containing all the Control Panels. Double-click the **Network** Control Panel.

2. From the Network Control Panel, choose the **Services** tab to display all services that are installed on the computer.

3. To add a new service, click the **Add...** button. This opens a dialog box showing all the services that are available to be installed.

4. Choose the service you want to add and click **OK**. The system starts copying files. You might need to insert the *Windows NT* CD-ROM to install some services.

5. After the service has been installed, you must rerun the most recent service pack to ensure that all components are the most recent. When you finish doing that, restart the computer.

installing Windows NT

| 70-067 | Windows NT Server (Core) | *Installation and Configuration* |
| 70-073 | Windows NT Workstation | *Installation and Configuration* |

To begin setting up *Windows NT*, you will use one of two commands (winnt or winnt32), depending on the *operating system* on the destination computer. When you run one of these commands, the computer accesses files on either a local CD-ROM or a network share. The winn32 command is used to upgrade from an existing version of *Windows NT Workstation*. The winnt command is used to install Windows NT on a computer that is running *MS-DOS, Windows 3.1x,* or *Windows 95*. During the installation process, all the files required during the installation process are copied over to the local computer so the installation can continue even if a network connection is unavailable after the computer is rebooted.

After the files are copied over to the local computer, the Setup program begins its text mode portion of the setup. During the text mode portion of setup, the files are copied from the temporary directory to the final destination directory. Also, the setup application detects the hardware in the machine.

After the text mode portion, the setup program begins its *GUI* portion. During the GUI portion of setup, the user is prompted for information that is used to customize the installation. This includes the name of the user, the name of the organization, and the product ID. The user is also asked what additional software he or she wants to install. After the accessory software is installed, the user is prompted to install networking components and to join a *domain* or workgroup.

Integrated Services Digital Network

See *ISDN.*

interactive debugging

70-068 Windows NT Server (Enterprise) *Troubleshooting*

During the *troubleshooting* process, you might need more information than is available from a *blue screen*. One of the ways you can get this information is to interactively debug the computer by using another computer remotely or via a null modem cable. A *kernel* debugger is located in the \support\debug directory on the *Windows NT* distribution CD. In addition, there is a separate debugger for each hardware platform.

The steps to setting up an interactive debugging session are outlined here:

1. Set up a serial connection between the computer that is crashing and the computer that is going to be used as the diagnosing computer. This connection can be made via a null modem cable or a modem.

2. Configure the computer that is crashing. You do this by editing the BOOT.INI file as outlined in the section entitled BOOT.INI.

3. Copy the symbol tree off the installation CD or from the most current service pack, and then place it on the diagnosing computer.

4. Set up and start the debugger on the computer that is crashing.

5. Start the debugger on the diagnosing computer. You can then begin diagnosing the problems on the computer.

It is important to note that this process is not used frequently. It is often easier to diagnose the problems by using a *memory dump* file or to rebuild the *operating system*.

Internet Control Message Protocol

See *ICMP*.

Internet Control Panel

70-067   NT Server (Core)   *Installation and Configuration*

The Internet Control Panel is used to configure *Internet Explorer* options. These options include how the computer interacts with the Internet and which applications are used in conjunction with Internet Explorer. This Control Panel contains six tabs of options: *General*, *Security*, *Content*, *Connection*, *Programs*, and *Advanced*.

- **General**. This tab is used to configure the page that Internet Explorer automatically opens to when it starts, how the temporary Internet files are stored, and how long it keeps track of Internet sites that have been visited.

- **Security**. This tab is used to configure the security level for the computer. This includes which downloaded applications are run on the computer and how *ActiveX* components are handled.

- **Content**. This tab is allows you to edit information about yourself, view which security certificates are on the machine, and enable the content advisor. The content advisor enables you to control which Web pages are accessible via a ratings system.

- **Connection**. This tab allows you to configure how the computer will connect to the Internet. This includes choosing between dialing up, connecting via a LAN, or connecting manually.

- **Programs**. The options on this tab allow you to configure Internet Explorer to open different applications to work as mail readers and news readers.

- **Advanced**. This tab is used to configure options for accessibility, security, and browsing.

For more information, see the following sections:

- *Internet Explorer*. This is an application that can be used to access the Internet.

- *Control Panels*. This entry outlines a list of all the Control Panels available on *Windows NT* computers.

Internet Explorer

General information pertaining to all tests

Internet Explorer is an application that is designed to download and display Web pages from the Internet. With Internet Explorer, you can access not only Web pages, but also *FTP* and *Gopher* sites.

For more information, see the following sections:

- *HTML.* HTML is the language that is used to create Web pages.

- *FTP.* FTP is a protocol that is used to transfer files over the Internet.

Internet Service Provider

See *ISP.*

Internet Services Application Programming Interface

See *ISAPI.*

InterNIC

General information pertaining to all tests

The InterNIC, or Internet Network Information Center, is the closest thing to a ruling body that the Internet has. The InterNIC coordinates *domain* names and *IP addresses.* This organization can be contacted at `http://www.internic.net`.

Interrupt Request Line

See *IRQ.*

inverse query

See *DNS.*

I/O Manager

70-067   NT Server (Core)   *Installation and Configuration*

The I/O Manager is a portion of the Windows NT Executive Services that manages all the input and output of the system. The primary function of the I/O Manager is to manage communications between the drivers installed on the system. The I/O Manager supports the file system drivers, *device drivers*, and network drivers. In addition, the I/O Manager includes standard interface for all types of drivers, which enables it to communicate with all drivers in the same way, without any knowledge of how the devices they control actually work. This system enables you to easily replace file system and device drivers. It also allows multiple drivers to be active at the same time.

For more information, see the section entitled *Executive Services*, which describes the set of services that are integral to the operation of *Windows NT*.

IP address

70-059　TCP/IP　　　　　　　　　　　*IP Addressing*

An IP address is a unique logical address on a *TCP/IP* network that identifies every computer on the network. An IP address is a 32-bit number. It is commonly represented in a format that is expressed as four numbers between 0 and 255 separated by periods (known as dotted decimal format). Each IP address consists of two parts. The first part of the address is the network ID. The network ID identifies all hosts on the same network. The second part of the address is the host ID. The host ID identifies individual computers in the network. When configuring an IP address, a *subnet mask* is used to distinguish the network ID from the host ID.

Table I.3 outlines the five different classes of IP addresses. Class D addresses are used for multicasting over the Internet, and Class E addresses are experimental.

Table I.3　**The Five Classes of IP Addresses**

Class	First Octet Start	First Octet End	Number of Networks	Number of Hosts
Class A	1	126	126	16,777,214
Class B	128	191	16,384	65,534
Class C	192	223	2,097,152	254
Class D	224	239		
Class E	240	247		

For more information, see the following sections:

- *Subnet mask.* This is a number that is used to distinguish between the network ID and the host ID.
- *TCP/IP.* This is a protocol stack that uses IP addresses.

IRQ

General information pertaining to all tests

An IRQ, or Interrupt Request Line, is a hardware line through which hardware devices send signals to get the attention of the processor. The devices do this when they are prepared to send or receive data. Normally, every device that is attached to the computer must have its own IRQ.

ISAPI

70-067　NT Server (Core)　　　　　　*Installation and Configuration*

ISAPI (Internet Server Application Programming Interface) is an *API* that was created for developing extensions for IIS. Instead of relying on *CGI* to request information from other applications, IIS uses ISAPI, which can take advantage of both the Win32 API and ODBC. ISAPI applications are implemented as *dynamic link libraries*. These libraries are loaded once to service multiple requests and are unloaded if they remain unused for a long period of time. This increases performance as the DLL is loaded within the process of IIS, speeding up the server performance by eliminating the need for the server to switch between multiple processes.

For more information, see the following sections:

- *API.* An API is a set of prewritten functions available to programmers.
- *ODBC.* ODBC is a way to communicate with databases.
- *CGI.* CGI offers another way of implementing extra functionality into a Web server.

ISDN

70-058   Networking Essentials   *WAN Technologies*

ISDN, or Integrated Services Digital Network, is a standard that was developed to provide high-speed data, video, and voice transmission services on digital telephone networks. ISDN separates bandwidth into six types of channels, as outlined in Table I.4.

Table I.4   **The Six ISDN Channels**

Channel	Transmission Rate	Service Type	Description
A Channels	4KHz	Analog	Telephone service.
B Channels	64Kbps	Digital	Data transmission services.
C Channels	8 or 16Kbps	Digital	Commonly used for out-of-band signaling.
D Channels	16 or 64Kbps	Digital	Used for out-of-band signaling. These channels are broken up into subchannels that add support for call setup, low bandwidth packet data, and telemetry data.
E Channels	62Kbps	Digital	Used for internal ISDN signaling.
H Channels	384, 1,536, or 1,920Kbps	Digital	Data transmission services.

Basic ISDN uses three channels: two B channels and a D channel. Basic rate ISDN is frequently known as 2B+D, and a computer can transmit data on both B channels at the same time at a maximum data rate of 128Kbps per channel. Primary rate ISDN consists of 23 B Channels and one D Channel, providing a total data rate of 1.54Mbps.

For more information, see the following sections:

- *ADSL.* This is another form of WAN connection service.
- *SONET.* This is another form of WAN connection service.
- *Frame relay.* This is another form of WAN connection service.

Isochronous Ethernet

See *IEEE 802.9.*

IsoNet

See *IEEE 802.9.*

ISP

General information pertaining to all tests

An ISP, or Internet service provider, is a commercial service that allows users to dial up by using a modem and access the Internet. This type of access usually provides a maximum throughput of about 56Kbps. This is usually the best way to get Internet connectivity without spending a large amount of money on special hardware and cabling.

iterative query

See *DNS.*

kernel

70-067   NT Server (Core)   *Installation and Configuration*

The kernel is the portion of *Windows NT* that controls the computer's processor. The kernel schedules the threads in and out of the processor in order to maximize performance. The kernel also ensures that all other executive services remain synchronized. These services include the *I/O Manager* and the *Process Manager*.

For more information, see the section titled *Executive Services*, which outlines the different executive services.

kernel mode

70-067   Implementing and Supporting Microsoft Windows NT Server 4.0
         Monitoring and Optimization

Kernel mode is the highly privileged mode of operation in which processes have complete and direct access to memory and hardware. This access also allows kernel mode applications to access the memory space of applications running in *user mode*.

Processes that are integral to the operating system are run in kernel mode. Kernel mode applications run at priority levels between 16 and 31. The memory space for these applications is strictly protected by the processor, so these applications will never be swapped out of memory. Applications cannot directly access the memory and hardware of any process running in kernel mode. Kernel mode is commonly known as "protected mode" and "ring 0."

For more information pertaining to kernel mode, see the section on *Executive Services*.

Keyboard Control Panel

70-067   Implementing and Supporting Microsoft Windows NT Server 4.0
         Installation and Configuration

The Keyboard Control Panel is used to configure how the keyboard responds and which language the keyboard layout uses. The Keyboard Control Panel contains three tabs: **Speed**, **Input Locals**, and **General**.

The **Speed** tab enables you to configure the speed at which the keyboard responds. The Repeat Delay slider controls the amount of time the computer waits before putting a second character on the screen when you hold down a key. The Repeat Rate slider controls the speed at which the third and following characters are placed on the screen. The Cursor Blink Rate controls the speed at which the cursor flashes on the screen when you are editing text.

The **Input Locals** tab enables you to configure keyboard layouts. From this tab, you can add additional keyboard layouts, which are loaded into memory when the computer is started. This allows you to switch between layouts without having to restart the computer.

The **General** tab enables you to change the keyboard driver that is loaded on the computer.

For more information regarding the Keyboard Control Panel, see the *Control Panel* section.

K

L

LAN

70-058 Networking Essentials   *Standards and Terminology*

A LAN, or local area network, is a group of computers that are connected in a relatively close space, such as a single floor in a building. LANs are usually characterized by the following:

- Relatively high speed
- Limited area
- Relatively inexpensive to implement

For more information, see the following sections:

- *Ethernet.* This is a type of LAN.
- *Token–ring network.* This is a type of LAN.
- *Star topology.* This is a type of topology that is used in LAN implementations.
- *Bus.* This is a type of topology that is used in LAN implementations.

license logging service

70-067   NT Server (Core)   *Managing Resources*

The license logging service is used to keep track of and log licensing information for the *License Manager* and to monitor the licensing options in the Control Panel in *Windows NT.* Within the License Manager application, you can set up the license logging service on a specific server to replicate its licensing information to a single server called an enterprise server. This enables you to view all licensing information for an entire domain or group of domains from a single server.

For more information regarding the license logging service, see the following sections:

- *Client access licenses.* A client access license is the actual license that allows clients to use resources on the computer.
- *License Manager.* A utility that allows you to view license usage statistics.

117

License Manager

70-067   NT Server (Core)   *Managing Resources*

License Manager is a utility that allows you to view all per-seat and per-server licenses across your organization. You also use License Manager to add and remove licenses, view usage statistics, and balance the license replicate load. This application is available only on *Windows NT* Server.

For more information regarding License Manager, see the following sections:

- *Client access licenses.* A client access license is the actual license that allows clients to use resources on the computer.

- *License logging service.* This is the Windows NT Server service that tracks license usage.

Licensing Control Panel

70-067   NT Server (Core)   *Installation and Configuration*

The Licensing Control Panel is used to configure the licensing mode on the server you are working on. This includes setting the type of licensing and the number of licenses available. For more information, see the following sections:

- *License Manager.* This application is used to view data about the licenses used on every computer in the domain.

- *License logging service.* This service gathers information about the licenses used.

L

Line Printer Daemon

See *LPD service.*

Line Printer Queue

See *LPQ.*

Line Printer Router

See *LPR.*

LLC

See *OSI Model.*

LMHOSTS

70-059   TCP/IP   *Name Resolution*

The LMHOSTS file is a text file used to map *NetBIOS* computer names to *IP addresses* for Windows networking computers outside of the local *subnet.* This file is read when the NetBIOS name cache does not contain the requested name and *WINS* or broadcast name resolution fails. After a name has been read from the LMHOSTS file, the name is stored in local cache for future use.

This file is stored in the %systemroot%\system32\drivers\etc directory. A sample file, called LMHOSTS.SAM, is added during the installation of *TCP/IP.* These entries are read in order, so the most frequently used entries should appear at the beginning of the file. This file includes several tags that allow computers to send requests to other computers that are running specific services. Table L.1 outlines the tags used in LMHOSTS.

Table L.1   **Tags Allowed in the LMHOSTS File**

Tag	Description
`#DOM:domain_name`	Indicates that the computer is a *domain controller* and gives the name of the *domain* that it controls.
`#PRE`	Tells the computer to preload the entry into cache during initialization. Entries with the `#PRE` tag are loaded as static, meaning they are always in cache.
`#INCLUDE`	Specifies the location of a central LMHOSTS file. This file is specified by using a UNC name. The name of this computer must be able to be resolved into an IP address, must be included in the local LMHOSTS file as a preloaded entry in a line before the `#INCLUDE` line, and must use the `#PRE` tag.
`#NOFNR`	Prevents the use of NetBIOS-directed name queries in the LAN Manager for a *UNIX* environment.
`#MH`	Tells the computer that the entry is a multihomed computer that can appear in the list more than once. Without this tag, multiple entries are ignored.
`#BEGIN_ALTERNATIVE`	Used in conjunction with the `#INCLUDE` tag, this specifies alternative locations of the central LMHOSTS file, which are useful in the event that the main central file is not available. Only one copy of the central LMHOSTS file is used.
`#END_ALTERNATIVE`	Specifies the end of the list of alternative central LMHOSTS servers. These servers are checked in order, and the names must be able to be resolved into IP addresses.

For more information regarding LMHOSTS, see the following sections:

- *NetBIOS name resolution.* Explains the steps involved in resolving NetBIOS computer names.
- *NBTSTAT command.* Displays statistics and current NetBIOS connections.
- *NetBIOS names.* Explains what a NetBIOS name is and how it is implemented.

L

local accounts

70-067   NT Server (Core)   *Managing Resources*

A local account is a noninteractive account that can be created in a *domain* for a user that resides in a *trusted domain.* A *user account* that has been created as a local account cannot log in to any other machine in the domain using that account.

Local accounts can be assigned permissions to resources in the domain. If a user that has not logged in to the domain tries to access a resource, he or she is prompted for a username and password. The user with the local account can then supply this username and password to gain access to only this resource.

To create a local user account, start User Manager for Domains, choose the **Account** button, and select the **Local Account** option from the **Account Type** area.

For more information regarding local accounts, see the following sections:

- *Global accounts.* These are normal interactive accounts in a domain.
- *User Manager for Domains.* This utility enables you to create and manage user accounts.

local area network

See *LAN.*

local groups

70-067   NT Server (Core)   *Managing Resources*

A local group can take one of two forms, depending on the *operating system* that you are running.

For *Windows NT Workstation* and *Windows NT* Server *member servers*, this is a group that can be granted permissions and rights on the local workstation only. This group can contain users from the local workstation, as well as user accounts and global groups from its own *domain* and from trusted domains if the workstation participates in a domain.

For Windows NT Server, this is a group that can be granted permissions and rights for the *domain controllers* in its own *domain* only. These groups can contain *user accounts* and *global groups* both from its own domain and from trusted domains.

For more information regarding local groups, see the section on *global groups*.

Local Procedure Call facility

70-067   NT Server (Core)   *Installation and Configuration*

Applications communicate with environmental subsystems in a client-server relationship. The application, known as the client, makes requests of the subsystem, known as the server. The Local Procedure Call, or LPC, facility is what allows the different levels to communicate. The LPC facility implements communication between the subsystems and the applications and hides the complexity of the calls from the application.

For more information, see the section entitled *Executive Services*, which outlines the different executive services.

local profiles

70-067   NT Server (Core)   *Managing Resources*

A local profile is a profile created automatically on the computer when a user logs in to a *Windows NT* computer. This profile contains user-specific information including desktop settings, application settings, and personal folder information. This profile information is local to the computer and is stored in the %systemroot%\profiles directory.

For more information, see the section:

- *Roaming profiles*. These profiles are not stored on the local computer; rather, they follow the user wherever he or she logs in.

LocalTalk network

70-058   Networking Essentials   *Standards and Terminology*

A LocalTalk network is one that was designed by Apple Computer and is based on all the networking hardware that is installed in every *Macintosh* computer. The LocalTalk specification includes the cables and connector boxes that connect components, as well as network devices that are part of the *AppleTalk* network system. This network uses the AppleTalk protocol to communicate.

For more information, see the following sections:

- *AppleTalk*. This is a routable protocol that is used in AppleTalk networks.

- *Macintosh*. This is the type of computer that uses LocalTalk networks.

logon scripts

70-067   NT Server (Core)   *Installation and Configuration*

Logon scripts are batch files that are run when a user logs in to the network. These scripts can be used to configure the user environment by making network connections and starting applications. Logon scripts can be created for individual users or for groups of users to use. Logon scripts can be assigned to users using the *User Manager for Domains* application. The logon scripts are located in the %Systemroot%\system32\repl\import\scripts directory.

For more information, see the following sections:

- *User Manager for Domains.* This is an application that is used to add and configure users in a domain.

- *Directory replication.* This is a service that can be used to make sure all servers have the same versions of the logon scripts.

LPD service

70-059   TCP/IP   *Connectivity in a Heterogeneous Environment*

The LPD service is also known as the TCP/IP Printing Services. This service allows remote *TCP/IP* hosts, such as *UNIX* hosts, to connect to *printers* that are available on *Windows NT* Servers. When you install the TCP/IP Printing Services, the services are set to start manually. To make the service start automatically when the computer is rebooted, you must set the service to automatic in the *Services Control Panel.*

For more information, see the following sections:

- *LPR.* A utility that is used to send print jobs to computers that are running the *LPD service.*

- *LPQ.* The command that is used to check the print queue on a server running the LPD service.

LPQ

70-059   TCP/IP   *Connectivity in a Heterogeneous Environment*

The LPQ utility is a command line function that allows you to check the status of a print queue on a computer that is running an LPD server. The syntax of the command is as follows:

```
LPQ -S server_name -P printer_name -I
```

The LPQ command uses the following options:

Option	Description
-S	Specifies the name of the computer to which the printer is attached.
-P	Specifies the name of the printer for which you want to check the queue.
-I	Requests that detailed information be returned.

Note that all the options and parameters you can pass into the command are case sensitive, including the name of the *printer.*

For more information regarding LPQ, see the following sections:

- *LPD service.* The service that allows TCP/IP hosts to connect to printers on Windows NT Servers.

- *LPR.* A utility that is used to send print jobs to computers running the LPD service.

LPR

The LPR utility is a command line program used to send a print job to a computer running an *LPD*. The *LPD service* can be running on any type of computer. In order to run LPR, you must know the host name and the *printer* name. The syntax of this command is as follows:

```
lpr -S Server -P Printer [-C Class] [-J Jobname] [-O option] filename
```

The LPR command uses the following options:

Option	Description
-S	Specifies the name of the computer to which the printer is attached.
-P	Specifies the name of the printer to which you are going to send the job.
-C	Specifies the content that will be placed on the banner page in the class section.
-J	Specifies the name of the job.
-O	Specifies the type of file you are sending to the printer. By default, this is text. Use the –Ol option for binary files.

Note that all the options and parameters you can pass into the command are case sensitive, including the name of the printer.

For more information regarding LPR, see the following sections:

- *LPD service.* The service that allows *TCP/IP* hosts to connect to printers on *Windows NT* Servers.

- *LPQ.* The command that is used to check the print queue on a server running the LPD service.

L

m-node

70-059 TCP/IP *Windows Internet Name Service*

M-node name resolution is a *NetBIOS* over *TCP/IP* implementation that combines *b-node* and *p-node* name resolution. In an m-node environment, computers will first try to register and resolve names by using broadcasts. If the broadcast fails, the computer will direct its request to a *WINS* server. The biggest advantage to this is that m-node can cross over a *router* to resolve and register names.

For more information on m-node, see the following sections:

- *WINS.* A way of automatically mapping NetBIOS names to *IP addresses*.

- *B-node.* Type of node that can be used to provide name resolution.

- *P-node.* Type of node that can be used to provide name resolution.

- *H-node.* Type of node that can be used to provide name resolution.

MAC address

70-058 Networking Essentials *Networking Standards*

MAC addresses are unique 48-bit numbers assigned to *network interface cards* by the manufacturers. Every MAC address is unique. The MAC address is the actual physical address of the card on the network and is used to map all network communications at the Data Link layer of the *OSI Model.*

For more information on MAC addresses, see the following sections:

- *OSI Model.* The OSI Model describes how network communication takes place.

- *Network interface card.* This is a piece of hardware used to connect the computer to the network.

Macintosh

General information pertaining to all tests

A Macintosh client is a computer that was originally based on a Motorola processor and has since been expanded to run both Motorola and PowerPC processors. Macintosh computers run MacOS from Apple Computer, Inc. Macintosh computers ship with the capability to connect to a network by utilizing the *AppleTalk* protocol. The makes Macintosh computers extremely easy to network. Macintosh computers can be made clients of *Windows NT* Servers by installing the Services for Macintosh component on the server.

For more information, see the following sections:

- *AppleTalk*. This protocol stack was developed so that Macintosh computers could be easily networked.

- *Services for Macintosh*. Services for Macintosh allows a Windows NT Server to become a file and print server that is accessible by Macintosh clients.

Mail and Fax Control Panel

70-067   NT Server (Core)   *Installation and Configuration*

The Mail and Fax Control Panel is used to configure the Microsoft Windows Messaging Profiles. This Control Panel looks different depending on what messaging applications are installed on a computer. The best way to learn more about the Mail and Fax Control Panel is to open it up and look at the options that are available to you on your computer.

MAN

See *IEEE 802.6.*

mandatory user profile

70-067   NT Server (Core)   *Managing Resources*

A mandatory user profile is a *user profile* created by the *administrator* and assigned to users. These profiles are used to create consistent user settings such as desktop and *printer configurations*. These profiles cannot be changed by the user and will remain the same every time the user logs in. A mandatory user profile is created by renaming the NTUSER.DAT file to NTUSER.MAN. All user profiles are assigned to the user within the *User Manager* application.

For more information, see the following sections:

- *Roaming user profile*. This profile follows a user to whatever workstation he logs in to.

- *Profile Editor*. This application is used to create profiles.

master browser

70-067   NT Server (Core)   *Installation and Configuration*

The master browser is the computer that maintains a list (called the *browse list*) of all computers on the network that have File and Print Sharing installed on them. The master browser propagates this list to all backup browsers on the network, and the browse list is available to any computer on the network that requests it. Every time a computer logs in to the network, the browse list is updated on the master browser. If the master browser is offline for any reason, a *browser election* is held to select a new master browser.

For more information on master browsers, see the following sections:

- *Browser election*. A browser election is initiated when any computer on the network cannot contact the master browser.

- *Browse list*. The browse list is a list of all computers on the network that have File and Print Services turned on.

master domain

See *trusted domain.*

master file table

70-067 NT Server (Core)   *Plan Hard Drive Configurations*

When a partition is formatted as or converted to *NTFS*, the system creates a set of files called the Master File Table, or MFT, that contains information used to keep track of the file system. The first portions of the file describe the MFT itself. The rest of the MFT contains records that outline every file on the volume. The attributes of the file, such as "read-only" and "hidden," are also written to the MFT.

For more information on the master file table, see the following sections:

- *NTFS.* This is the file system that utilizes an MFT.
- *Convert utility.* This convert utility is used to convert a FAT file system to an NTFS file system.

MAU

See *hub.*

Media Access Control

See *MAC address.*

M

member server

70-067 NT Server (Core)   *Installation and Configuration*

A member server is a computer that has *Windows NT Server* installed on it but that does not perform any functions of a *domain controller*, such as account validation. As such, these machines do not receive copies of the user database. Commonly, these servers perform the roles of file and print servers and application servers.

For more information, see the following sections:

- *PDC.* This is another role that a Windows NT Server can perform.
- *BDC.* This is another role that a Windows NT Server can perform.

memory dump

70-068 NT Server Enterprise   *Troubleshooting*

One way to troubleshoot a stop message, or *blue screen*, is to configure *Windows NT* to create a memory dump. A memory dump is a file that contains an exact copy of everything that was in physical memory when the error occurred. You can then use the Dump Exam and Dump Check utilities to examine the file. The biggest problem with having Windows NT create a memory dump is that you must have enough space on a hard drive to create the file. The file will be the same size as the amount of RAM you have in your computer. For example, if your computer has 128 megabytes of RAM, the file that is created will be 128 megabytes. The other requirement for creating a memory dump is that you must have a page file on your system partition that is at least the same size as the amount of RAM in the system.

By default, Windows NT creates a memory dump file whenever a blue screen occurs. To configure Windows NT to create a memory dump file, choose **Start**, **Settings**, **Control Panel**, **System**. This opens the System Control Panel. You can then configure the memory dump options located in the Recovery section of the **Startup/Shutdown** tab.

For more information on memory dumps, see the following sections:

- *Interactive debugging*. Interactive debugging is another way to troubleshoot a blue screen on a Windows NT computer.

- *Dump Check utility*. This utility is used to verify a memory dump file.

- *Dump Exam utility*. This utility is used to extract information from a memory dump file.

mesh topology

70-058   Networking Essentials   *Standards and Terminology*

The mesh topology is commonly used in WANs. One of the best examples of a mesh network is the Internet. Mesh topologies connect many remote sites over telecommunications links. *Routers* are used to provide connectivity between different portions of the mesh, determining the best route to send the data at that particular time.

For more information, see the following sections:

- *Bus*
- *Star topology*
- *X.25*
- *Frame relay*

M

Metropolitan Area Network

See *IEEE 802.6.*

MFT

See *master file table.*

MIPS

70-067   NT Server (Core)   *Installation and Configuration*

MIPS is a *RISC*-based processor that can be used with *Windows NT*. RISC-based processors are faster and more efficient than some other processors because they rely on a smaller set of instructions in the processor.

modem

General information pertaining to all tests

A modem is a piece of hardware that can be used to send data over a standard telephone system. Because the phone system is based on analog signaling, the digital data used by the computer must be converted before it is sent. The modem takes the data from the computer and modulates it into an analog signal that can be understood by the phone system. When the data is received, the modem demodulates it back into digital data for the computer. This MOdulating and DEModulating is how the modem gets its name. For more information, see the following sections:

- *POTS.* This is the standard telephone system.

- *RAS.* This is the Windows NT service that supports dialup by using modems.

Modems Control Panel
70-067 NT Server (Core)   *Installation and Configuration*

The Modems Control Panel is used to add, remove, and configure modems on the computer. From this Control Panel, you can set defaults for the modem including the connection speed, data bits, and stop bits. Most of these options are correct by default. The best way to get a handle on the different options is to open the Control Panel and look at the options available.

Mouse Control Panel
70-067 NT Server (Core)   *Installation and Configuration*

The Mouse Control Panel is used to control the characteristics of the mouse, or other pointing device, that you have installed on your computer. In this Control Panel, you can configure whether the mouse is right- or left-handed, the speed of the double-click, any different mouse pointers that you use, and the type of mouse you have installed on the computer.
For more information on the Mouse Control Panel, see the *Control Panels* section.

MSAU
See *hub.*

M

multilink
70-067 NT Server (Core)   *Install and Configure Remote Access Server*

Multilink is a feature that enables a computer to connect to a remote computer by using multiple phone lines and modems. This creates one logical connection for the computer to communicate through, increasing the total bandwidth that is available to the computer. To utilize multilink, you must have one phone line for every modem that you are planning to use.
For more information, see the following sections:

- *RAS.* This is the *Windows NT* service that supports multilink.

- *Modem.* This is the piece of hardware that is used to communicate over phone lines.

Multimedia Control Panel
70-067 NT Server (Core)   *Installation and Configuration*

The Multimedia Control Panel is used to change the settings of *multimedia devices*, including sound cards, video playback devices, and CD-ROM drives on the system. These settings include the volume of the playback devices, the size of the window that is used to display video, and the properties of the devices themselves.
For more information, see the following sections:

- *Control Panels.* This outlines all the Control Panels that are normally found on a *Windows NT* computer.

- *Sound Control Panel.* This Control Panel is used to set up sounds that are triggered by events on the system.

Multiple Master Domain Model

70-068   Windows NT Server (Enterprise)   *Planning*

The Multiple Master Domain Model is one in which there is more than one master domain. Each master domain contains user and global group accounts that are used by all other *domains* in the model. This domain model is extremely scalable because each master domain can contain the maximum number of user accounts. Because there is no limit to the number of master domains, this can be used to expand the network to allow for an unlimited number of users.

The Multiple Master Domain Model requires much more planning than any other domain model. Each master domain must be identified, and the administrative method for each must be identified. You can achieve centralized administration by assigning the global domain admins group to all the local admins groups and all the other domains.

The trust relationships in the model are configured in basically the same way as in the *Single Master Domain Model.* Each of the resource domains trusts each of the master domains. Each of the master domains establishes *two-way trusts* with all the other master domains. A basic multiple master domain is outlined in Figure M.1.

For more information about the Multiple Master Domain Model, see the following sections:

- *Domain.* A domain is a group of computers that are logically grouped together.

- *Single Master Domain Model.* This is another form of domain model.

- *Trust relationship.* This is the basis for creating domain models.

- *Two-way trust.* This is a form of a trust in which both domains trust each other.

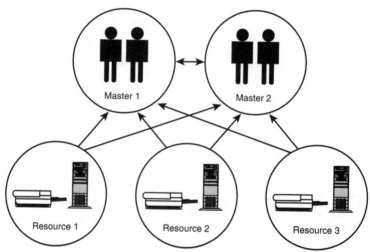

Figure M.1   The Multiple Master Domain Model contains many trusts.

Multiport Repeater

See *hub.*

multiprocessing

70-067   NT Server (Core)   *Installation and Configuration*

Multiprocessing is the capability to use more than one processor in a computer. Multiprocessing allows threads from any process to run any processor that is available. *Windows NT* is a multiprocessing *operating system.* Windows NT's implementation of multiprocessing is known as symmetric multiprocessing.

For more information, see the following sections:

- *Multithreading.* This is a process that is made available when you have a multiprocessing operating system.

- *Multitasking.* This is a process that is sped up when you have a multiprocessing operating system.

Multistation Access Unit

See *hub.*

multitasking

70-067   NT Server (Core)   *Installation and Configuration*

Multitasking is the capability of the computer to run more than one task at any given time. There are two types of multitasking: cooperative and preemptive.

Cooperative Multitasking

A cooperative multitasking *operating system* is one in which the applications that are using a computer's processor give up control of the processor voluntarily so other processes can use it. This type of multitasking requires that all applications on the computer are written in such a way that they do give up control. It is possible for a poorly written application to take control of the processor and not release it, causing any other applications that are running on the computer to become processor starved. Windows 3.11 is an example of a cooperative multitasking environment.

Preemptive Multitasking

A preemptive multitasking operating system is one in which the operating system will interrupt a running process if another process needs to use the processor. In this way, any application can be multitasked. When another application needs to use the processor, the operating system simply suspends the processing of the first application and turns control over to the second. This type of multitasking is made possible by scheduling. The *kernel* is responsible for scheduling threads in and out of the processor. *Windows NT* uses preemptive multitasking.

For more information, see the following sections:

- *Multithreading.* This is the capability of an application to have more than one thread scheduled in and out of the processor.

- *Multiprocessing.* This is the capability to support more than one processor in a single computer.

M

multithreading

70-067   NT Server (Core)   *Installation and Configuration*

Multithreading enables applications running on a computer to use more than one thread of execution. This allows the application's threads to be scheduled in and out of the processor more often, thus giving it more processor time. *Windows NT* allows applications to be multithreaded.

For more information, see the following sections:

- *Thread.* This is a single set of instructions the processor works with.

- *Process.* Every application that runs on the computer creates a process.

- *Multiprocessing.* This is the capability to support more than one processor in a single computer.

- *Multitasking.* This is a process that is sped up when you have a multiprocessing operating system.

M

NBTSTAT command
        NetBIOS over TCP/IP

NBTSTAT is a command-line utility used to display statistics about current *TCP/IP* connections using *NetBIOS* over *TCP/IP*. This command is available when TCP/IP is installed on the machine. The syntax of the command is as follows:

```
nbtstat [-a remotename] [-A IP address] [-c] [-n] [-R] [-r] [-S] [-s]
[interval]
```

The options include the following (note that all options are case sensitive):

Option	Description
-a remotename	Specifies the name of a remote computer on which you want to view the information.
-A IP address	Specifies the *IP address* of a remote computer about which you want to view the information.
-c	Specifies that you want to view all the names in the name cache, as well as the IP addresses.
-n	Specifies that you want to view the NetBIOS names registered by the local computer. This will also indicate whether the name was registered by using broadcasts (b-node) or with WINS (other node types).
-R	Forces the computer to reload the LMHOSTS file.
-r	Lists statistics on name resolution. On computers configured to use *WINS*, this will return the number of names registered with the WINS server versus those registered by using broadcasts.
-S	Displays both client and server sessions using the IP addresses of the remote computers.
-s	Displays both the client and server sessions. This attempts to convert the remote computer's IP address into a name.
interval	Causes the computer to display the selected statistics, pausing between displays for the interval specified.

NDIS
70-058 Networking Essentials   *Standards and Terminology*

NDIS (Network Device Interface Standards) is the Microsoft and 3Com specification for interfacing with network cards. NDIS is designed to provide two functions. First, NDIS provides a vendor-neutral boundary between the network adapter and the *protocol*. This way, any NDIS-compliant protocol stack can communicate with the network adapter. Second, NDIS provides a way to bind multiple protocols to a single adapter, allowing the computer to simultaneously support communications under multiple protocols. NDIS is similar to the Novell ODI specification.

For more information, see the following sections:

- *Protocol*. This is a set of rules for sending and receiving data on the network.
- *ODI*. ODI is another specification that is similar to NDIS.

NET command

General information pertaining to all tests

The NET command is used to perform many *Windows NT* functions from a command line, including creating user accounts, sharing resources on the network, viewing shared resources on the network, and accessing shared resources. Table N.1 outlines information on the different NET commands. To view specific options that can be passed into each command, type NET HELP [COMMAND]. For example, to get extra information on the NET USER command, you would type NET HELP USER at the command prompt.

Table N.1 **NET Commands**

Command	Description
NET ACCOUNTS	Updates the user accounts database and displays the logon requirements for all accounts.
NET CONFIG SERVER	Displays and configures the Server service on the local machine.
NET CONFIG WORKSTATION	Displays or changes configuration of the Workstation service.
NET CONTINUE	Restarts a service that was paused by using the NET PAUSE command.
NET FILE	Closes a file that is open on a server and removes any locks from it.
NET GROUP	Enables you to add, modify, and delete global groups on servers.
NET HELP	Displays help information on any of the other NET commands.
NET HELPMSG	Displays information about Windows NT network error messages.
NET LOCALGROUP	Enables you to add, modify, and delete local groups on computers.
NET NAME	Enables you to add and delete messaging aliases used with the NET SEND command.
NET PAUSE	Pauses any of the pausable services on Windows NT. This keeps users from accessing a service until it is restarted by using the NET CONTINUE command.
NET PRINT	Displays print jobs and print queues on a server.
NET SEND	Sends messages to other users or computers on the network. Computers that you are sending messages to must be active in order to receive the messages.
NET SESSION	Enables you to view and disconnect sessions between the local computer and other computers on the network.
NET SHARE	Enables you to share a resource on the computer to make it available to other users on the network.
NET START	Starts network services.

Command	Description
NET STATISTICS SERVER	Displays the statistics log for the Server service on the local computer.
NET STATISTICS WORKSTATION	Displays the statistics log for the Workstation service on the local computer.
NET STOP	Stops network services.
NET USE	Connects shared resources to the local computer.
NET USER	Enables you to add, modify, and delete users from any computer on which you have privileges to do so.

NetBEUI

70-067 NT Server (Core)   *Installation and Configuration*
70-058 Networking Essentials   *Implementation*

NetBEUI, the NetBIOS Extended User Interface, is an extremely fast, small, and efficient protocol best suited for use on small *LANs*. NetBEUI is an extension of *NetBIOS*. This protocol should primarily be used on workgroup-size LANs of 2–200 workstations. NetBEUI is not a routable protocol, which means it cannot pass across a router to connect to computers on other network segments. In most installations, Microsoft recommends the use of some other protocol besides NetBEUI because it operates mainly through the use of broadcasts and has a tendency to bog down the network.

NetBIOS

70-067 NT Server (Core)   *Installation and Configuration*
70-058 Networking Essentials   *Implementation*

NetBIOS, the Network Basic Input/Output System, is an application interface that provides users and applications a single way to access the network. NetBIOS is closely related to *NetBEUI*; NetBEUI was the original implementation of NetBIOS. Other implementations of NetBIOS have been released, making NetBIOS independent of the lower protocols. These other implementations include NetBIOS over TCP/IP and NetBIOS over IPX.

For more information, see the following sections:

- *NetBEUI.* This is a protocol that is designed around NetBIOS.

- *NetBIOS naming scheme.* Provides information on how NetBIOS computers must be named.

N

NetBIOS naming scheme

70-067 NT Server (Core)   *Installation and Configuration*
70-058 Networking Essentials   *Implementation*

When setting up a *NetBIOS* network, you must be careful to follow specific rules for naming the computers. It is important to note that any *Windows NT* or *Windows 95* computer is a NetBIOS computer. The following list outlines the NetBIOS naming conventions:

- **Uniqueness.** All computer names in the network must be unique.

- **Length.** A NetBIOS computer name can consist of no more than 15 characters.

- **Characters.** NetBIOS computer names can contain any alphanumeric characters. They can also contain any of the following special characters:

  ! @ # $ % ^ & ( ) - _ ' { } . ~

  NetBIOS names cannot contain any spaces.

- **Character case.** NetBIOS computer names are not case sensitive.

When naming NetBIOS computers, you should attempt to name them something you will recognize later. This could include naming each one with the name of the person that will be using the computer, by the location of the computer, or by some other convention you decide on. If you choose names that are difficult to decipher, such as Computer1 and Computer2, it could become difficult to discern where each computer is in the event of trouble.

For more information, see the following sections:

- *NetBIOS.*

- *NetBEUI.* This is the simplest implementation of NetBIOS.

Netlogon service

70-067   NT Server (Core)   *Installation and Configuration*

The primary function of the Netlogon service is to validate user logons. When a user logs in to a *Windows NT domain*, the Netlogon service checks the users login credentials (the username and password) to see whether he or she has permission to log in. The Netlogon service is also responsible for replicating the user accounts database between the primary domain controller (*PDC*) and the backup domain controllers (*BDC*) and for providing pass-through authentication to a trusted domain.

N

netstat command

70-059   TCP/IP   *Connectivity*

The netstat command is used to display protocol statistics for *TCP/IP* network connections. This utility is installed when you install TCP/IP. The syntax of the command is as follows:

```
netstat [-a] [-e] [-n] [-s] [-p protocol] [-r] [interval]
```

The netstat command takes the following options:

Option	Description
-a	Displays all connections and listening ports.
-e	Displays *Ethernet* statistics.
-n	Displays addresses and port numbers in numerical form.
-s	Displays per-*protocol* statistics. The protocols shown are TCP, UDP, *ICMP*, and IP.
-p protocol	Limits the connections shown to a specific protocol. The protocols can be specified as ip, tcp, udp, or icmp.
-r	Displays the contents of the route table.
interval	Causes the computer to display the selected statistics, pausing between displays for the specified interval.

NetWare

General information pertaining to all tests

NetWare is a network *operating system* designed and developed by Novell. In the late 1980s and early 1990s, this was the operating system of choice for network installations. NetWare's market share has since been taken over by *Windows NT*.

For more information, see the following sections:

- *NWLink IPX/SPX.* This is the protocol that NetWare runs on.

- *CSNW.* This is the client service that can be installed on a Windows NT Workstation computer to enable access to a NetWare computer.

- *GSNW.* This is a service that can be installed to allow multiple Windows NT clients to connect through a single connection.

network adapter card

70-058   Networking Essentials   *Network Adapter Cards*

A network adapter card is a piece of hardware that fits into one of the expansion slots of a computer. This piece of hardware provides a connection between the computer itself and the physical wiring of the network. Network adapter cards are also frequently known as Network Interface Cards and NICs. The network card must perform three functions:

- **Prepare data for transmission.** The network adapter must convert the data the computer sends it into a form that is compatible with the network.

- **Send data.** The network adapter must actually place the data on the network.

- **Control the flow of data from the PC to the transmission medium.** The network adapter negotiates with any other network cards to determine how the transmissions will occur. This includes data rate and the amount of time between packets.

It is extremely important to note what resource settings Microsoft recommends for the network adapter cards. If you're manually configuring the card, Microsoft recommends that the *IRQ* be set to IRQ 5 if it is available. On older cards, this is often the default IRQ setting. On newer multimedia PCs, however, you will often run into problems placing a network card on IRQ 5 because most sound cards are set to use it. Other settings that you will have to be concerned with are the base memory address and the I/O port. The recommended setting for the base memory address is 300-3FF. The recommended setting for the I/O port is D8000.

Network Control Panel

70-067   NT Server (Core)   *Installation and Configuration*

The Network Control Panel is used to install and configure network services, hardware, and software. The Network Control Panel is divided into five tabs: **Identification, Services, Protocols, Adapters,** and **Bindings**.

- **Identification.** From the Identification tab, you can configure the *NetBIOS* name of the computer and what *domain* or workgroup the computer participates in.

- **Services.** From the Services tab, you can install and configure services on the computer. These services include information such as the *SNMP service, Remote Access Service,* and the *TCP/IP printing service.*

- **Protocols.** From the Protocols tab, you can install and configure the network protocols on which the computer will communicate.

- **Adapters.** The Adapters tab is used to view and configure the resources of any network adapters installed in the computer.
- **Bindings.** From the Bindings tab, you can configure the order in which network protocols and services are bound to network cards. A *binding* is a connection between the network service or protocol and the network card. These connections are used to optimize the protocols you want the network card or service to use first.

For more information on the Network Control Panel, see the section titled *Control Panels*.

network interface card

See *network adapter card.*

Network layer

See *OSI Model.*

Network Monitor

70-068   NT Server Enterprise   *Monitoring Network Traffic*

Network monitor is a tool that can be used to capture and analyze network traffic. A scaled-down version of this tool ships as part of *Windows NT* Server, and the full version ships with Systems Management Server. Using this tool, it is possible to filter and view packets that are being sent to a particular computer or to view the overall network traffic. The version of Network Monitor that ships with Windows NT Server allows you to capture only packets that are coming in and out of the machine it is running on; the version that comes with Systems Management Server allows you to capture all packets on the local segment.

For more information, see the following sections:

- *Performance Monitor.* This tool allows you to capture and view data about the performance of the server.
- *Baseline.* This is a basic outline of the system performance that can be used to compare data that is gathered later.

Network Neighborhood

General information pertaining to all tests

The Network Neighborhood is an icon on the desktop of *Windows NT* and *Windows 95* computers that provides a way to browse the network. This browse list is pulled from one of the backup browser computers on the network. When a computer first requests a copy of the browse list, it actually requests a list of three backup browsers from the master browser. It receives a copy of the browse list from one of the computers on that list.

For more information, see the following sections:

- *Master browser.* The master browser is a computer that maintains a list of all computers on the network that have network services, such as File and Print Sharing, turned on.
- *Browse list.* The browse list is a list of all computers on the network that have network services, such as File and Print Sharing, turned on.

network share

70-067   NT Server (Core)   *Managing Resources*

A network share is a resource made available on the server for clients to access. This can be a directory, a *printer*, or some other resource such as a CD-ROM or *modem*. The *administrator* can assign permissions as to who can access and use the information or resource that is shared.

For more information, see the section titled *assigning NTFS permissions*, which outlines assigning permissions on an *NTFS* partition.

NIC

See *network adapter card.*

NSLOOKUP

70-059   TCP/IP   *Implementing Microsoft DNS Servers*

NSLOOKUP is a tool that can be used to view information from a *DNS* server and make sure that the DNS server is resolving names correctly. When it is run, this application contacts the primary DNS server listed in the DNS section of the *TCP/IP* protocol. From there, it can query the DNS for information. The syntax of the command is this

```
nslookup [-option ...] [computer-to-find ¦ [server]]
```

where the options include the following:

Option	Description
-help	Gives a summary of the nslookup commands.
-finger	Connects with the finger server on the current computer to attempt to identify a user.
-ls	Lists information stored in the DNS server for the specified user.
-server	Changes the default server to the specified DNS server.
-set	Enables you to configure settings for how nslookup functions.
-view	Sorts and lists the output of the ls commands.
computer-to-find	Indicates the name of the computer you are trying to look up.
server	Specifies which DNS server you are going to use to look up the computer.

For more information, see the section titled *DNS*, which describes a service that is used to convert host names into *IP addresses* that can be used by the system.

NT Hardware Qualifier

70-073   NT Workstation   *Installation and Configuration*

The NT Hardware Qualifier tool (NTHQ) is a tool you can use to verify that all the equipment in your computer is NT compatible before you install *Windows NT*. This tool is located in the \support\hqtool directory on the Windows NT Workstation CD.

To run the NT Hardware Qualifier, you must first run the batch file named MAKEDISK.BAT, which makes a special bootable floppy. NTHQ detects and identifies the hardware in the machine and then presents you with a report you can compare to the *HCL* to see whether the hardware is supported by Windows NT. The information NTHQ returns is separated into four areas: System, Video, Motherboard, and Other.

The most important area of the system that you need to investigate is the Other area. This section contains information about hardware components NTHQ could not identify. This report is also useful for finding hardware conflicts such as *IRQ* and base memory. One thing you need to be extremely careful about is that this utility will not detect any hardware that has been added since Windows NT was originally released, and the utility has not been updated in the service packs.

For more information, see the section on *HCL*, which describes a list of all hardware that has been approved for use with Windows NT.

NT virtual DOS machine

See *Win16 NTVDM*.

NTDETECT

See *boot process, Intel*.

NTFS

General information pertaining to all tests

NTFS, or the NT File System, is an advanced high-performance file system that ships with *Windows NT*. This file system is the preferred file system for use with NT. The following list describes some of the features of NTFS:

- **Long filenames.** NTFS supports long filenames (up to 255 characters long).

- **Recoverability.** NTFS is a recoverable file system that uses transaction logging to log all file and directory updates. If a power failure occurs when the system is in the middle of writing to the disk, the information in the transaction log can be used to repeat or complete the failed operation.

- **Security.** NTFS enables the user to secure files and directories on the computer.

- **Compression.** NTFS enables the user to compress files and directories on the partition to optimize space.

- **Size.** NTFS partitions can be as large as 16 exabytes in size. An exabyte is a little bit larger than one billion gigabytes.

For more information, see the following sections:

- *Master file table.* The master file table replaces the file allocation table of a FAT partition in an NTFS partition.

- *FAT.* FAT is another type of partition that is supported by Windows NT.

NTLDR

See *boot process, Intel*.

NTOSKRNL.EXE

See *boot process, Alpha* and *boot process, Intel*.

NTVDM
See *Win16 NTVDM.*

NWLink IPX/SPX
70-058   Networking Essentials   *Planning*

NWLink IPX/SPX is Microsoft's implementation of Novell's IPX/SPX protocol stack. *Windows NT* uses this protocol stack to communicate with Novell *NetWare* servers. The NWLink IPX/SPX protocol is a small but relatively fast *protocol* that is routable. This protocol suite will automatically detect the *frame type* that is in use on the network and will set the frame type accordingly. If it detects a *frame type* other than the 802.2 frame type, NWLink defaults to the 802.2 frame type. For example, if Windows NT detects the 802.3 frame type, the NWLink frame type default would still be 802.2. This protocol suite consists of two primary portions: IPX and SPX.

IPX
The IPX (Internetwork Packet Exchange) protocol resides at the Network layer of the *OSI Model.* IPX provides connectionless service that is responsible for routing and maintaining network addresses. IPX relies on hardware addresses to provide network device addresses.

SPX
The SPX (Sequenced Packet Exchange) protocol resides at the Transport layer of the OSI Model. SPX extends the functionality of IPX by providing connection-oriented service and reliable delivery, retransmitting packets in the event of an error. SPX sequences the packets of data. On the receiving end, missing packets are immediately detected, and retransmission of those packets is requested.

For more information, see the section *installing network protocols*, which provides an overview of the procedure for installing network protocols.

N

O

Object Manager

70-067   NT Server (Core)   *Installation and Configuration*

The Object Manager is the component of the *Windows NT Executive Services* that is responsible for naming and setting security on objects. An object is a software component that consists of a data type, attributes, and a set of operations the object performs. The Object Manager is also responsible for tracking the creation and use of all objects on the system.

For more information, see the section titled *Executive Services*, which contains a list of all the executive services.

ODBC

General information pertaining to all tests

ODBC, or Open Database Connectivity, is a technology that allows developers to create database applications that are independent of the backend database. ODBC is implemented through a series of drivers loaded on the client machine. For example, suppose a developer creates an application that uses ODBC to access a Microsoft *SQL Server* database. Without changing the way the front-end code works, the developer could easily port this application over to an Oracle backend.

O

ODI

70-058   Networking Essentials   *Standards and Terminology*

ODI, or Open Data-Link Interface, was developed by Novell and Apple and serves the same function that *NDIS* does in NetWare and Macintosh environments. ODI is a set of rules that provide a vendor-independent interface between a *protocol* stack and the *network adapter*. Much like NDIS does, this interface allows multiple network drivers to support multiple protocol stacks.

one-way trust

70-067   NT Server (Core)   *Installation and Configuration*
70-068   NT Server Enterprise   *Planning*

A one-way trust, as shown in Figure O.1, is a trust in which the *trusting domain* relies on the *trusted domain* to authenticate users. All user accounts remain in the trusted domain. Administrators in the trusting domain can then assign those users permissions to local resources.

For more information related to one-way trusts, see the following sections:

- *Single Domain Model*
- *Single Master Domain Model*
- *Multiple Master Domain Model*
- *Complete Trust Domain Model*
- *Two-way trust*

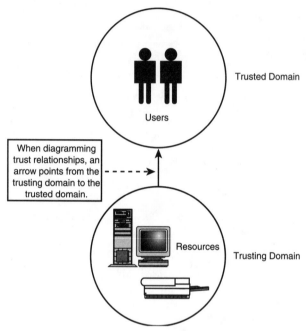

Figure O.1   In a one-way trust, the trusting domain relies on the trusted domain to validate user accounts. Note that in a diagram of a trust, the arrow always
points toward the trusted domain.

Operating System
General information pertaining to all tests

An operating system is an application that is written to perform all the low-level functions of reading and writing to devices and allowing other applications to run. Operating
systems are usually defined by what processor type they run on.
Several operating systems are discussed in this book, including the following:

- *Windows NT*
- *Windows 95/98*
- *Windows 3.11*
- *DOS*
- *NetWare*
- *OS/2*

oscilloscope

70-058 Networking Essentials   *Troubleshooting*

An oscilloscope is a tool used to measure and view fluctuations in signal voltage and strength to assist in finding broken or damaged networking cables.

For more information related to oscilloscopes, see the section *TDR*.

OSI Model

70-058 Networking Essentials   *Networking Standards*

The OSI Model, or Open Standards Interface Model, defines and describes the different processes of open systems networking. The OSI Model is a seven-layer standard that divides the functions of a communications protocol. Each layer addresses a specific function that is performed during the communication process (see Figure O.2).

How Layers Communicate

In order to communicate, each layer of the communicating computer's protocol stack talks to the corresponding layer on the other computer. For this to work, each protocol layer on the sending computer adds information (in the form of a header) to the data being sent. When the receiving computer gets the packet, each layer strips off the appropriate header information. (The Physical layer does not add a header to the packet.)

When creating products that map directly to one of the layers of the OSI Model, developers need only be concerned with communicating with the layers directly above and below that with which they are working. For example, if the product communicates at the Transport layer, it needs to communicate with only the Network and the Session layers (see Figure O.3).

Physical Layer

The Physical layer is concerned with all aspects of transmitting and receiving bits of data on the network media. This layer defines the physical structure of the network, the specifications for using the network media, and bit transmission and encoding. Although the Physical layer does not specify the transmission media to be used, it does specify several requirements the transmission media must meet. These requirements change based on the media.

O

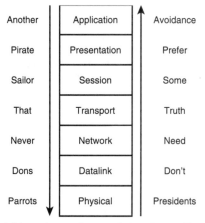

Another	Application	Avoidance
Pirate	Presentation	Prefer
Sailor	Session	Some
That	Transport	Truth
Never	Network	Need
Dons	Datalink	Don't
Parrots	Physical	Presidents

Figure O.2 The OSI Model is made up of seven distinct layers. You will need to know the different layers of the OSI Model when you take the Networking Essentials test; use either of these mnemonic phrases if you have trouble remembering the order of the layers.

As data is sent, each layer of the OSI model adds a header to the data packet.

When data is received, the header information is stripped off in the same order that it was added.

Original Data (Application Layer)					
Original Data (Application Layer)	Presentation Layer Header				
Original Data (Application Layer)	Presentation Layer Header	Session Layer Header			
Original Data (Application Layer)	Presentation Layer Header	Session Layer Header	Transport Layer Header		
Original Data (Application Layer)	Presentation Layer Header	Session Layer Header	Transport Layer Header	Network Layer Header	
Original Data (Application Layer)	Presentation Layer Header	Session Layer Header	Transport Layer Header	Network Layer Header	Data Link Layer Header
Original Data (Application Layer)	Presentation Layer Header	Session Layer Header	Transport Layer Header	Network Layer Header	Data Link Layer Header	Physical Layer Header

Figure O.3   Each layer of the OSI Model communicates directly with corresponding layers by adding and removing headers from the packet.

Data Link Layer

The Data Link layer resides on top of the Physical layer. The primary responsibilities of the Data Link layer are to take data passed from the upper levels and disassemble it into bits for transmission by the Physical layer and to reassemble information passed to it from the Physical layer. The Data Link layer is also responsible for addressing, error control, and flow control. The *IEEE 802.3* standard divides the Data Link layer into two distinct layers described as follows:

- *Media Access Control (MAC)*. The MAC layer is responsible for providing a method by which multiple devices can share the same media channel. This layer also provides a means of addressing information between network devices.

- *Logical Link Control (LLC)*. The LLC layer is responsible for establishing and maintaining connections between devices.

Network Layer

The Network layer handles communications between devices on logically separate networks, called internetworks. These internetworks can be very large and can consist of different types of networks. The Network layer uses routing algorithms to pass data back and forth between the source and destination networks. Each network is assigned a network ID, which is used to perform the routing.

Transport Layer

The Transport layer allows the upper portions of the OSI Model to communicate with the network while hiding the complexities of network operations from it, and it is also responsible for breaking down large messages into smaller segments for delivery by the network. In some cases, the Transport layer can take steps to ensure reliable delivery of messages to the destination address. This does prevent errors during transport; however, if errors do occur, they are detected and corrected.

Session Layer

The Session layer is responsible for managing communications by establishing, managing, and terminating connections between computers. These connections can take three forms: simplex, half-duplex, and full-duplex.

- *Simplex.* Simplex communications are simple one-way communications. A simple example of this is a doorbell. When a doorbell is pushed, it sends a signal down the wire. The doorbell button does not receive a message back from the inside of the house.

    In a network, an example of a simplex message is an *SNMP* message. The client computer sends a message to the management station but does not receive any sort of message back.

- *Half-duplex.* Half-duplex communications are two-way communications, but communication travels in only one direction at a time. An example of this type of communication is a two-way radio. When two people communicate over a two-way radio, one person must stop transmitting and free the channel before the second person can begin transmitting.

    A network example of a half-duplex message is the way in which a Web browser and a Web server interact. The Web browser requests an item from the server, and then the server responds by providing the requested item.

- *Full-duplex.* Full-duplex communications are two-way communications in which information travels both ways at once. This type of communication provides each device with its own separate channel for communication. An example of this is a telephone, which allows both users to communicate at the same time. Similarly, modems use full-duplex methods to communicate with one another.

Presentation Layer

The Presentation layer is responsible for dealing with the grammatical rules needed for communication between computers. This layer takes application-specific data from the Application layer and translates it into machine-independent data that will be supported by the lower layers.

Application Layer

The Application layer provides upper-level network support for applications, including file and print services, *email* services, and database services. The Application layer also advertises these services to all computers on the network.

For more information, see the following section:

- *TCP/IP Layered Model.* Explains how TCP/IP maps to the OSI Model.

OS/2

General information pertaining to all tests

OS/2 is a 32-bit operating system that was originally designed by Microsoft and IBM. After version 1.0, Microsoft left the venture, but IBM continued to build and market it. OS/2 does not hold a significant amount of the *operating system* market share, which makes it difficult for companies that are using OS/2 to find software to run on it. Windows NT provides an OS/2 subsystem to provide compatibility between the operating systems.

p-node

70-059 TCP/IP   *Windows Internet Name Service*

P-node name resolution is a *NetBios* over *TCP/IP* implementation that solves many problems that can occur when using *b-node* name resolution.

Computers using p-node name resolution do not create or respond to broadcast messages. Rather, every computer on the network contacts a WINS server to register its name. The WINS server keeps track of all names and addresses and ensures that no duplicate names exist on the network. When one computer wants to contact another, it must first contact the WINS server to find out the *IP address* of the destination computer. Those queries go straight to the WINS server, reducing the overall amount of broadcast traffic on the network.

The biggest problems with using p-node name resolution are that every computer on the network must be configured with the address of the *WINS* server and, if the WINS server is unavailable for any reason, no clients will be able to resolve names.

For more information, see the following sections:

■ *WINS*. This service automatically maps NetBIOS names to IP addresses.

■ *B-node*.

■ *P-node*.

■ *M-node*.

P

Packet Assembler/Disassembler

See *PAD*.

Packet Internetwork Groper

See *PING*.

packet sniffer

70-058 Networking Essentials   *Troubleshooting Equipment*

A packet sniffer is a piece of hardware used to analyze network traffic, track performance, and analyze packets on the network. A packet sniffer can track down malfunctioning network hardware such as *hubs* and network cards, identify *bottlenecks*, and discover *protocol* problems. Packet sniffers are extremely expensive, and for smaller networks, software-based solutions may fulfill your needs. Packet sniffers are also known as *protocol analyzers*.

For more information, see the following sections:

- *Hub.* This is a piece of network hardware used to connect computers.
- *Network adapter cards.* This is a piece of hardware put in a computer to allow the computer to connect to the network.

PAD

70-058 Networking Essentials   *Standards and Terminology*

A PAD, or Packet Assembler/Disassembler, is a piece of hardware used in *X.25* networks to receive input from a terminal and assemble it into packets for transmission over the network. The PAD also disassembles packets received from the network for delivery to the terminal.

PC Card (PCMCIA) Control Panel

70-067 NT Server (Core)   *Installation and Configuration*

The PC Card (PCMCIA) Control Panel is used to control PC card settings and enable PCMCIA sockets on the computer. A PCMCIA card is a removable device about the size of a credit card that is used in laptop computers. These cards can function as *hard drives,* modems, *network adapter cards,* and memory cards. This Control Panel can be used to view configuration settings, including the memory address and IRQ, of a card.

PCMCIA

General information pertaining to all tests

PCMCIA (the Personal Computer Memory Card International Association) has become the standard for removable devices that can be installed in portable computers. PCMCIA cards are about the size of a credit card. These cards can function as memory, *hard drives, modems* and fax, network, and *wireless* communication devices.

For more information, see the section titled *PCMCIA Control Panel,* which describes the Control Panel that can be used to install and configure PCMCIA cards.

P

PDC

70-067 NT Server (Core)   *Installation and Configuration*
70-068 NT Server Enterprise   *Server Roles*

The PDC, or primary domain controller, is a server that resides in a *Windows NT domain* that is responsible for keeping the master copy of all accounts in the domain. Any changes that are made to the accounts are replicated out to all *BDCs* on the domain. The PDC authenticates some of the users that log in to the domain. Because of the number of other tasks the PDC has to do, however, the BDC performs most user authentication. A domain can have only one PDC; but if the PDC goes down for any reason, a BDC in the domain is promoted to perform the functions of the PDC. If this occurs, any changes to user accounts that were not replicated out to the BDCs will be lost.

For more information on PDCs, see the following sections:

- *BDC.* This type of domain controller provides backup for the PDC.
- *Domain.* A domain is a logical grouping of computers.

Peer Web Services

70-073   NT Workstation   *Connectivity Issues*

Peer Web Services allow you to publish Web pages on a small scale by using *Windows NT Workstation* 4.0 and *Windows 95*. Frequently, Peer Web Services are used to develop and test Web-based applications without loading Windows NT Server and *Internet Information Server* on the client computer. All extensions and filters, such as *ISAPI*, are supported by Peer Web Services.

peer-to-peer network

70-073   NT Workstation   *Connectivity Issues*

In a peer-to-peer network, any computer can connect to and use files on any other computer on the network (not just to specialized servers). One of the best reasons to use peer-to-peer networking is that you can reduce the cost of the servers. The downside to using it is that users have control over which resources on their machines are shared and who has access to those resources. Because of this, peer-to-peer networks provide a significantly less-secure environment than traditional server-based networks do. When considering peer-to-peer networking, it is important to remember that *Windows NT Workstation* is limited to 10 concurrent inbound connections.

Performance Monitor

70-068   NT Server Enterprise   *Monitoring*

Performance Monitor is an application that monitors the performance of *Windows NT* Servers and Workstations. This tool allows *administrators* to track statistics and view trends on users' computers. By using Performance Monitor, administrators can perform the following tasks:

- Analyze server operations in real and recorded time.
- Identify trends over time.
- Identify server *bottlenecks*.
- Monitor the effects of configuration changes.
- Determine capacity.
- Monitor local and remote computers running Windows NT.
- Isolate and track individual portions of the system including processors, *hard drives*, memory, and network cards.
- Perform monitoring functions separately or simultaneously.

For more information, see the following sections:

- *Counters*. Performance Monitor uses these to track system performance.
- *Baseline*. This is a measurement over an average period of time that can be used to determine overall system performance.
- *Bottlenecks*. A bottleneck is a resource that is not performing up to expectations.

P

physical address

See *MAC address.*

Physical layer

See *OSI Model.*

PING

70-059 TCP/IP   *Connectivity*

The PING command is one of the most useful commands in the *TCP/IP* suite of protocols. This command sends a series of *ICMP* packets to another computer, which then
returns a response. This information can be used to troubleshoot connectivity between
two computers.

The syntax of the PING command is as follows:

```
ping [-t] [-a] [-n count] [-l size] [-f] [-i TTL] [-v TOS][-r count] [-s
count] [[-j host-list] ¦ [-k host-list]][-w timeout] destination-list
```

PING takes the following options:

Option	Description
-t	Pings the specified host until interrupted.
-a	Resolves addresses to host names.
-n count	Indicates the number of echo requests to send.
-l size	Sends the buffer size.
-f	Sets the Don't Fragment flag in the packet.
-i TTL	Enables Time To Live.
-v TOS	Specifies Type Of Service.
-r count	Records the route for count hops.
-s count	Displays the timestamp for count hops.
-j host-list	Indicates a loose source route along host-list.
-k host-list	Indicates a strict source route along host-list.
-w timeout	Specifies the timeout in milliseconds to wait for each reply.

P

Plain Old Telephony System

See *POTS.*

Point-to-Point Tunneling Protocol

See *PPTP.*

Policy Editor

70-067 NT Server (Core)   *Managing Resources*

Policy Editor is a utility that creates rules governing what a user sees and what portions
of the configuration settings the user has access to. These policies, known as *user policies*,
can be set up on a per-user, per-group, and per-machine basis. They are applied to the

computer during startup. A user policy can control anything from the default wallpaper that is displayed on the desktop to removing the Run... command from the Start menu. User policies are saved in the netlogon shared folder on the *PDC* under the name NTCONFIG.POL. User policies are applied to the computer by modification of the client computer's Registry.

The following steps outline the procedure by which user policies are applied to the computer:

1. The computer first checks to see whether any computer polices need to be applied.

2. Group policies are checked and applied to the computer. If the user logging in to the computer is a member of several groups, the computer relies on the priority of each group policy as set by the administrator.

3. Finally, checks for and applies any individual user policies that are present. The last policy that is applied will override any conflicting settings. For example, if the group policy specifies that the user cannot access the Run... command but the user policy specifies that the user can access it, the group policy information will be overridden by user policy.

Ports Control Panel

70-067   NT Server (Core)   *Installation and Configuration*

The Ports Control Panel is used to install and configure serial ports on your computer. Any *serial port* that is detected on the computer is automatically installed and will appear in the Ports Control Panel. If you do not want a built-in serial port to be installed on the *Windows NT* computer, you must first disable it in the *BIOS* of the machine.

POTS

70-058   Networking Essentials   *Standard and Terminology*

POTS, or Plain Old Telephony System, is the standard telephone service. This is simply the regular telephone service that most people have running into their homes and businesses.

PPP

70-059   TCP/IP   *TCP/IP and Remote Access*

PPP, or Point-to-Point Protocol, is a *protocol* used for communications between two computers over a serial interface, such as a *modem*. PPP was developed as a replacement for *SLIP* and provides many advances that were not available to SLIP users. The biggest advantage is that PPP provides for the use of *DHCP* to assign *IP addresses* to client computers. Other advances include password *encryption* and the capability to transport protocols other than *TCP/IP*.

Windows NT uses PPP to provide remote access services to other computers, enabling them to connect to other servers that use SLIP or PPP. Windows NT Remote Access Service, or *RAS*, also provides two extensions to PPP. Those extensions are *Multilink* and use the Point-to-Point Tunneling Protocol, or *PPTP*. Multilink enables client computers to connect to a server using multiple connections, which increases the throughput of the total connection. Each connection that is made to the server requires an individual phone line and modem. This can provide an inexpensive solution to allow higher bandwidth connections to remote sites or offices that have a single modem.

For more information, see the following sections:

P

- *PPTP.* This is a remote access protocol used to connect to a server over public networks such as the Internet.
- *DHCP.* This is a protocol used to dynamically assign IP addresses to computers.
- *SLIP.* This is a protocol that was replaced by PPP.

PPTP

70-059 TCP/IP   *TCP/IP and Remote Access*

PPTP (the Point-to-Point Tunneling Protocol) is a *protocol* that allows for the creation of virtual private networks, or VPNs, across public *TCP/IP* networks such as the Internet. A VPN allows client computers to make secure and *encrypted* connections to servers on a remote network. PPTP is most frequently used to enable client computers to connect to a local Internet service provider, or *ISP*, and then use the ISP's network as a *gateway* for communicating with a remote network. When the client computer connects to the remote server, the two computers negotiate a 40-bit key that will be used to encrypt all packets sent over the Internet. PPTP then encapsulates all the data—no matter what protocol is being used—as *PPP* packets. This makes it possible for any protocol on the remote network to be sent over the Internet.

PPTP is implemented as part of the Remote Access Service (*RAS*) of *Windows NT Server.*

For more information, see the following sections:

- *VPN.* This is the process of connecting to private networks by using public networks such as the Internet.
- *PPP.* This is a dial-up protocol that can be used to connect to a *Windows NT Server.*

Presentation layer

See *OSI Model.*

P

primary domain controller

See *PDC.*

print devices

70-067 NT Server (Core)   *Managing Resources*

A print device, in *Windows NT* terminology, is simply the physical device that prints. A printer takes information passed to it from a computer and produces hard copy output on paper, film, or some other form of media. Print devices are installed on Windows NT computers through the *Printers Control Panel.*

print pools

70-067 NT Server (Core)   *Managing Resources*

A print pool consists of two or more identical *print devices* that are associated with a single *Windows NT* printer. This allows multiple devices to handle the print requests that are passed to a single printer, speeding up the output of large numbers of print requests.

printer

70-067   NT Server (Core)   *Managing Resources*

A printer is a software interface between the operating system and a *print device*. A single printer on a *Windows NT* computer can control several print devices, thus creating a *print pool*. Printers are installed through the *Printers Control Panel*. The printer defines where the print job will go before it is printed, when it will actually print, and other physical options related to the print device, such as printer resolution and maximum paper size. The printing process is described in the following steps:

1. The client computer alerts the server computer that it is going to send a print job. The server computer checks the version of the printer driver installed on the client computer. If the client computer has an older version of the printer driver, the server downloads the newest version of the driver to the client machine.

2. The printer driver spools the print job to a file on the local machine. The local machine then contacts the server computer and transmits the print job to the server print spooler.

3. The server print spooler holds the data until it is ready to print and then sends it to the local print provider.

4. The local print provider sends the data to the print processor. The print processor renders the data into information that can be used by the print device and then passes it on to the print monitor.

5. The print monitor sends the data to the print device for printing.

Printers Control Panel

70-067   NT Server (Core)   *Managing Resources*

The Printers Control Panel is used to install, configure, and remove *printers* on *Windows NT* computers. To access the Control Panel, click **Start**, **Settings**, **Control Panel**. This opens the Control Panel window where you can choose **Printers**. From the Printers window, you can perform three functions: install a printer, remove a printer, or check the status of a printer.

To install a printer, double-click on the **Add Printer** button. This starts a wizard that will allow you to add the printer and make it available to client computers.

To check the status of an existing printer, double-click on the name of the printer. This displays a window showing any print jobs that are being sent or are waiting to be sent to the printer. If you are logged in as an *administrator*, or if you have permissions to manage print jobs, you can choose any job in the window and either delete or pause it. Deleting a print job stops it from being printed and deletes it from the server computer. Pausing a print job also stops it from being printed, but does not delete it from the server. This allows the job to be restarted later.

Finally, to delete a printer, choose the printer name from the window and press the **Delete** key. This removes the printer from the list of printers available to client computers and removes it from the server computer. If any print jobs are waiting to be printed, the printer will not be deleted until after the jobs have been completed.

P

priority boost

70-073   NT Workstation   *Running Applications*

On a *Windows NT* computer, many background applications, such as services, run at a high priority. Although this improves response time to client computers using these services, it can cause applications running in the foreground to respond more slowly. To help resolve this issue, Windows NT provides any application that is running in the foreground a priority boost of 2, making it run at a base priority of 10 instead of 8. This improves response time for those applications.

The priority boost settings are located on the **Performance** tab of the **System Control Panel**. If you set the slider to Maximum, you will get the best overall response time for foreground applications. However, this setting will cause background applications to slow down slightly. If you set the slider to the middle value, which is the default setting, you will increase the response time of background programs but still give more processor time to the foreground program. If you set the slider to None, all applications will get equal amounts of processor time.

private IP space

70-059   TCP/IP   *IP Addressing*

A private IP space is a range of non-Internet routable *IP addresses* that is given to a group of computers on a private network. The fact that the IP addresses are nonroutable is a built-in security feature. The problem that arises from this, however, is that networks that employ private IP spaces must also use a *firewall* or proxy server to allow the client computers to access the Internet. Table P.1 lists the private IP spaces.

Table P.1   **Ranges of Private IP spaces**

Class	Beginning Address	Ending Address
Class A	10.0.0.0	10.255.255.255
Class B	172.16.0.0	172.16.255.255
Class C	192.168.0.0	192.168.255.255

process

70-073   NT Workstation   *Running Applications*

Every application run on a *Windows NT* system creates a process. A process is the executable portion of the application—a set of memory addresses and one or more threads. The process is simply a container for these individual portions.

Process Manager

70-067   NT Server (Core)   *Installation and Configuration*

The Process Manager is the portion of the *Windows NT Executive Services* that is responsible for creating and destroying processes and keeping track of process and thread objects. This subsystem also contains services used for creating and using threads and processes.

For more information, see the following sections:

- *Process*. This is created whenever an application is executed.
- *Executive Services*. This section describes the purpose of the Executive Services.

protocol

70-058   Networking Essentials   *Standards and Terminology*

At the most basic level, a protocol is a set of rules for sending information over the network. These rules control the content of the message, how the message is formatted, the timing of the message, how the message is sequenced, and how errors are handled if they should occur. For two computers to communicate, they must speak the same protocol.

For more information, see the following sections:

■ *TCP/IP*

■ *NetBEUI*

■ *NWLink IPX/SPX*

protocol analyzers

See *packet sniffer.*

P

R

RAID

RAID (Redundant Array of Inexpensive Disks) is a method used to enable several fault-tolerant disk systems. There are six levels of RAID, 0 through 5, each of which provides a different level of fault tolerance, performance, and cost. Of the six levels of RAID, only three are supported by *Windows NT* Server. The following sections outline the different RAID levels supported by Windows NT Server.

RAID 0

RAID 0, or *disk striping*, does not truly provide any data redundancy at all. Rather, RAID 0 divides the data into 64KB blocks and writes the data across different physical drives. This process can greatly increase disk read and write performance of your *hard drives*, but there is no method for recovering data if one of the drives crashes. A minimum of two hard drives are required, and you can have a maximum of 32 drives. The set of drives that you set up is known as a stripe set. Aside from not having any sort of data redundancy, the biggest limitation of using stripe sets is that neither the *system partition* nor the *boot partition* can be contained in a stripe set.

RAID 1

RAID 1, or *disk mirroring*, is the process of duplicating all writes made to a single logical drive to two separate hard drives. Information is written to both drives in a mirror set at the same time. Another version of RAID 1, called *disk duplexing*, is created when each disk in a mirror is controlled by a separate hard drive controller. Unlike in RAID 0, all drives and partitions in a Windows NT Server can be mirrored, including the boot and system partitions. The biggest drawback to using RAID 1 is that it has the highest cost, per megabyte, of all fault-tolerance systems because only 50 percent of the total available disk space is available for use.

RAID 5

RAID 5, or disk striping with parity, provides the best data redundancy. Disk striping with parity uses a process similar to RAID 0. It breaks up the data into 64KB chunks and writes it across several drives. The difference lies in the fact that RAID 5 requires a third hard disk drive that is used to store parity information. A RAID 5 array can have a maximum of 32 hard drives. Windows NT uses the three hard drives to spread out the data and the parity information. Because Windows NT has to calculate the parity information every time it writes to the disk, RAID 5 slows down write performance. If any one of the hard disk drives in the set fails, the information that was lost can be regenerated from the parity information. Neither the system nor the boot partition can be located in a RAID 5 partition.

For more information on RAID, see the section titled *Disk Administrator*.

157

RAS

70-067   NT Server (Core)   *Install and Configure Remote Access Service*

RAS, or Remote Access Service, provides access to a *Windows NT* network from any location that has a phone line. RAS allows users that are traveling or that work at remote locations to connect to a network and fully utilize all resources that are available to them on the network. Both Windows NT Server and Workstation can act as RAS servers and clients. On the server side, Windows NT Server supports 256 inbound RAS connections, and *Windows NT Workstation* supports one inbound RAS connection.

RAS primarily supports the *PPP* line protocol, but it can connect to other servers that are running *SLIP*. RAS users can use any protocol that is supported on the network over a RAS connection, including *TCP/IP*, *NetBEUI*, and IPX/SPX. RAS can communicate over Public Switched Telephone Network, also known as standard phone lines; *ISDN*; null modem (which is a serial cable linking two computers); and *X.25*. RAS can also use the *PPTP* protocol to connect to servers over the Internet. PPTP encrypts all data that is sent.

RDISK

See *ERD*.

recursive query

See *DNS*.

Redundant Array of Inexpensive Disks

See *RAID*.

RegEdit

See *Registry Editor.*

R

Regional Settings Control Panel

70-067   NT Server (Core)   *Installation and Configuration*

The Regional Settings Control Panel is used to edit specific information about the locale from which you are currently operating. This includes the way that numbers, currency, date, and time are displayed on the machine.

For more information regarding the Regional Settings Control Panel, see the *Control Panel* section.

Registry

General information pertaining to all tests

The Registry is a hierarchical database used to store information pertaining to hardware, *device drivers*, *operating system* settings, and applications installed on the computer. The

Windows NT Registry is divided into five subtrees that contain different information on a per-computer and per-user basis. The per-computer sections contain information about the hardware and software that is installed on the machine. The per-user sections contain information that outlines each individual user's settings including the desktop wallpaper, *printers*, and network settings. The Registry can be modified directly by using the Registry Editor or indirectly by using the Control Panels. Table R.1 outlines the keys in the Windows NT Registry.

Table R.1   **Windows NT Registry Keys**

Key	Description	Abbreviation
HKEY_LOCAL_MACHINE	This key contains information that pertains to the computer itself. This includes information such as installed hardware, operating system, device drivers, and startup information.	HKLM
HKEY_CLASSES_ROOT	This key contains information used to associate file types to applications by the filename extension. For example, by default, any file ending in .TXT is opened with the Notepad application. This also contains information that is used for object linking and embedding (OLE). These values are the same as those in HKEY_LOCAL_MACHINE ➥ \Software\Classes.	HKCR
HKEY_CURRENT_CONFIG	This subtree contains information about the hardware configuration currently running on the computer. These are changes to the default settings that are pulled from HKEY_LOCAL_MACHINE.	HKCC
HKEY_CURRENT_USER	This key contains user information about the person currently logged in to the computer. This information includes the desktop settings, network connections, and printer settings, as well as user-specific application settings.	HKCU
HKEY_USERS	This key contains information about all the user profiles stored on the computer. This includes the user that's currently logged in and the default user profile. When a user logs in, his user settings are copied from this key into the HKEY_CURRENT_USER key.	HKU

R

For more information regarding the Registry, see the following sections:

- *Registry Editor*. This is a tool that is used to directly modify the Registry.
- *Policy Editor*. This is a tool that is used to indirectly modify the Registry.
- *Control Panels*. These are small applications used to indirectly modify the Registry.

Registry Editor
General information pertaining to all tests

The Registry Editor in *Windows NT* takes two different forms. Regedt32 is the traditional Registry Editor that ships with Windows NT. Regedit is a newer version that was written for *Windows 95*, but will also run on Windows NT. Both versions of the tool are known as the Registry Editor and are installed when you set up Windows NT. The biggest reason to use one over the other is that regedt32 has a read-only mode that allows you to view settings in the *Registry* without making any changes. When Windows NT is installed, it does not create an icon to start either of these tools. To start the Registry Editor, click on the **Start** menu and choose **Run...**. In the Run dialog box, type either **regedt32** or **regedit**.

Remote Access Administrator
70-067   NT Server (Core)   *Install and Configure Remote Access Service*

The Remote Access Administrator is used to view the status of any *RAS* servers that are installed in a *domain*. This includes which servers are running, the total number of ports on the computer, and the number of ports in use on the server. From this window, you can also choose which users have permissions to dial in to the server. If you double-click on the name of the server, it will show you all the ports on the computer and which users are logged in to each of those ports.

For more information on the Remote Access Administrator, see the *RAS* section.

Remote Access Service
See *RAS*.

remote administration
70-067   NT Server (Core)   *Installation and Configuration*

Remote administration is the ability to manage a computer without having to physically sit in front of it. Microsoft provides several tools that allow administrators to remotely administer a *Windows NT Server* from a *Windows NT Workstation* or *Windows 95* computer. These utilities include:

- System policies
- System Policy Editor
- *User Manager*
- *User profiles*
- *Systems Management Server*
- *Performance Monitor*

remote procedure call
See *RPC*.

repeaters

70-058 Networking Essentials   *Connectivity Devices*

A repeater is a piece of networking hardware that is used to regenerate and pass a signal on to another portion of the network, effectively increasing the overall length of the network. Because a repeater must read every packet and regenerate it, repeaters introduce some delays in to the network. These delays explain why a network cannot be extended indefinitely: It would be impossible for computers on the network to know when other computers are communicating on the network. A repeater does not filter or interpret any portion of the packet. Its job is to merely repeat the signal that is received on one port and pass that signal on to another port. The repeater transmits all packets it receives on to the other segments of the network. This includes corrupt packets and broadcast storms.

resource domain

See *trusting domain.*

RG-8

See *coax.*

RG-58

See *coax.*

RIP

70-059 TCP/IP   *Implementing IP Routing*

RIP, the Routing Information Protocol, is a *protocol* that is used to build dynamic routing tables. RIP allows routers to exchange routing information between themselves. Using RIP, routers broadcast their route tables to other routers and listen for broadcast route tables. In this way, eventually all routers on the network will know where to send data to get it to another network. RIP has been implemented on *Windows NT* to handle IP and IPX traffic.

For more information, see the section on *routers,* which describes a piece of networking hardware that can be used to send data to other networks.

RISC

General information pertaining to all tests

RISC, or Reduced Instruction Set Computing, is a processor architecture that utilizes a smaller number of instructions on the processor itself. This type of computing generally produces faster processors. *Windows NT* supports RISC processors such as Alpha, PPC, and *MIPS.*

R

roaming user profiles

70-067 NT Server (Core) *Managing Resources*

A roaming user profile is a *user profile* that follows the user to whatever computer he or she logs in to on the network. This profile contains information about the user's personal settings, including desktop settings, application information, and *printer* settings. Roaming profiles are usually stored on a centralized server and are activated when the *administrator* enters a profile path under the user account profile in User Manager. The first time the user logs off, the local user profile is copied to the location specified in the profile path. After that, every time the user logs on, the profile is copied down to the local machine and is updated on the server when the user logs off. If for some reason the server is not available when the user logs on, the computer will use a local cached copy of the profile.

For more information on roaming user profiles, see the section titled *local profiles*.

routers

70-058 Networking Essentials *Connectivity Devices*

A router is a piece of network hardware that is used, much like a *bridge*, to connect large networks. Routers organize large networks into logical segments in which each segment, known as a *subnet*, is assigned an address. Routers build tables of network locations and use complex algorithms to determine the most efficient path for sending packets to the destination address. Unlike bridges, routers create redundant paths to different networks. If one of the connections along the most efficient path between the originating network and the destination network is down, routers along the way will frequently know another way to get the packet to the destination network.

In addition to being used to create redundant network paths, routers can also be used to connect dissimilar networks. For example, by using a router, it is possible to connect a *token-ring* network to an *Ethernet* network. In order for a router to work, however, the networks being connected must be using routable *protocols*. Routable protocols include *TCP/IP*, IPX, and *AppleTalk*.

Routing and Remote Access Server

See *RRAS*.

R

Routing Information Protocol

See *RIP*.

RPC

70-067 NT Server (Core) *Installation and Configuration*

An RPC, or remote procedure call, is a facility that enables distributed applications to call services on other computers in a networked environment. RPCs are primarily used during the remote administration of computers.

For more information, see the section titled *local procedure call,* which describes the message-passing function that is performed on local machines.

RRAS

70-067   NT Server (Core)   *Installation and Configuration*

RRAS, or Routing and Remote Access Server, a service that can be installed on a *Windows NT* computer to provide not only dialup access, but also the capability to perform routing and provide secure connections to the computer. RRAS is an add-on for *Windows NT Server* that replaces the Remote Access Service. Some of the major advances of RRAS are listed here:

- **Dynamic routing.** RRAS enables Windows NT to utilize dynamic routing protocols including *RIP, OSPF*, and RIP for IPX.

- **Demand dial.** RRAS can provide demand-dial services for standard telephone systems and *ISDN* lines.

- **Tunneling.** RRAS enables networks to create tunnels over the Internet and allows users to connect to the server by using those tunnels.

- **Static routing.** RRAS allows the use of static routing.

R

SAM

70-067   NT Server (Core)   *General Information*

The SAM, or Security Accounts Manager, is a subsystem *of Windows NT* that maintains the security accounts database. This database, also called the directory database, contains all the user account information and the *user policy* settings. The SAM provides user validation services and an *API* that can be used by developers to access the directory database. This database is stored in a protected area of the *Registry* accessible only by the SAM subsystem.

SCSI

70-067   NT Server (Core)   *Install and Configure SCSI Devices*
70-073   NT Workstation   *Configure Peripherals and Devices*

SCSI, or Small Computer Systems Interface, is a high-speed parallel interface that connects computers to peripheral devices such as *hard drives* and CD-ROMs. These devices are primarily used in high-performance workstations and servers. SCSI devices are installed on *Windows NT* computers using the *SCSI Control Panel*.

SCSI Adapters Control Panel

70-067   NT Server (Core)   *Installation and Configuration*

The SCSI Adapters Control Panel allows you to add and remove SCSI adapters and view the devices attached to those controllers. It is important to note that all drive controllers, whether they are SCSI adapters or not, show up in this Control Panel. From this Control Panel, you can also view information about the devices attached to a particular controller, including the SCSI ID of the device.

For more information regarding the SCSI Adapters Control Panel, see the section titled *SCSI*.

S

Security Accounts Manager

See *SAM*.

Security ID

See *SID*.

Security Reference Monitor

70-067   NT Server (Core)   *Installation and Configuration*

The Security Reference Monitor is a portion of the *Windows NT Executive Services*. This service checks to see if a user has permission to access an object and perform whatever action the user is attempting. The Security Reference Monitor enforces access validation and generates *audit* messages where they are required. This feature provides services to both *kernel* and user mode services.

For more information, see the following sections:

- *Auditing*
- *Executive Services*

Serial Line Internet Protocol

See *SLIP*.

serial port

General information pertaining to all tests

A serial port is a hardware location through which data passes in and out of a computing device. Serial ports are usually used to connect devices such as external modems and plotters. Serial ports are installed and configured via the *Ports Control Panel*.

For more information, see the following sections:

- *Modems*. These devices are used to send and receive data through phone lines.
- *Control Panels*. This section outlines the different Control Panels and their uses.

Server Control Panel

70-067   NT Server (Core)   *Installation and Configuration*

The Server Control Panel is used to view and manage the properties of the computer. The Server Control Panel consists of five tabs: **Users**, **Shares**, **In Use**, **Replication**, and **Alerts**.

From the **Users** tab, you can view the users connected to the server and see what resources they are using. From the **Share** tab, you can view all the shares on the server and see which users are using those shares. From the **In Use** tab, you can view any resource on the server that is being used. From the **Replication** tab, you can configure *Windows NT* Server import and export directories. On a *Windows NT Workstation*, you can set up the machine as an import directory only. From the **Alerts** tab, you can view the list of users and computers that are notified when administrative alerts occur on this computer.

For more information on the Server Control Panel, see the following sections:

- *Alerts*. This is an event that can occur on a Windows NT computer that generates a message to the *administrator*.
- *Directory replication*. This is a process in which files and directories are moved between computers.
- *Control Panels*. This section lists the control panels that normally appear on a Windows NT computer.

Services Control Panel

70-067   Windows NT Server (Core)   *Installation and Configuration*

The Services Control Panel is used to view the current status of the services on the computer as well as to start and stop services. From this *Control Panel*, you can also choose any service and click the **Startup** button to change the way that particular service starts.

For more information on the Services Control Panel, see the *Control Panels* section.

Services for Macintosh

70-067   Windows NT Server (Core)   *Managing Resources*

Services for Macintosh, or SFM, is a software component that allows *Macintosh* computers to connect to *Windows NT* Servers and use the resources available on them. This service allows PCs and Macintosh computers to share resources such as files and *printers*. The *AppleTalk* protocol is installed on the Windows NT Server when SFM is installed.

When working with SFM, you need to be aware of the primary group. A primary group is the group in which a Macintosh user usually shares documents. You specify a user's primary group when you set up the user account. Whenever a user creates a document or folder on the server, the primary group is assigned as the object's associated group.

For more information, see the following sections:

■ *AppleTalk*. This is a protocol suite that was designed for Macintosh computers.

■ *Macintosh*. This is a type of computer that uses the AppleTalk protocol.

Session layer

See *OSI Model.*

shared folders

70-067   NT Server (Core)   *Managing Resources*

A shared folder is a folder that has been made available on a server for use through the network by client computers. Depending on the level of access a user has, the client computer can connect to this share and use resources available.

shielded twisted-pair

See *twisted-pair.*

SID

70-067   NT Server (Core)   *Managing User Accounts*

A SID, or Security ID, is a unique identifier that is assigned to a *user account* or group when it is created. A SID is also assigned to every *Windows NT* computer when it joins the *domain*. The SID is completely unique. This identifier is used to assign permissions to a specific user. If you rename the user account, all the permissions that were assigned to it will remain the same. If you delete a user account and then re-create it with the same name, all the permissions that were assigned to the original account will be lost and must be reassigned. When you delete a user account, the SID is lost and can never be re-created.

Simple Network Management Protocol

See *SNMP.*

Single Domain Model

70-068   NT Server Enterprise   *Planning*

A Single Domain Model (see Figure S.1) is one in which all user accounts and resources reside in a single *domain.* This domain model is the simplest form to install and provides centralized administration of both users and resources. No *trust relationships* are established in a Single Domain Model. If you're considering a Single Domain Model, you must take into consideration the maximum size your domain will grow to be. A Single Domain Model can effectively handle only 20,000 users.

For more information related to the Single Domain Model, see the following sections:

- *Single Master Domain Model*
- *Multiple Master Domain Model*
- *Complete Trust Domain Model*

Single Master Domain Model

70-068   NT Server Enterprise   *Planning*

In a Single Master Domain Model (see Figure S.2), all user account information is stored in one master domain, and all the resources are stored in separate *domains.* To create this model, you need a minimum of two domains. In one domain, you create all the *user accounts* and *global groups* you need. In the second domain, you place all your resources. These resources could include file and print servers, application servers (such as email servers and database servers), and any other type of resources (such as CD-ROM servers and shared *modems*). The domain with the resources in it, known as the resource domain, then creates a *trust relationship* with the domain with the accounts in it, known as the *accounts domain.* The accounts domain is known as the *trusting domain*, and the accounts domain is known as the *trusted domain.*

This domain model allows for centralized administration of user accounts while allowing departmental administration of resources. The major limitation of the Single Master Domain Model is that you are limited to about 20,000 user accounts.

Figure S.1   A Single Domain Model consists of one domain.

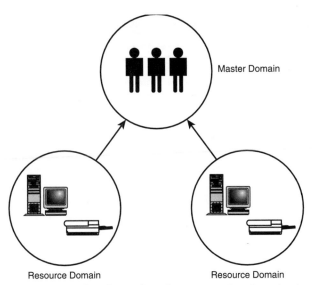

Figure S.2   A single master domain consists of one master domain and at least one
resource domain.

For more information regarding the Single Master Domain Model, see the following
sections:

■ *Single Domain Model*

■ *Multiple Master Domain Model*

■ *Complete Trust Domain Model*

SLIP

70-059 TCP/IP	*Configure RAS and Dial-Up Networking for Use on a TCP/IP Network*
70-067 NT Server (Core)	*Install and Configure Remote Access Service (RAS)*

SLIP, or Serial Line Internet Protocol, is an older remote access protocol that was used
before *PPP* was developed. SLIP is the industry standard *protocol*, but it has many limitations when compared to PPP:

■ SLIP supports only *TCP/IP*. SLIP does not support other protocols such as IPX
or *NetBEUI*.

■ SLIP requires that all computers dialing in be assigned a static *IP address*. It does
not support *DHCP*.

■ SLIP does not support *encryption*. All passwords are transmitted in clear text.

■ It requires scripting to complete the logon process.

For more information regarding SLIP, see the following sections:

■ *PPP.* This is another protocol that supports dialup access.

■ *RAS.* A portion of *Windows NT* that allows for client computers to dial up and
access the network.

Small Computer Systems Interface

See *SCSI.*

SMS

See *Systems Management Server.*

SNA Server

General information pertaining to all tests

SNA Server is a BackOffice product that can be installed on *Windows NT Server.* SNA, or System Network Architecture, is a communications framework that was developed by IBM for communications between IBM mainframes. This application provides a *gateway* connection from Windows NT networks to IBM mainframe and AS/400 hosts.

SNMP

70-059 TCP/IP   *Configure SNMP*

SNMP, or Simple Network Management Protocol, is a *TCP/IP*-based management protocol. SNMP is used to manage and monitor devices such as *hubs, routers,* and computers on a network. SNMP can be configured to respond to almost any event on a piece of networking hardware or a client workstation.

SNMP consists of two parts. The agent, or client, station is the piece of hardware that SNMP gathers information from. The management station is a centralized computer that gathers information from the SNMP agents on the network. The agent portion of SNMP is installed when you install SNMP on a *Windows NT* computer. The management portion of SNMP is implemented in the form of a third-party application.

SNMP Management Station

The SNMP management station is a workstation running one of the third-party applications that can be used to collect information from the agent computers. Some of the more common SNMP management utilities include the following:

- HP OpenView
- IBM NetView
- Sun Net Manager

These applications are used to query the agent computers. Usually there is only one management computer in a group of SNMP hosts. This group is called an SNMP community, and it also serves in terms of functionality as the password for accessing the information.

SNMP Agent

The SNMP agent is a computer, router, or hub that can answer the queries asked of it by the management station. The management station can ask a predefined number and type of questions. These questions are outlined in the form of a Management Information Base, or MIB. A MIB is simply a hierarchical database of all the information the computer will collect. MIBs are pairings of numbers that form a tree where the information is stored. For example, the Microsoft LAN Manager MIB is 1.3.6.1.4.1.77. Any specific information under that becomes a piece of information the computer will gather. The MIBs are available to both the agent and the management station. Primarily, the agent

S

station is passive, responding only to the questions that the management station asks of it. There are instances, though, in which the agent becomes active and initiates communication with the management computer. This instance is known as a trap. A trap is a predefined event that can occur on the agent computer. When the trap is triggered, the agent computer sends an alert to the management station telling it that the event has occurred. For example, some events that cause a trap to be sent are client *hard drives* filling up, certain application errors, and routers or hubs reaching a certain level of activity. These traps can be configured based on any of the values available in a MIB.

For more information regarding SNMP, see the following sections:

- *TCP/IP.* TCP/IP is the underlying protocol for SNMP.

- *Hub.* This is a piece of networking hardware that can use SNMP.

- *Router.* This is a piece of networking hardware that can use SNMP.

SONET

70-058 Networking Essentials   *WAN Transmission Technologies*

SONET, or Synchronous Optical Network, is a standard that was developed by Bell Labs. SONET is a standard that uses *fiber-optic cable* for communications. SONET can provide extremely high data rates that are measured based on the OC hierarchy. The basic OC rate is 51.84Mbps. With SONET, higher rates are available based on multiples of the OC rate. For example, OC 12 would be approximately 622Mpbs.

For more information, see the following sections:

- *Fiber-optic cable.* This is the type of transmission medium that is used in SONET.

- *ATM.* This is a transmission type that is similar to SONET.

Sounds Control Panel

70-067 NT Server (Core)   *Installation and Configuration*

The Sounds Control Panel is used to configure *Windows NT* to play sounds in conjunction with certain operating system events. These events include login and logoff, errors, and system notifications. In order for you to hear these sounds, you must have a sound card installed and configured on your system.

For more information regarding the Sounds Control Panel, see the following sections:

- *Multimedia Control Panel.* This Control Panel is used to configure playback levels.

- *Control Panels.* This section provides a list of available Control Panels on a Windows NT computer.

S

SQL Server

General information pertaining to all tests

SQL Server is a Relational Database Management System, or RDBMS, that is used to host and share databases. These databases can be extremely large. Using this type of scenario, it is possible for large numbers of users to access data and retrieve only the data in which they are interested.

star topology

70-058 Networking Essentials   *Network Topologies*

In the star network topology, shown in Figure S.3, all nodes on the network are connected to a central *hub*. This hub is responsible for receiving signals from one device on the network and transmitting them to the proper device. Multiple hubs can be connected to form a *cascaded star* topology. The most common type of network that utilizes the star topology is *10BASE-T*.

For more information regarding the star topology, see the following sections:

- *Bus*. In a bus topology, all computers are connected to a shared piece of cabling.
- *Cascaded star*. In this topology, several hubs are connected.
- *Mesh topology*. In this topology, all computers are connected in a mesh form.

STOP screens

See *blue screen*.

STP

See *twisted-pair*.

subnet

70-059 TCP/IP   *Subnetting*

A subnet is a small network on a larger *TCP/IP* network. Subnets are defined by subnet masks. The subnet mask tells the computer whether a specific host lies on its own subnet or another one by telling which portion of the *IP address* is the network ID and which portion is the host IP. Take, for example, the IP address of 198.218.247.11 with the subnet mask of 255.255.255.0. This tells the computer that the network ID is 198.218.247 and the host ID is 11.

For more information, see the following sections:

- *IP address*. This is an address that is assigned to each computer on a TCP/IP network.
- *TCP/IP*. This is a protocol used on networks.

S

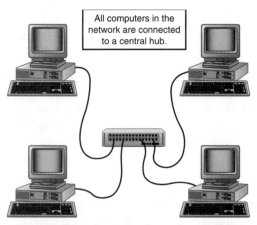

All computers in the network are connected to a central hub.

Figure S.3   In a star network topology, all nodes on the network are connected to a central hub.

subnet masking

70-059 TCP/IP   *Subnet Masking*

Subnet masking is the process of creating a subnet by dividing up a *TCP/IP* network by using subnet masks. Subnetting a network is a five-step process:

1. Determine the number of network IDs required currently and for future use.
2. Determine the maximum number of host addresses on each subnet, again allowing for future growth.
3. Define one subnet mask for the entire network that gives the desired number of subnets and allows enough hosts per subnet.
4. Determine the resulting subnet network IDs that are used.
5. Determine the valid host IDs and assign *IP addresses* to the hosts.

For more information regarding subnet masking, refer to either of these companion texts offered by New Riders and Sams, respectively:

■ *MCSE Training Guide: TCP/IP, Second Edition* (October 1998)

■ *Sams Teach Yourself TCP/IP Network Administration in 21 Days*

switch

70-058 Networking Essentials   *Connectivity Devices*

A switch is a connectivity device that reduces network traffic on an *Ethernet* segment. This piece of equipment functions like a combination of a *bridge* and a *hub*. Like a hub, the switch connects multiple computers on the network. Like a bridge, a switch forwards packets to the correct network segment based on the destination address of the packet. The switch learns the location of all computers on the network as it transmit packets. When a computer transmits packets to a computer that has transmitted on the network before, the switch simply reads the destination address of the packet and forwards it to that computer. If the destination address of the computer is not known to the switch, it broadcasts the packet to all computers attached to the switch.

For more information, see the following sections:

■ *Hub.* This is a piece of hardware that is used to connect computers to a network.

■ *Bridge.* This is a piece of equipment that is used to connect two network segments and reduce overall network traffic.

S

sysdiff

70-073 NT Workstation   *Installation and Configuration*

The sysdiff utility offers one way of automating the installation of applications on *Windows NT* computers. When used in conjunction with an *answer file* and a *uniqueness database file*, sysdiff can create a totally automated installation of Windows NT and all applications on the system. Using sysdiff requires three steps: creating a snapshot, creating a difference file, and applying the difference file.

Creating a Snapshot

After the initial installation of Windows NT, the first step in using sysdiff is to create a snapshot of the system. A snapshot records the original configuration of the machine and is used as a comparison when you create a difference file.

The command line for creating a snapshot file is

```
sysdiff /snap [/log:logfile.txt] snapshot file
```

where the options are as follows:

Option	Description
/snap	Instructs the sysdiff application to make a snapshot of the system in its current state.
/log:logfile.txt	Specifies the location of an optional log file that can be created during the process.
snapshot file	Specifies the name and location of the file that will contain the snapshot of the system.

Create a Difference File

After you create a snapshot of the system, you must install all the applications on the system and then create a difference file. To create a difference file, sysdiff checks the snapshot file to see what has changed on the computer since the snapshot was taken. It then notes the locations of the files and *Registry* entries that have changed, recording them in a difference file that can be applied to other machines.

The command line for creating a difference file is

```
sysdiff /diff [/c:title] [/log:logfile.txt] snapshot file different file
```

where the options are as follows:

Option	Description
/diff	Instructs the sysdiff application to make a difference file.
/c:title	Specifies the optional title of the difference file.
/log:logfile.txt	Indicates the location of an optional log file that can be created during the process.
snapshot file	Specifies the name and location of the file that contains the snapshot.
difference file	Specifies the name and location of the file that will contain the difference file.

Applying the Difference File

The last step is to apply the difference file to a computer that has a fresh installation of Windows NT. This copies all the files into the correct directories and places all Registry settings in the Registry. When that is complete, all the applications will run as if they were directly installed on the machine.

The command line for applying a difference file is

```
sysdiff /apply [/m] [/log:logfile.txt] different file
```

where the options are as follows:

Option	Description
/apply	Instructs the sysdiff application to apply the changes recorded in the difference file to the computer.
/m	Instructs sysdiff to make all changes that have been made to the Start menu to the Default User Start menu and not to that of the currently logged in user.
/log:logfile.txt	Indicates the location of an optional log file that can be created during the process.
difference file	Specifies the name and location of the file that contains the difference information.

System Control Panel

70-067   NT Server (Core)   *Installation and Configuration*

The System Control Panel provides information about the computer and allows you to change environmental settings. This Control Panel is divided into six tabs, each of which has a different role in configuring how the system works. The six tabs are outlined here:

- **General.** Provides information about the system itself. This information includes the *operating system* installed on the computer, registration information, the type of processor, and the amount of RAM in the computer.

- **Performance.** Allows you to change the *priority boost* of the foreground application and allows you to configure virtual memory settings.

- **Environment.** Allows you to configure any environment variables, including the location of the TEMP directory and the search path.

- **Startup/Shutdown.** Allows you to configure the default operating system and the amount of time *Windows NT* will wait before starting it. From this tab, you can also configure how Windows NT will react when a *STOP screen* occurs.

- **Hardware Profiles.** Contains options for configuring Windows NT to work with different hardware profiles. This is useful when you have installed Windows NT on a laptop computer that may or may not be in a docking station.

- **User Profiles.** Enables you to view, delete, and change the type of *user profiles* on the local machine.

For more information regarding the System Control Panel, see the following sections:

- *Control Panels*
- *Memory dump*
- *Blue screen*

System Log

70-067   NT Server (Core)   *Installation and Configuration*

The system log contains information about *Windows NT* itself. This information includes messages about services that are started and stopped, individual portions of the operating system that are initialized, and any errors that occur. The information displayed in the system log is broken into three categories, as outlined in Table S.1.

S

Table S.1   **Types of Information Displayed in the System Log**

Category	Description
Informational messages	Informational messages are displayed by using a blue circle icon with a white I in the middle. These messages are usually errors that tell you about specific portions of the operating system initializing, as well as general information about the goings on of the operating system.
Warnings	Warnings are messages that let you know about possible problems that are occurring or are getting ready to occur. These messages are marked with a yellow exclamation point icon.
Errors	Errors are exactly that: actual problems with the *operating system* that have occurred. These include failure of device drivers and hardware errors. These messages are marked with a red stop sign icon.

system partition

70-067 NT Server (Core)   *Installation and Configuration*

The system partition on a *Windows NT* computer contains all the files that are required to boot the computer. This system partition is very easy to confuse with the *boot partition*. The boot partition contains all the *operating system* and support files.

system policies

70-067 NT Server (Core)   *Managing Resources*

A system policy is a way of controlling user environments and actions, customizing settings, and enforcing system configuration on computers running *Windows NT Workstation*, *Windows NT* Server, and *Windows 95*. A system policy is used to overwrite certain parts of the *Registry* on the client computer and can be implemented to make changes for specific users, groups, or computers or for all users.

A system policy is created by using the *Policy Editor*. This tool allows you to create policies that restrict what a user can see and do from the desktop, restrict options in the *Control Panel*, and configure network settings. To enforce system policies on a Windows NT computer, you simply create the policy by using Policy Editor and save it in the netlogon directory with the filename NTCONFIG.POL. For Windows 95 clients, save the file with the name CONFIG.POL.

For more information regarding system policies, see the following sections:

■ *Policy Editor*. This tool is used to create system policies.

■ *Registry Editor*. This tool is used to view and modify the Registry directly.

Systems Management Server

General information pertaining to all tests

Systems Management Server, or SMS, is a portion of the BackOffice suite that is designed to make administration easier. SMS includes desktop management software, inventory capabilities, and software that automates the distribution of software.

S

Tape Devices Control Panel

70-067   NT Server (Core)   *Installation and Configuration*

The Tape Devices Control Panel is used to detect tape drives installed on the computer. From this *Control Panel*, you can also specify a tape drive device driver to install.

For more information on this feature, see the *Control Panels* section.

Task Manager

General information pertaining to all tests

The Task Manager is an application that allows you to monitor your computer and see what is running on it. The Task Manager contains three tabs: **Applications**, **Processes**, and **Performance**.

On the **Applications** tab, you can see which programs are running on your computer. You can also end, switch to, and start a new program. From the **Processes** tab, you can view every *process* that is running on the computer, including services and all applications that are running on the computer. From this tab, you can also end any process that is running. On the **Performance** tab, you can get a dynamic overview of the system status. This includes graphs displaying CPU usage and memory, as well as displays that outline the amount of memory in use on the computer.

For information related to the Task Manager, see the *Performance Monitor* section.

TCP/IP

General information pertaining to all tests

TCP/IP (Transmission Control Protocol/Internet Protocol) is a suite of *protocols* that can be used to provide communications between different applications and hardware platforms. TCP/IP is the primary protocol used on the Internet. TCP/IP was developed by the United States Department of Defense to provide service on large internetworks. TCP/IP consists of three elements—IP, TCP, and UDP—which provide a foundation for all other protocols associated with TCP/IP.

T

IP

The Internet Protocol, or IP, is a connectionless protocol that provides datagram service. IP is a packet-switching protocol that performs IP addressing and route selection. When a packet is transmitted, an IP header is appended to it. These packets are then routed through the network by way of dynamic route tables that are checked at each hop. IP performs packet assembly and disassembly service as required by the Physical and Data Link layers of the *OSI Model*. IP also performs error checking on the header by using a checksum.

TCP

The Transmission Control Protocol, or TCP, is an extremely robust protocol that provides full-duplex end-to-end connections. TCP establishes and maintains a logical connection between the two communicating computers, maintaining the integrity of the transmission. During the transmissions, TCP detects any problems that arise and attempts to resolve them by retransmitting. When TCP is used in conjunction with IP, it provides connection-oriented servers and sequencing by adding sequence numbers at the byte level.

UDP

UDP, the Universal Datagram Protocol, is a connectionless protocol that resides at the Transport layer of the OSI Model. UDP provides datagram service, meaning that it sends a packet but does not expect a reply from the receiving computer. UDP is used when the speed of data transmission is more important than the reliability of the delivery. Unlike TCP, UPD does not establish, maintain, and close connections to a remote host. However, UPD can decrease the overall amount of network traffic and frequently performs faster than TCP does.

For more information on TCP/IP, see the following sections:

- *IP address.* The actual address on the TCP/IP network. Each computer must have a unique IP address.

- *ARP.* A protocol used to determine the physical address of a destination computer.

- *DNS.* A system of resolving computer names, such as www.mcp.com, into IP addresses.

- *FTP.* A protocol that can be used to transfer files between computers.

- *HTTP.* The protocol the World Wide Web runs on.

- *FQDN.* The full host name of a computer.

- *ICMP.* The protocol that is used to transfer messages and control information between computers.

- *Subnet masking.* The process of dividing a single TCP/IP network into multiple logical networks.

TCP/IP layered model

70-059 TCP/IP   *Overview of the TCP/IP Suite*

The TCP/IP suite maps to a four-layer model. This model is known as the Internet Protocol Suite and consists of the Network Interface, Internet, Transport, and Application layers. Each of these layers corresponds to at least one layer of the *OSI Model*, as shown in Table T.1.

Table T.1   **Internet Protocol Suite Versus OSI Model**

Internet Protcol Suite Layer	OSI Model Layer(s)
Application	Application, Presentation, and Session
Transport	Transport
Internet	Network
Network Interface	Data Link and Physical

Each layer of the Internet Protocol Suite performs the same functions as the corresponding layer(s) of the OSI Model.

For more information, see the section titled *OSI Model*.

TCP/IP Printing Services

See *LPD*.

Telephony Control Panel

70-067   NT Server (Core)   *Installation and Configuration*

The Telephony Control Panel is used to configure the dialing properties for any *modems* installed on the computer. These settings include the area code you are dialing from, any extra digits you must dial to access the lines, and settings for disabling call waiting. You can also set the computer to use a calling card.

For more information on the Telephony Control Panel, see the *Control Panels* section.

terminator

70-058   Networking Essentials   *Transmission Media*

A terminator is a piece of equipment that is used in *bus* topology networks. This piece of equipment is a resistor that is used to absorb signals that reach the end of the cable. Both ends of a bus network must be terminated.

Thicknet

70-058   Networking Essentials   *Transmission Media*

Thicknet is a type of *coax* cable about one-half inch in diameter that is used in the *10BASE5* cabling topology. This cable type falls into the *RG-8* family of coaxial cable. This type of cable has a very thick core that can carry signals over a distance of up to 1,650 feet. This type of cable is often used to connect two smaller *Thinnet* networks. The biggest drawbacks to using Thicknet are that it is relatively expensive to run and difficult to work with.

Refer to Appendix A for more information about Thicknet.

Thinnet

70-058   Networking Essentials   *Transmission Media*

Thinnet cable is a type of coaxial cable that is used in the *10BASE2* cabling topology. Thinnet falls into the *RG-58* family of cables, and it has a 50-ohm impedance and a diameter of 0.25 inch. This type of cabling is frequently used to create smaller networks, which are then connected with *Thicknet* cables. The biggest problem with running thinnet is that it can carry a signal over a short distance only.

Refer to Appendix A for more information about Thinnet.

time domain reflectometer

70-058   Networking Essentials   *Troubleshooting Equipment*

A time domain reflectometer, or TDR, is used to check cables for breaks or imperfections that could lead to problems in transmission. It does this by sending sound waves down the cable and measuring the amount of time it takes for the sound waves to bounce back.

token passing
70-058   Networking Essentials   *Standards and Terminology*

Token passing is an access control method that is used on *token-ring networks*. A token is a special type of frame that circulates around the network. Only the computer that holds the token can transmit data on the network. When the computer completes the transmission, it releases the packet and allows other computers to transmit data.

token-ring network
70-058   Networking Essentials   *Network Topologies*

A token-ring network uses a *token passing* architecture as outlined in the *IEEE 802.5* standard. Each node on the network is attached to a *concentrator* called a multistation access unit (also known as an *MAU* or MSAU). An MAU adds *fault tolerance* to the network by detecting computers that have crashed on the network and bypassing them. Token-ring networks can run at either 4 or 16 megabits per second over *STP* cabling, but only one speed at a time.

A token-ring network operates in a logical ring topology. This means that all data passes around the network in a circle before returning to the sending computer. Because a physical ring is extremely difficult to implement, a token-ring network operates using a physical *star topology*. All computers in the network are connected to the MAU.

Each node on a token-ring network serves as a *repeater* for tokens and data frames from the nearest upstream active neighbor (NUAN). After the local node processes the frame, the frame is transmitted to the next node. Each token makes at least one trip around the ring before it returns to the originating workstation. If a workstation detects an error, it begins *beaconing* to identify the address of the failed node.

Transmission Control Protocol/Internet Protocol
See *TCP/IP*.

Transport layer
See *OSI Model*.

T

trust relationship
70-068   NT Server Enterprise   *Planning*

A trust relationship is a link between *domains*. These allow pass-through authentication where the *trusting domain* honors the authenticated users from the *trusted domain*. When a trust relationship is set up, any *user account* and *global group* that is set up can be assigned permissions to resources in the trusting domain.

For more information, see the following sections:

- *Trusted domain*. In a trust relationship, this is the domain that contains user accounts.
- *Trusting domain*. In a trust relationship, this is the domain that contains resources.
- *Single Master Domain Model*.
- *Multiple Master Domain Model*.
- *Complete Trust Domain Model*.

trusted domain

70-068   NT Server Enterprise   *Planning*

The trusted domain in any sort of a *trust relationship* is one that authenticates users. These users are then assigned permissions in a *trusting domain*. The trusted domain is frequently known as the *accounts domain*.

For more information related to trusted domains, see the following sections:

- *One-way trust*. This is a trust model in which there is a trusting domain and a trusted domain.

- *Two-way trust*. This is a trust model in which each *domain* participating in the trust is trusted by all other domains.

- *Multiple Master Domain Model*. This is a domain model in which there are multiple master, or accounts, domains.

- *Single Master Domain Model*. This is a domain model in which there is only one master, or accounts, domain.

trusting domain

70-068   NT Server Enterprise   *Planning*

A trusting domain is one that contains resources that can be assigned to users who have been authenticated by a *trusted domain* in a trust relationship. The trusting domain assigns permissions to any user account that is located in its own *SAM* and that of any user that is located in the SAM of a trusted domain. This setup makes it easier for departments to manage the resources in their local resources.

For more information regarding trusting domains, see the following sections:

- *One-way trust*. This is a trust model in which there is a trusting domain and a trusted domain.

- *Two-way trust*. This is a trust model in which each domain participating in the trust is trusted by all other domains.

- *Multiple Master Domain Model*. This is a domain model in which there are multiple master, or accounts, domains.

- *Single Master Domain Model*. This is a domain model in which there is only one master, or accounts, domain.

twisted-pair

70-058   Networking Essentials   *Transmission Media*

Twisted-pair cabling has become the de facto standard for networks that use copper cabling. The primary reason for the popularity of twisted-pair cabling is that it is extremely inexpensive to run.

Essentially, twisted-pair cabling consists of one or more pairs of copper wires that are twisted together. Because the wires are twisted together, the individual pairs are less sensitive to electromagnetic interference (*EMI*). Two basic types of twisted-pair cable are used in *LAN* installations: shielded twisted-pair and unshielded twisted-pair.

T

Shielded Twisted-Pair

Shielded twisted-pair cabling consists of one or more twisted pairs wrapped in foil and a copper braid. Shielded twisted pair, or STP, was used in IBM Token Ring networks. Early IBM network designers used STP cabling to reduce the amount of EMI. It is more expensive to run STP cable than it is to run unshielded twisted-pair, but STP is less costly than *Thicknet* or *fiber-optic cable*. STP cabling has a theoretical capacity of 500 megabits, but the most common data rate that is supported is 16 megabits per second in IBM Token Ring networks.

Unshielded Twisted-Pair

Like STP, unshielded twisted-pair consists of one of more twisted pairs of wire. Unshielded twisted pair, or UTP, does not have any shielding around the wires at all. UTP has recently become the de facto standard for network installations. Nearly all copper-based network installations use UTP. UTP cabling has a capacity of about 100 megabits and is the cheapest type of cable to run. There are five grades of UTP: Category 1 through Category 5.

For more information, see the following sections:

- *Category 1 UTP.*
- *Category 2 UTP.*
- *Category 3 UTP.*
- *Category 4 UTP.*
- *Category 5 UTP.*
- *IBM cabling system.* This is a cable grading system that was outlined by IBM.
- *Appendix A* has more information regarding STP, UTP, and other cable types.

two-way trust

70-068   NT Server Enterprise   *Planning*

A two-way trust, as shown in Figure T.1, is one in which the partners in the trust both trust and are trusted by each other. This type of trust is sometimes referred to as a bidirectional trust. This means that a user can log in to any computer in either *domain* and access resources in both domains to which he or she has access. It is important to note that a two-way trust is, in reality, two *one-way trusts*.

When diagramming trust relationships, you should note that arrows are used to indicate the direction of the trust. The domain that the arrow points to is the trusted domain.

T

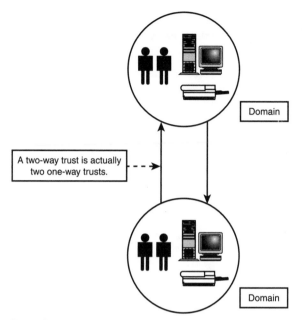

Figure T.1   A two-way trust is actually two one-way trusts.

T

UDF

70-073   NT Workstation   *Installation and Configuration*

A UDF, or uniqueness database file, is a text file containing information that is used during an *unattended install* that makes each individual workstation different from all others present. When used in conjunction with an *answer file*, a UDF makes it possible to install *Windows NT* without any user intervention. The UDF merges with or overrides sections of the answer file during the *GUI* portion of the setup program. This allows you to create one answer file and one or more UDFs that specify unique settings for the computer. When setting up a UDF, you use the same section IDs that are outlined in the section on answer files.

The format of a UDF is shown here:

```
[UniqueIDs]
User1 = UserData, GuiUnattended, Network
User2 = UserData, GuiUnattended, Network
[User1:UserData]
FullName = "User Number One"
OrgName = "Any Company, Inc."
ComputerName = "NTW0201"
ProductId = "123-456789012345"
[User2:UserData]
FullName = "User Number Two"
OrgName = "Any Company, Inc."
ComputerName = "NTW0202"
ProductId = "234-567890123456"
[GuiUnattended]
TimeZone = "(GMT-06:00) Central Time (US & Canada)"
[User1:Network]
JoinDomain = "ACIDOM1"
[User2:Network]
JoinDomain = "ACIDOM2"
```

Note that following the [UniqueIDs] section are the sections referenced in Table A.1 in the *answer file* entry. The section names can take two forms. First, the sections can take the form of exactly what is shown in the [UniqueIDs] section. Like the [GuiUnattended] preceding section, that section will be used for all users that reference it. Second, the section names can take the form of the unique ID followed by a colon and then the section name. As a result, you can include different settings for each user in the file.

For more information regarding the UDF, see the following sections:

- *Answer file.* A file used in conjunction with a UDF to perform an unattended install.

185

- *Unattended install.* An installation of Windows NT that uses a UDF and an answer file to minimize user interaction during setup.

UDP

70-059 TCP/IP   *General Information*

UDP (the Universal Datagram Protocol) is a *protocol* that offers connectionless datagram service but does not guarantee delivery or correct packet sequencing errors. UDP is the complement of TCP. Frequently, higher-level protocols or applications add reliability to the UDP protocol. It is possible to use checksums with UDP, which will force UDP to check the integrity of the header and the data. UDP is frequently used to support applications that stream data from one sender to multiple receivers.

For more information regarding UDP, see the *TCP/IP* section.

unattended install

70-073 NT Workstation   *Installation and Configuration*

When preparing a large rollout of *Windows NT Workstations,* an administrator must find a way to make the job as easy as possible. Using an unattended installation can make the job much easier and quicker for the team performing the rollout. Setting up an unattended installation takes more time in the beginning, but it saves a great deal of time in the long run.

Three types of files are used to perform an unattended installation:

- **Answer file.** An *answer file* is a text file that contains the answers to the prompts Windows NT Setup will ask.
- **Uniqueness database file (UDF).** A *UDF* contains information that will make an installation of Windows NT unique. This includes information such as the computer name, the *domain* name, and the *IP address*.
- **Sysdiff.** *Sysdiff* is a utility that allows you to install applications to the destination machine. This process involves making before and after images of the software on the computer. When you get to the point of the before image (after the initial installation of Windows NT), you apply the patch generated by Sysdiff to get to the after image (when all applications are installed). This application is not installed with Windows NT.

The syntax for running an unattended installation of Windows NT using an answer file and a UDF can take two formats:

```
winnt.exe /u:answer_file /s:x:\ /udf:userid,x:\udf.txt
```

or

```
winnt32.exe /u:answer_file /s:x:\ /udf:userid,x:\udf.txt
```

In either case, the following options are used:

Option	Description
/u:answer_file	Specifies the name of the answer file that will be used during the installation. Replace answer_file with the name of the file.
/s:x:\	Specifies the location of the Windows NT installation files.
/udf:userid,x:\udf.txt	Specifies the unique ID that is used with the UDF file and the path of the UDF.

For more information related to unattended installations, see the following sections:

U

- *Answer file.* Used in conjunction with a UDF to perform an unattended install.
- *UDF.* Used in conjunction with an answer file to perform an unattended install.

UNC

70-058   Networking Essentials   *Standards and Terminology*
70-073   Windows NT Workstation   *Use Various Methods to Access the Network*

UNC, or Universal Naming Convention, is a *Windows NT* convention for naming and identifying resources on remote computers. Under this convention, the name begins with two backslashes (\\). This tells the computer that the particular resource resides on a remote computer. Following the backslashes is the name of the server that the resource resides on, followed by another backslash. The next portion is the name of the resource that is shared on the server. This resource can be a shared directory, a *printer*, or some other type of resource (such as a named pipe). After the resource is added, directories or files can be appended.

Bringing it all together, a UNC name looks like this:
\\servername\sharename\directoryname\file. Usually, though, a UNC pathname will look like this: \\servername\sharename.

Unicode

70-067   Windows NT Server (Core)   *General Information*

The Unicode standard was developed to address the problem of multiple coding schemes and character sets. The Windows standard 8-bit coding scheme can represent a maximum of 256 characters. While this standard works well for Western character sets (such as English, French, Spanish, and German), it is insufficient for Eastern languages that can employ thousands of characters. To get around this limitation, Unicode was developed. Unicode consists of a 16-bit coding scheme, which can represent 65,536 characters. This is enough to accommodate all languages currently in use in computer commerce (including punctuation marks and mathematical symbols) and leaves room for expansion.

uninterruptible power supply

See *UPS.*

uniqueness database file

See *UDF.*

Universal Naming Convention

See *UNC.*

UNIX

General information pertaining to all tests

UNIX is an extremely powerful multitasking and mutiuser operating system that was developed in the late 1960s by AT&T Bell Laboratories. UNIX is a highly portable operating system that will run on most hardware platforms. UNIX is still a major competitor in the network operating system world, and many corporations still run it.

unshielded twisted-pair

See *twisted-pair.*

UPS

70-067   NT Server (Core)   *Installation and Configuration*

A UPS (uninterruptible power supply) is a battery you can hook up to your computers to keep them running in the event of a power failure. During a power failure, *Windows NT* can monitor your UPS battery life and, in the event that battery power drops too low, shut down the computer gracefully.

The amount of time between the initial power failure and system shutdown depends on several factors. The two main considerations are total battery capacity and the number of devices attached to the UPS. The more devices that are plugged in, the shorter the battery life. When sizing a UPS for your system, try to get at least 10 to 30 minutes of battery life. After you have received the UPS, you should test it during off hours by unplugging the UPS from the wall. This will allow you to see how much time you have before the servers are shut down.

UPS Control Panel

70-067   NT Server (Core)   *Installation and Configuration*

The UPS Control Panel enables you to configure how your system will utilize a *UPS*, as well as any characteristics of the UPS itself. Most of the configuration settings are available in the documentation that comes with the UPS when you purchase it.

One of the most important options that must be configured correctly is the polarity of the signal the UPS sends the computer when a power failure occurs. It is very easy to misconfigure this option, resulting in unexpected server shutdown.

Another important option that must be configured correctly is the Execute Command File option. This is a batch file that is run after the UPS reaches the point at which it is going to shut down the computer. This command file can be used to stop services, terminate user connections to the server, or send a message to the systems administrator. The catch in configuring this option is that the command file must run in less than 30 seconds, or you can jeopardize the safe shutdown of the computer.

U

user account

70-067   NT Server (Core)   *Managing Resources*

A user account consists of all the information that defines a user to *Windows NT.* This information includes the user name, password, groups the user belongs to, and rights and permissions the user has.

For more information, see the following sections:

■ *User Manager.* This is the application that is used to create user accounts.

■ *Local user.*

■ *Global user.*

User Datagram Protocol

See *UDP*.

User Manager

70-067 NT Server (Core) *Managing Resources*

User Manager is an administrative utility installed on *Windows NT Workstation* and *Windows NT* Server *member servers* that is used to administer users, groups, and security policies. This utility can be used only to create and administer users and groups on the local computer and set up audit policies. *User Manager for Domains* is used to administer domain users and groups.

For more information regarding User Manager, see the following sections:

- *User account.* A user account is all the information that defines a user on a Windows NT system.

- *Local group.* This is a group that can be granted permissions only on the local machine or within the local *domain*.

User Manager for Domains

70-067 NT Server (Core) *Managing Resources*

User Manager for Domains is an administrative tool installed on *Windows NT* Server domain controllers that is used to add, edit, and delete *user accounts*, groups, and security policies.

For more information regarding User Manager for Domains, see the following sections:

- *Global account.* These accounts are normal user accounts created in a Windows NT *domain*.

- *Local account.* This is a user account that can be created to assign permissions to users in untrusted domains.

- *Global group.* This is a group of users on servers and workstations in its own domain and in trusting domains.

- *Local group.* This is a group that can be granted permissions only on the local machine or within the local domain.

user profiles

70-067 NT Server (Core) *Managing Resources*

U

A user profile is the configuration setting for a specific user. By default, this information is stored as a *local profile*, but it can be configured as a *roaming profile* that follows the user wherever he goes. A local profile contains user information stored only on the local computer. If the user logs in to another computer, the changes he makes on that computer will not be available to him if he logs in to another computer.

Most of the configuration settings include color schemes, desktop wallpaper, screen savers, and mouse and keyboard layouts. Other configuration settings include access to program groups, *printers*, and Internet settings.

For more information regarding user profiles, see the following sections:

- *Local profile.* A local profile is one that is stored on a single local computer.

- *Mandatory profile.* A mandatory profile is one that is automatically applied to users when they log in to the computer.
- *Roaming profile.* A roaming profile is one that follows the user to whatever workstation he or she logs in to.

UTP

See *twisted-pair.*

video adapters

A video adapter is the piece of hardware that interprets graphical and textual information from the computer and writes it to the monitor. *Windows NT* does not communicate with the video adapter directly. Rather, Windows NT communicates with the video adapter through the *video driver*.

For more information, see the following sections:

- *DirectX*. This is a technology developed to speed access to the video adapter.

- *HAL*. This is the layer used to hide the underlying hardware platform from the operating system.

video driver

General information pertaining to all tests

A video driver is a software component that you install on the computer to allow the *operating system* to communicate with the hardware. Like any other piece of hardware you install on a *Windows NT* computer, you should first check to see whether it is on the Windows NT Hardware Compatibility List (*HCL*).

For more information, see the following sections:

- *Video adapters*. These are hardware components that produces video output from the computer to the monitor.

- *GDI*. This is the *Executive Service* that is used to produce video output on the monitor.

Virtual Memory Manager

V

The Virtual Memory Manager is a portion of the *Windows NT Executive Services*. The Virtual Memory Manager maps virtual addresses in a process's address space to physical pages in memory. This subsystem hides the organization of memory from the process's threads to make sure the thread can access only its own memory space. This way, the thread does not know whether the actual memory pages lie in physical memory or in the page file.

Virtual Private Networking

See *VPN*.

VPN

70-059 TCP/IP

Configure a RAS Server and Dial-Up Networking for Use on a TCP/IP Network

A VPN, or Virtual Private Networking, is an on-demand connection between two computers in different locations that tunnel, or route, information over either public or private networks. Data that is transmitted between the computers is *encrypted* to ensure privacy, and it is transmitted over the network by using *PPTP*. In order to use Virtual Private Networking on a *Windows NT* network, you must install the *Remote Access Service* or *Routing and Remote Access Service*. These products allow you to create VPN RAS devices on the server that client computers can connect to.

For more information, see the following sections:

- *RAS*. This is a service that you can install on *a Windows NT* computer to allow other computers to dial up and access resources on it.

- *PPTP*. This protocol is used to create VPNs.

- *RRAS*. This service can be installed on a Windows NT computer as an upgrade to RAS.

V

Web service

The Web service is installed as a part of the Internet Information Server. The Web service uses the Hypertext Transfer Protocol, or *HTTP*, to allow users to access information on the Internet.

For more information related to Web service, see the following section:

- *HTTP*

Win16 NTVDM

See *WOW*.

Win16 on Win32

See *WOW*.

Window Manager

The Window Manager is a portion of the *Windows NT Executive Services* that is used to create interfaces. It is also responsible for processes that use windows functions without opening windows or affecting the user interfaces.

Windows 3.11

General information pertaining to all tests

Windows 3.11 was one of the original versions of Windows that was widely embraced and implemented by the public. Windows 3.11 was a 16-bit shell for MS-DOS that featured cooperative multitasking. Cooperative multitasking is a form of multitasking that allows the application in the foreground to release control of the processor and other resources when it is ready to (however, the *operating system* could not force it to relinquish that control).

W

Windows 95

General information pertaining to all tests

Windows 95 is the 32-bit *operating system* that replaced *Windows 3.11* as the operating system of choice. This operating system is more reliable and faster than Windows 3.11. Table W.1 outlines some of the general advantages and disadvantages of Windows 95.

Table W.1 **An Overview of Windows 95**

Feature	Description
User interface	The Windows 95 interface is extremely easy to learn and use. It was designed to be easy to set up, simple to learn and use, and much easier to manage and support than previous versions of Windows.
32-bit system architecture	Windows 95 uses a 32-bit architecture to create a much more stable operating system overall. The 32-bit protected subsystems make it much more crash resistant. Windows 95 uses a combination of 32-bit code for speed and reliability and 16-bit code for maintaining compatibility with existing applications and drivers.
Preemptive multitasking	Windows 95 supports preemptive multitasking, which means the operating system can smoothly carry on several tasks at the same time.
Plug and Play	Windows 95 supports Plug and Play technologies that allow for easy installation of hardware devices into the computer. This allows the user to install hardware without worrying about the resource configuration.
Network support	Windows 95 ships with networking components that make it compatible with Microsoft, Novell, and Banyan networks.
Mail, fax, and telecommunications	Windows 95 ships with software that allows it to send and receive email and faxes and to dial in to dialup systems.
Support for remote access	Windows 95 enables users to dial in to remote networks with a minimum of configuration.
Backward compatibility for devices and applications	Windows 95 is backward compatible with most existing 16-bit applications that were designed for use with DOS and previous versions of Windows.
Multimedia capability	Windows 95 has extended support for multimedia. This includes technologies such as video and audio playback.
Long filenames	Windows 95 supports filenames of up to 255 characters using a Virtual FAT System. The VFAT system allows mixed-case characters, numbers, and spaces within a filename.

Windows Internet Naming Service

See *WINS.*

W

Windows NT

General information pertaining to all tests

Windows NT is a high-performance *operating system* that is designed for a corporate environment. Windows NT is divided into two separate operating systems: *Windows NT Server* and *Windows NT Workstation.*

For more information, see the following sections:

- *Windows NT Server.* This is a version of Windows NT used to provide resources for other users to access.

- *Windows NT Workstation.* This is a version of Windows NT that is used as a client operating system.

Windows NT Backup program

70-067   NT Server (Core)   *Managing Resources*

The Windows NT Backup program is an application that ships with *Windows NT.* This application allows you to make backups of your data to a tape drive. The use of this application is outlined in the section titled *Backing Up.*

Windows NT Server

General information pertaining to all tests

Windows NT Server is a specialized *operating system* that is designed and optimized to be a file, print, and application server for organizations of various sizes. Windows NT Server is required for use with all the other BackOffice components including *SQL Server,* Exchange Server, *SMS,* and *SNA Server.* Table W.2 outlines the major advantages of using Windows NT Server.

Table W.2   **Advantages of Using Windows NT Server**

Feature	Advantage
Performance	Windows NT Server is specifically tuned for file, print, and application services. NT Server can support as many as four processors out of the box; OEM versions can support up to 32 processors.
Fault tolerance	Windows NT implements built-in software support for *RAID* as a form of data protection.
NT Directory Services (NTDS)	The Windows NT Directory Services provides a secure distributed directory database.
Network Services	Windows NT Server supports additional network services including *DNS* Server, *DHCP,* and *WINS.*
Macintosh support	Windows NT Server can provide file and print sharing services to *Macintosh* clients.
RAS connections	Windows NT Server can support up to 256 inbound *RAS* connections.
Administrative wizards	Windows NT Server includes several *wizards* that assist the administrator in performing common tasks.
Internet Information Server	Windows NT Server integrates Internet Information Server. This means that a Web server is simply another portion of the operating system.

For more information, see the following sections:

- *Installing Windows NT.* This section outlines the steps required to install Windows NT.

- *RAID.* This is a form of hard disk fault tolerance that is supported by Windows NT Server.

- *RAS.* Windows NT Server supports RAS, which allows users to log in to the server remotely.

W

Windows NT Workstation

General information pertaining to all tests

Windows NT Workstation is an *operating system* that provides a subset of the functionality of *Windows NT Server*. Windows NT Workstation can function as a standalone operating system, as a member of a workgroup, or as a member of a Windows NT domain. Windows NT Workstation provides support for multiple processors, provides security for directories and files, and is an extremely stable operating system. Workstation supports fewer types of devices than *Windows 95* does.

WINS

70-059	TCP/IP	*Windows Internet Name Service*
70-067	NT Server (Core)	*Installing and Configuring Windows NT*
70-068	NT Server Enterprise	*Planning*

The Windows Internet Name Service, or WINS, is a service that maps *NetBIOS* computer names to *IP addresses*. A WINS server provides a dynamic way for WINS clients to register, renew, release, and resolve computer names on a network. This service offers a definite improvement over each individual computer on the network broadcasting to all clients; instead, each client sends a directed request to the WINS server to resolve a computer name, and the WINS server responds directly to the client. WINS can also be used in place of *LMHOSTS* files on networks by using a *DHCP* server to assign IP addresses to clients. The WINS service is installed on the computer from the Services tab of the *Network Control Panel*.

The WINS server provides four basic services: registration, renewal, release, and resolution of computer names.

Name Registration

The name registration process occurs when a WINS client computer starts. The client computer communicates with the server to handle the registration process. This process is automatic, allowing the WINS database to be maintained without user intervention.

During startup, the client machine automatically sends its name and IP address to the WINS server. If the server responds to the client computer's registration request and the client computer's name is not already registered, the server responds with an acknowledgment of the request. Contained in the acknowledgment is the registration's "time to live," or TTL.

If the name the client computer is attempting to register is already registered in the WINS database, the server computer attempts to challenge the computer that is currently holding the name. If the computer does not respond to the challenge, the registration process continues. If the other computer responds to the challenge, the client that is attempting to register the name receives a negative acknowledgment, or NACK, in response to its registration request. Communication over NetBIOS is disabled for the client computer for the rest of the session.

Name Renewal

After a client computer has registered in the WINS database, it is assigned a time to live. When the time to live expires, the name will be removed from the database. So that clients don't have to reregister their names, however, a client can renew its registration of the name before the TTL expires.

Suppose that after one-eighth of the time-to-live value has passed, the client computer attempts to renew its name registration. If the primary WINS server is not available, the client will attempt to renew its name every two minutes until half of its time-to-live value has expired. If the server has still not received a response from the primary WINS

W

server, the client tries to communicate with the secondary WINS server. If, after one-half of the remaining time to live has expired, the client has not yet received a response, the client attempts to communicate with the primary WINS server again until the name is renewed or the name expires. After the name is renewed, the client receives a new time-to-live value.

Name Release
When a WINS client has completed its session and has begun a normal and orderly shutdown, it sends a release request to the WINS server. If a computer is not shut down correctly, the WINS server does not release the name until the record expires or is challenged. This request instructs the WINS server to remove the client IP address and name from the database. When the server receives the release request, it verifies that the IP address and name are stored in the database. If both the IP address and name are in the database and they match up, the information is removed from the database, and the client request is acknowledged. If an error occurs, the client computer will receive a NACK.

Name Resolution
When a WINS client attempts to resolve a computer name, it sends a resolution request to the WINS server. Name resolution normally occurs when a client computer attempts to access a resource on a remote network. The name resolution process varies depending on the node type that is chosen. Four node types use broadcasts, the WINS server, and LMHOSTS or the DNS server to provide name resolution. The four types of nodes are *b-node, h-node, m-node,* and *p-node.*

WINS Manager

70-059	TCP/IP	*Windows Internet Name Service*
70-067	NT Server (Core)	*Installing and Configuring Windows NT*
70-068	NT Server Enterprise	*Planning*

The WINS Manager is a utility that is used to add, administer, and configure WINS server and to view WINS server statistics. When you install WINS on a computer, the WINS Manager is automatically installed, and an icon for it is placed in the Administrative Tools (Common) group. To start the WINS Manager, click **Start, Programs, Administrative Tools (Common), WINS Manager**. If WINS is installed on the same computer on which you are starting the WINS Manager, WINS will automatically be opened for administration. The title bar of the WINS Manager displays the *IP address* of the server that is currently selected for administration. Statistics for the current server are displayed in the right pane of the window.
   For more information regarding the WINS Manager, see *WINS.*

WINS replication

70-059	TCP/IP	*Windows Internet Name Service*
70-067	NT Server (Core)	*Installing and Configuring Windows NT*
70-068	NT Server Enterprise	*Planning*

W

In scenarios that require more than one *WINS* server, it is important to set up the different WINS servers to share their databases. This is accomplished through WINS replication. Each server that participates in WINS replication is a push partner, a pull partner, or both.
   A push partner in a WINS replication scenario is one that sends a message to its partner when changes occur to its WINS database. The replication partners respond with a replication request. The push partner then sends the changes that have occurred to the database over to the partner. In order to keep WINS databases on primary and secondary

WINS servers current, it is imperative that both must be push and pull partners with each other. Replication is initiated by the push partner when a certain number of changes have occurred.

A pull partner is one that pulls replicas of changes from its partner by requesting replication and then accepting the changes that are sent. The pull partner initiates replication by waiting a predetermined amount of time before it simply requests that replication begin. Replication is carried out only between push and pull partners in a scenario, not every server.

Replication begins when one WINS server polls another to obtain a replica. Polling first begins at system startup and continues at specified intervals after that. Replication can also be triggered when a WINS server reaches a specified number of changes and registrations, called an update count. When the server reaches the update count, it sends out a notification to the other servers. The other servers then decide whether or not to pull the changes.

For related information, see the following:

- *WINS*

- *WINS Manager*

wireless

70-058 Networking Essentials   *Networking Media*

Wireless networking media enables computers to participate in a network without being tied to a single location by wires. A company might employ a wireless network for several reasons. These include setting up a network where cabling would be impossible or inconvenient to set up, providing for users that move around within their work environment, and setting up temporary installations. When you're setting up a wireless network, several technologies are available, including infrared, laser, narrow-band radio, spread-spectrum radio, and microwave.

Infrared

Infrared networking technology transmits coded data over pulses of infrared light. Infrared transmissions are limited to about 100 feet supporting data speeds of up to 10 megabits per second. Infrared is divided into four categories:

- **Scatter infrared.** Scatter transmissions are reflected off walls, floors, and ceilings until, eventually, the signals reach the receiver. Because this process can take a great deal of time, scatter infrared has extremely slow data rates.

- **Reflective infrared.** With reflective infrared, signals are directed toward a central point that, in turn, sends the signals to different nodes.

- **Broadband optical telepoint.** Broadband optical telepoint uses broadband transmissions, which results in high-speed data rates.

- **Line-of-sight infrared.** Line-of-sight infrared requires that transmissions occur over clear line-of-sight paths.

Laser

Laser transmissions require high-power lasers to transmit data several thousand yards by using line-of-sight transmissions. Laser provides data rates similar to those of infrared.

Narrow–Band Radio

Narrow-band radio transmissions occur at a single frequency and provide a higher range than infrared technology. Narrow-band radio signals can bounce off walls, buildings, and

W

other obstacles, which greatly increases the range of coverage. Heavier obstacles and walls, such as those made of steel or concrete, effectively block narrow-band signals.

Spread-Spectrum Radio

Spread-spectrum radio transmissions occur at several frequencies to transmit messages. Spread-spectrum radio employs two different techniques: frequency hopping and direct sequence modulation.

- **Frequency hopping**. Frequency hopping switches between different frequencies, staying on each frequency for a specified amount of time. For effective transmission to occur, the transmitter and the receiver must stay in sync at all times.

- **Direct sequence modulation**. Direct sequence modulation relies on a technique in which the data to be sent is broken up into small pieces, called chips, and then transmitted simultaneously on different frequencies. The receiving station knows which frequencies are valid and how to reorder the chips to re-create the data.

Microwave

Microwave technologies employ frequencies in the lower gigahertz range that take two distinct forms: terrestrial microwave and satellite links.

- **Terrestrial microwave**. Terrestrial microwave requires the use of Earth-bound transmitters and receivers operating in a line-of-sight fashion. Terrestrial microwave uses licensed frequencies that require a license obtained from the FCC. The capacity of land-based microwave signals can be extremely high, but normally they operate between 1 and 10 megabits. Terrestrial microwave signals are highly susceptible to weather interference.

- **Satellite microwave**. Satellite microwave transmissions are relayed through satellites that operate in geosynchronous orbit 22,300 miles above the Earth. Satellite communications are extremely expensive and require licensing from the FCC. Typical data rates using satellite transmissions are between 1 and 10 megabits per second.

Refer to Appendix A for a detailed breakdown of these wireless methods.

wizard

70-067   NT Server (Core)   *Installation and Configuration*

A wizard is an application that simplifies the procedure required to perform a particular task. For example, *Windows NT* offers wizards to assist you in adding and creating new users, adding *printers*, and assigning permissions.

workgroup

70-058   Networking Essentials   *Planning*

A workgroup is a group of computers put on a network for the purpose of sharing resources. Usually, the term workgroup is used to define a *peer-to-peer* network. These types of networks do not usually have a dedicated server.

WOW

70-067   NT Server (Core)   *Installation and Configuration*

WOW is an acronym for Win16 on Win32. WOW is also known as the *Win16 NTVDM*. This subsystem allows for the translation of Windows 3.1x-based applications so they can be run in standard mode or 386-enhanced mode for Intel-based computers and standard mode for *RISC*-based computers.

Windows NT runs each 16-bit Windows application as a single NT virtual DOS machine, or *NTVDM*, but all of those applications share one address space. The WOW subsystem is a multithreaded *process* in which each *thread* in the process is a different 16-bit application. By using a 486 emulator, the WOW subsystem also allows 16-bit Windows applications to run on *RISC* processors. The entire process is multitasking, but only one thread in the process can run at any one time. All other threads in the process are blocked. If the WOW subsystem is preempted, the *kernel* resumes processing with the thread that was preempted.

Within the WOW subsystem are two system threads and one thread for each 16-bit application that is running. The first system thread is the WOWEXEC.EXE. This thread starts the Win16 applications. The other system thread is the heartbeat thread that simulates system interrupts to the application.

For more information regarding WOW, see the following sections:

- *Thread*
- *Process*

W

X.25

70-058   Networking Essentials   *WAN Technologies*

X.25 is a network standard developed by the International Telecommunications Union, formerly known as the Consultative Committee for International Telephony and Telegraphy (CCITT). X.25 is a packet-switching standard commonly used for permanent or switched virtual WAN circuits. A device known as a packet assembler/disassembler, or *PAD*, is used to translate input from the computer into packets that are suitable for use on the network.

Normally, these networks run at a maximum speed of 64Kbps and can run on public data communications networks (see *POTS*). Because of this, X.25 incorporates extensive error correction and detection.

For more information regarding X.25, see the *PAD* section.

X

APPENDIX **A**

Comparison Tables

Appendix A shows several tables that contain important information that compares similar topics and technologies.

Table A.1 **10BASE Types**

	10BASE2	10BASE5	10BASE-T
Topology	Bus	Bus	Star Bus
Cable types	Thinnet	Thicknet	Cat 3, 4, 5 STP, and UTP
Type of connection to card	BNC T connectors	AUI or DIX connectors	RJ-45 connectors
Termination resistance	50ohm	50ohm	N/A (10BASE-T networks do not require termination)
Maximum segment length	185 meters	500 meters	100 meters
Minimum segment length	0.5 meter	2.5 meters	100 meters
Maximum computers per segment	30	100	1 (Each computer is on its own network cable, or physical segment)
Maximum overall network length	925 meters	2500 meters	N/A
Maximum computers per network	90	300	1,024
Maximum connected segments	5 segments using 4 repeaters; only 3 segments can contain computers	5 segments using 4 repeaters; only 3 segments can contain computers	N/A

Table A.2 **Cable Types**

Cable Type	Max Length	Min Length	Max Nodes	Connection Hardware	Cost	Bandwidth	EMI Sensitivity
Thinnet	185m	0.5m	30	BNC barrel connectors	< STP	10Mbps	< UTP
Thicknet	500m	2.5m	100	DIX or AUI connectors	> STP < fiber	10Mbps	< UTP
UTP	100m	2.5m	1,024	RJ-45 connectors	Cheapest	10–100Mbps	Very sensitive
STP	100m	2.5m	1,024	IBM data connector	> UTP < Thicknet	4–16Mbps	< UTP
Fiber	5Km	5m	1,024	ST, SC, FC, and FDDI connectors	Expensive	100Mbps +	Not sensitive

Table A.3 **File Systems**

	FAT	FAT32	NTFS
Operating systems supported	DOS, Windows 3.11, Windows 95, Windows NT	Windows 95 OSR2 and Windows 98	Windows NT
Maximum partition size	2 Gigabytes	2 Terabytes	16 Exabytes
Maximum cluster size	64K	32K	64K
Recommended partition sizes with Windows NT	Less than 511Mb	Not supported in Windows NT	Greater than 512Mb
Supports compression	Yes (DriveSpace)	No	Yes (built in)

A

Table A.4 **Networking Hardware**

	Repeater	Hub	Switch	Bridge	Router
OSI Layer	Physical	Physical	Data Link	Data Link	Network
Function	Reads packets from one network segment and passes them on to the next.	Reads packets from one network segment and passes them to all connected segments.	Reads packets from one segment, examines the destination address, and sends them to the correct computer.	Reads packets from one segment, examines the destination address, and sends them to the correct segment.	Reads packets from a local network segment, examines the destination network address and forwards it to the correct network.
Redundant paths	No	No	No	No	Yes
Uses route tables	No	No	Yes	Yes	Yes
Works only with specialized protocols	No	No	No	No	Yes
Reduces network traffic	No	No	Yes	Yes	Yes
Can eliminate broadcast storms	No	No	Sometimes: If the destination address is a valid address, it will be sent on.	Yes	Yes
Connects unlike networks	No	No	No	Yes	Yes
Connects unlike physical media	Yes	Yes	Yes	Yes	Yes
Speed	Very fast	Very fast	< Hub > Bridge	< Switch > Router	Slowest
Cost	Relatively inexpensive	Relatively inexpensive	> Hub < Bridge	> Switch < Router	Very expensive

Table A.5 **WAN Transmission Technologies**

	X.25	Frame Relay	ISDN	FDDI	T1	T3	T4	ATM
Type of service	Analog	Digital	Digital	Digital	Digital	Digital	Digital	Digital
Bandwidth available	56Kb	56Kb – 1.544Mbps	128Kb – 1.544Mbps	100Mbps	1.544 Mbps	44.736 Mbps	274.76 Mbps	155 Mbps – 622+ Mbps
Range	Unlimited	Unlimited	Unlimited	100Km	Unlimited	Unlimited	Unlimited	Unlimited
Hardware considerations	Requires a PAD	Requires a frame-capable router	Requires an ISDN modem	Requires special network cards and hubs	Requires a CSU/DSU (Channel Service Unit/ Digital Service Unit)	Requires a multi-plexer	Requires a multi-plexer	Requires ATM switches and network cards
Type of connections	Switched	Switched	Private virtual circuits	Token passing	Point-to-point	Point-to-point	Point-to-point	Switched
Cost	Infrequently implemented	> ISDN	Cheapest	High initial investment, low ongoing cost	High	Higher	Highest	High initial investment

Table A.6 **Windows Systems**

	Windows 3.11	Windows 95/98	Windows NT
System architecture	16-bit	Both 16-bit and 32-bit	32-bit
Processors supported	286, 386, 486, Pentium, Pentium Pro, and Pentium II	386DX, 486, Pentium, Pentium Pro, MIPS, and PowerPC	486, Pentium, Pentium Pro, Pentium II, Alpha, and Pentium II
Minimum memory required	2Mb	4Mb	12Mb
File systems supported	FAT	FAT and FAT32	FAT and NTFS
Security	Very low	Medium	Extremely secure
Device support	Fair	Very good	Relatively low
Multitasking type	Cooperative	Semi-preemptive	True preemptive
Multiprocessing	No	No	Yes
Multithreading	No	Yes	Yes
Speed	Slow	Relatively fast	Relatively fast

Table A.7 Computing Types

	Peer-to-Peer	Client/Server	Centralized (Mainframe)
Servers	All computers on the network can act as servers	Only specialized, usually high-power, computers on the network can act as servers	Only a single high-end computer acts as the server
Clients	All computers on the network act as clients	Less specialized computers on the network act as clients	Clients are dumb terminals that have no processor or hard disk and limited memory
Processing location	All processing is done on the client computer	The majority of the processing is done on the server	All processing is done on the server
Data storage	Data is stored on the client computers	The majority of the data is stored on the server computers	All data is stored on the server
Administration type	Every user has administrative control of his or her own machine	Centralized administration	Centralized administration
Network traffic	Very high	Medium	Very low
Cost	Relatively low	Medium	Very large initial cost

A

209

Index

B

⟍ Books for Networking
New Riders ⟍ Professionals

Windows NT Titles

Windows NT TCP/IP
By Karanjit Siyan
1st Edition Summer 1998
500 pages, $29.99
ISBN: 1-56205-887-8

If you're still looking for good documentation on Microsoft TCP/IP, then look no further— this is your book. *Windows NT TCP/IP* cuts through the complexities and provides the most informative and complete reference book on Windows-based TCP/IP. Concepts essential to TCP/IP administration are explained thoroughly, then related to the practical use of Microsoft TCP/IP in a real-world networking environment. The book begins by covering TCP/IP architecture, advanced installation and configuration issues, then moves on to routing with TCP/IP, DHCP Management, and WINS/DNS Name Resolution.

Windows NT DNS
By Michael Masterson, Herman L. Knief, Scott Vinick, and Eric Roul
1st Edition Summer 1998
325 pages, $29.99
ISBN: 1-56205-943-2

Have you ever opened a Windows NT book looking for detailed information about DNS only to discover that it doesn't even begin to scratch the surface? DNS is probably one of the most complicated subjects for NT administrators, and there are few books on the market that really address it in detail. This book answers your most complex DNS questions, focusing on the implementation of the Domain Name Service within Windows NT, treating it thoroughly from the viewpoint of an experienced Windows NT professional. Many detailed, real-world examples illustrate further the understanding of the material throughout. The book covers the details of how DNS functions within NT, then explores specific interactions with critical network components. Finally, proven procedures to design and set up DNS are demonstrated. You'll also find coverage of related topics, such as maintenance, security, and troubleshooting.

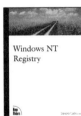

Windows NT Registry
By Sandra Osborne
1st Edition Summer 1998
500 pages, $29.99
ISBN: 1-56205-941-6

The NT Registry can be a very powerful tool for those capable of using it wisely. Unfortunately, there is very little information regarding the NT Registry, due to Microsoft's insistence that their source code be kept secret. If you're looking to optimize your use of the registry, you're usually forced to search the Web for bits of information. This book is your resource. It covers critical issues and settings used for configuring network protocols, including NWLink, PTP, TCP/IP, and DHCP. This book approaches the material from a unique point of view, discussing the problems related to a particular component, and then discussing settings, which are the actual changes necessary for implementing robust solutions. There is also a comprehensive reference of registry settings and commands, making this the perfect addition to your technical bookshelf.

Windows NT Performance Monitoring, Benchmarking, and Tuning

By Mark Edmead and Paul Hinsberg
1st Edition Fall 1998
400 pages, $29.99
ISBN: 1-56205-942-4

Performance monitoring is a little like preventative medicine for the administrator: No one enjoys a checkup, but it's a good thing to do on a regular basis. This book helps you focus on the critical aspects of improving the performance of your NT system, showing you how to monitor the system, implement benchmarking, and tune your network. The book is organized by resource components, which makes it easy to use as a reference tool.

Windows NT Terminal Server

By Ted Harwood
1st Edition Winter 1998
500 pages, $29.99
ISBN: 1-56205-944-0

It's no surprise that most administration headaches revolve around integration with other networks and clients. This book addresses these types of real-world issues on a case-by-case basis, giving tools and advice on solving each problem. The author also offers the real nuts and bolts of thin client administration on multiple systems, covering such relevant issues as installation, configuration, network connection, management, and application distribution.

Windows NT Security

By Richard Puckett
1st Edition Winter 1998
600 pages, $29.99
ISBN: 1-56205-945-9

Swiss cheese. That's what some people say Windows NT security is like. And they may be right, because they only know what the NT documentation says about implementing security. Who has the time to research alternatives; play around with the features, service packs, hot fixes, and add-on tools, and figure out what makes NT rock solid? Well, Richard Puckett does. He's been researching Windows NT Security for the University of Virginia for a while now, and he's got pretty good news. He's going to show you how to make NT secure in your environment, and we mean really secure.

Windows NT Administration Handbook

By Eric Svetcov
1st Edition Winter 1998
400 pages, $29.99
ISBN: 1-56205-946-7

Administering a Windows NT network is kind of like trying to herd cats—an impossible task characterized by constant motion, exhausting labor, and lots of hairballs. Author Eric Svetcov knows all about it— he's administered NT networks for some of the fastest growing companies around Silicon Valley. So we asked Eric to put together a concise manual of best practices, a book of tools and ideas that other administrators can turn to again and again in administering their own NT networks. Eric's experience shines through as he shares his secrets for administering users, for getting domain and groups set up quickly and for troubleshooting the thorniest NT problems. Daily, weekly, and monthly task lists help organize routine tasks and preventative maintenance.

Planning for Windows NT 5

By David Lafferty and Eric K. Cone

1st Edition Spring 1999

400 pages, $29.99

ISBN: 0-73570-048-6

Windows NT 5 is poised to be one of the largest and most important software releases of the next decade, and you are charged with planning, testing, and deploying it in your enterprise. Are you ready? With this book, you will be. *Planning for Windows NT 5* lets you know what the upgrade hurdles will be, informs you how to clear them, guides you through effective Active Directory design, and presents you with detailed rollout procedures. MCSEs David Lafferty and Eric K. Cone give you the benefit of their extensive experiences as Windows NT 5 Rapid Deployment Program members, sharing problems and solutions they've encountered on the job.

MCSE Core Essential Reference

By Matthew Shepker

1st Edition Fall 1998

500 pages, $19.99

ISBN: 0-7357-0006-0

You're sitting in the first session of your Networking Essentials class and the instructor starts talking about RAS and you have no idea what that means. You think about raising your hand to ask about RAS, but you reconsider—you'd feel pretty foolish asking a question in front of all these people. You turn to your handy *MCSE Core Essential Reference* and find a quick summary on Remote Access Services. Question answered. It's a couple months later and you're taking your Networking Essentials exam the next day. You're reviewing practice tests and you keep forgetting the maximum lengths for the various commonly used cable types. Once again, you turn to the *MCSE Core*

Essential Reference and find a table on cables, including all of the characteristics you need to memorize in order to pass the test.

BackOffice Titles

Implementing Exchange Server

By Doug Hauger, Marywynne Leon, and William C. Wade III

1st Edition Fall 1998

450 pages, $29.99

ISBN: 1-56205-931-9

If you're interested in connectivity and maintenance issues for Exchange Server, then this book is for you. Exchange's power lies in its ability to be connected to multiple email subsystems to create a "universal email backbone." It's not unusual to have several different and complex systems all connected via email gateways, including Lotus Notes or cc:Mail, Microsoft Mail, legacy mainframe systems, and Internet mail. This book covers all of the problems and issues associated with getting an integrated system running smoothly and addresses troubleshooting and diagnosis of email problems with an eye toward prevention and best practices.

SQL Server System Administration

By Sean Baird, Chris Miller, et al.

1st Edition Fall 1998

400 pages, $29.99

ISBN: 1-56205-955-6

How often does your SQL Server go down during the day when everyone wants to access the data? Do you spend most of your time being a "report monkey" for your co-workers and bosses? *SQL Server System Administration* helps you keep data consistently available to your users. This book omits the introductory information. The authors don't spend time explaining queries and how they work. Instead they focus on the information that you can't get anywhere else, like how to choose the correct replication topology and achieve high availability of information.

Internet Information Server Administration

By Kelli Adam, et. al.
1st Edition Winter 1998
300 pages, $29.99
ISBN: 0-73570-022-2

Are the new Internet technologies in Internet Information Server 4.0 giving you headaches? Does protecting security on the Web take up all of your time? Then this is the book for you. With hands-on configuration training, advanced study of the new protocols in IIS 4, and detailed instructions on authenticating users with the new Certificate Server and implementing and managing the new e-commerce features, *Internet Information Server Administration* gives you the real-life solutions you need. This definitive resource also prepares you for the release of Windows NT 5 by giving you detailed advice on working with Microsoft Management Console, which was first used by IIS 4.

Unix/Linux Titles

Solaris Essential Reference

By John Mulligan
1st Edition Winter 1998
350 pages, $19.99
ISBN: 0-7357-0230-7

Looking for the fastest, easiest way to find the Solaris command you need? Need a few pointers on shell scripting? How about advanced administration tips and sound, practical expertise on security issues? Are you looking for trustworthy information about available third-party software packages that will enhance your operating system? Author John Mulligan—creator of the popular Unofficial Guide to Solaris Web site (sun.icsnet.com)—delivers all that and more in one attractive, easy-to-use reference book. With clear and concise instructions on how to perform important administration and management tasks and key information on powerful commands and advanced topics, *Solaris Essential Reference* is the reference you need when you know what you want to do and you just need to know how.

Linux System Administration

By James T. Dennis
1st Edition Winter 1998
450 pages, $29.99
ISBN: 1-56205-934-3

As an administrator, you probably feel that most of your time and energy is spent in endless firefighting. If your network has become a fragile quilt of temporary patches and workarounds, then this book is for you. For example, have you had trouble sending or receiving your email lately? Are you looking for a way to keep your network running smoothly with enhanced performance? Are your users always hankering for more storage, more services, and more speed? *Linux System Administration* advises you on the many intricacies of maintaining a secure, stable system. In this definitive work, the author addresses all the issues related to system administration, from adding users and managing files permission to Internet services and Web hosting to recovery planning and security. This book fulfills the need for expert advice that will ensure a trouble-free Linux environment.

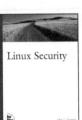

Linux Security

By John S. Flowers

1st Edition Spring 1999

400 pages, $29.99

ISBN: 0-7357-0035-4

New Riders is proud to offer the first book aimed specifically at Linux security issues. While there are a host of general UNIX security books, we thought it was time to address the practical needs of the Linux network. In this definitive work, author John Flowers takes a balanced approach to system security, from discussing topics like planning a secure environment to firewalls to utilizing security scripts. With comprehensive information on specific system compromises, and advice on how to prevent and repair them, this is one book that every Linux administrator should have on the shelf.

Linux GUI Application Development

By Eric Harlow

1st Edition Spring 1999

400 pages, $34.99

ISBN: 0-7357-0214-7

We all know that Linux is one of the most powerful and solid operating systems in existence. And as the success of Linux grows, there is an increasing interest in developing applications with graphical user interfaces that really take advantage of the power of Linux. In this book,

software developer Eric Harlow gives you an indispensable development handbook focusing on the GTK+ toolkit. More than an overview on the elements of application or GUI design, this is a hands-on book that delves deeply into the technology. With in-depth material on the various GUI programming tools, a strong emphasis on CORBA and CGI programming, and loads of examples, this book's unique focus will give you the information you need to design and launch professional-quality applications.

Lotus Notes and Domino Titles

Domino System Administration

By Rob Kirkland

1st Edition Winter 1998

500 pages, $29.99

ISBN: 1-56205-948-3

Your boss has just announced that you will be upgrading to the newest version of Notes and Domino when it ships. As a Premium Lotus Business Partner, Lotus has offered a substantial price break to keep your company away from Microsoft's Exchange Server. How are you supposed to get this new system installed, configured, and rolled out to all of your end users? You understand how Lotus Notes works—you've been administering it for years. What you need is a concise, practical explanation about the new features, and how to make some of the advanced stuff really work. You need answers and solutions from someone like you, who has worked with the product for years, and understands what it is you need to know. *Domino System Administration* is the answer—the first book on Domino that attacks the technology at the professional level, with practical, hands-on assistance to get Domino running in your organization.

Lotus Notes and Domino Essential Reference

By Dave Hatter & Tim Bankes
1st Edition Winter 1998
500 pages, $19.99
ISBN: 0-7357-0007-9

You're in a bind because you've been asked to design and program a new database in Notes for an important client that will keep track of and itemize a myriad of inventory and shipping data. The client wants a user-friendly interface, without sacrificing speed or functionality. You are experienced (and could develop this app in your sleep), but feel that you need to take your talents to the next level. You need something to facilitate your creative and technical abilities, something to perfect your programming skills. Your answer is waiting for you: *Lotus Notes and Domino Essential Reference*. It's compact and simply designed. It's loaded with information. All of the objects, classes, functions, and methods are listed. It shows you the object hierarchy and the overlying relationship between each one. It's perfect for you. Problem solved.

Networking Titles

Cisco Router Configuration and Troubleshooting

By Pablo Espinosa and Mark Tripod
1st Edition Winter 1998
300 pages, $34.99
ISBN: 0-7357-0024-9

Want the real story on making your Cisco routers run like a dream? Why not pick up a copy of *Cisco Router Configuration and Troubleshooting* and see what Pablo Espinosa and Mark Tripod have to say? They're the folks responsible for making some of the largest sites on the Net scream, like Amazon.com, Hotmail, USAToday, Geocities, and Sony. In this book, they provide advanced configuration issues, sprinkled with advice and preferred practices. You won't see a general overview on TCP/IP—we talk about more meaty issues like security, monitoring, traffic management, and more. In the troubleshooting section, the authors provide a unique methodology and lots of sample problems to illustrate. By providing real-world insight and examples instead of rehashing Cisco's documentation, Pablo and Mark give network administrators information they can start using today.

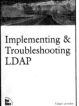

Implementing and Troubleshooting LDAP

By Robert Lamothe
1st Edition Spring 1999
400 pages, $29.99
ISBN: 1-56205-947-5

While there is some limited information available about LDAP, most of it is RFCs, white papers and books about programming LDAP into your networking applications. That leaves the people who most need information—administrators— out in the cold. What do you do if you need to know how to make LDAP work in your system? You ask Bob Lamothe. Bob is a UNIX administrator with hands-on experience in setting up a corporatewide directory service using LDAP. Bob's book is NOT a guide to the protocol; rather, it is designed to be an aid to administrators to help them understand the most efficient way to structure, encrypt, authenticate, administer and troubleshoot LDAP in a mixed network environment. The book shows you how to work with the major implementations of LDAP and get them to coexist.

Implementing Virtual Private Networks:

A Practitioner's Guide
By Tina Bird and Ted Stockwell
1st Edition Spring 1999
300 pages, $29.99
ISBN: 0-73570-047-8

Tired of looking for decent, practical, up-to-date information on virtual private networks? *Implementing Virtual Private Networks*, by noted authorities Dr. Tina Bird and Ted Stockwell, finally gives you what you need—an authoritative guide on the design, implementation, and maintenance of Internet-based access to private networks. This book focuses on real-world solutions, demonstrating how the choice of VPN architecture should align with an organization's business and technological requirements. Tina and Ted give you the information you need to determine whether a VPN is right for your organization, select the VPN that suits your needs, and design and implement the VPN you have chosen.

Next Generation Training

Get on board with New Riders Certification Series.

MCSE Covers Exam 70-068
Second Edition
Windows NT® Server 4 Enterprise

NEXT GENERATION TRAINING

Jason Sirockman

Engineered for test success. MCSE Training Guides, *Second Editions* are comprehensive guides that have been built by professionals who have passed the test and who have instructed hundreds of candidates. These guides are designed around the exam objectives, and include Study Strategies, Step-by-Step Exercises, Case Studies, Exam Tips, and Review Sections. Each *Training Guide* comes with a CD that contains New Riders Top Score software—a complete, fully functional test engine with over 150 sample questions, as well as a simulation feature, which allows you to get hands-on experience with the technology or operating environment. All *MCSE Training Guides* are Microsoft-approved study guides.

500 practice questions for MCSE success
Test Prep MCSE
Networking Essentials
Second Edition
Covers Exam: 70-058
PRACTICE, PRACTICE, PRACTICE, PASS!

Questions. Questions. Questions. Designed to help you cram for the exam. A new way to review: Our *MCSE TestPrep, Second Editions* have been completely revised to provide you with the practice you'll need to obtain certification—hundreds of questions and the explanations that make sense of it all. The #1 workbook to supplement any self-study program.

Fast Track MCSE
TCP/IP
Covers Exam: 70-059

Your accelerated path to MCSE success. If you already have the technical knowledge but need the essential information to pass the exam, then *MCSE Fast Tracks* will appeal to you. No superfluous information. Study for your exam—and pass—with the instructor-tested, classroom-proven approach designed for the advanced candidate.

Front cover image: Leeward Side, British Steel Global Challenge © Mark Pepper/PPL. With compliments PPL Limited: The Specialist Photo Source. 68 East Ham Road, Littlehampton, West Sussex BN177BE tel 44(0)1903-730618 ppl@mistral.ce.uk

**MCSE Fast Track:
Networking
Essentials**

1-56205-939-4,
$19.99, 9/98

**MCSE Fast Track:
TCP/IP**

1-56205-937-8,
$19.99, 9/98

**MCSE Fast Track:
Windows 98**

0-7357-0016-8,
$19.99, Q4/98

**MCSE Fast Track:
Internet Information
Server 4**

1-56205-936-X,
$19.99, 9/98

**MCSE Fast Track:
Windows NT
Server 4**

1-56205-935-1,
$19.99, 9/98

**MCSD Fast Track:
Solution
Architectures**

0-7357-0029-X,
$19.99, Q1/99

**MCSE Fast Track:
Windows NT Server
4 Enterprise**

1-56205-940-8,
$19.99, 9/98

**MCSD Fast Track:
Visual Basic 6,
Exam 70-175**

0-7357-0018-4,
$19.99, Q4/98

**MCSE Fast Track:
Windows NT
Workstation 4**

1-56205-938-6,
$19.99, 9/98

**MCSD Fast Track:
Visual Basic 6,
Exam 70-176**

0-7357-0019-2,
$19.99, Q4/98

TRAINING GUIDES

Complete, Innovative, Accurate, Thorough

Our next generation Training Guides have been developed to help you study and retain the essential knowledge that you need to pass the MCSE exams. We know your study time is valuable, and we have made every effort to make the most of it by presenting clear, accurate, and thorough information.

In creating this series, our goal was to raise the bar on how MCSE content is written, developed, and presented. From the two-color design that gives you easy access to content to the new software simulator that allows you to perform tasks in a simulated operating system environment, we are confident that you will be well-prepared for exam success.

Our New Riders Top Score Software Suite is a custom-developed set of full-functioning software applications that work in conjunction with the Training Guide by providing you with the following:

Exam Simulator tests your hands-on knowledge with over 150 fact-based and situational-based questions
Electronic Study Cards really test your knowledge with explanations that are linked to an electronic version of the Training Guide
Electronic Flash Cards help you retain the facts in a time-tested method
An Electronic Version of the Book provides quick searches and compact, mobile study
Customizable Software adapts to the way you want to learn

MCSE Training Guide: Networking Essentials, Second Edition

1-56205-919-X, $49.99, 9/98

MCSE Training Guide: Windows NT Server 4, Second Edition

1-56205-916-5, $49.99, 9/98

MCSE Training Guide: Windows NT Server 4 Enterprise, Second Edition

1-56205-917-3, $49.99, 9/98

MCSE Training Guide: Windows NT Workstation 4, Second Edition

1-56205-918-1, $49.99, 9/98

MCSE Training Guide: Windows 98

1-56205-890-8, $49.99, Q4/98

MCSE Training Guide: TCP/IP, Second Edition

1-56205-920-3, $49.99, 10/98

MCSE Training Guide: SQL Server 7 Administration

0-7357-0003-6, $49.99, Q1/99

TRAINING GUIDES
First Editions

Your Quality Elective Solution

MCSE Training Guide: Systems Management Server 1.2, 1-56205-748-0

MCSE Training Guide: SQL Server 7 Design and Implementation

0-7357-0004-4, $49.99, Q1/99

MCSE Training Guide: SQL Server 6.5 Administration, 1-56205-726-X

MCSE Training Guide: SQL Server 6.5 Design and Implementation, 1-56205-830-4

MCSE Training Guide: Windows 95, 70-064 Exam, 1-56205-880-0

MCSD Training Guide: Solution Architectures

0-7357-0026-5, $49.99, Q1/99

MCSE Training Guide: Exchange Server 5, 1-56205-824-X

MCSE Training Guide: Internet Explorer 4, 1-56205-889-4

MCSE Training Guide: Microsoft Exchange Server 5.5, 1-56205-899-1

MCSE Training Guide: IIS 4, 1-56205-823-1

MCSD Training Guide: Visual Basic 6, Exam 70-175

0-7357-0002-8, $49.99, Q1/99

MCSD Training Guide: Visual Basic 5, 1-56205-850-9

MCSD Training Guide: Microsoft Access, 1-56205-771-5

MCSD Training Guide: Visual Basic 6, Exam 70-176

0-7357-0031-1, $49.99, Q1/99

TESTPREP SERIES

Practice and cram with the new, revised Second Edition TestPreps

Questions. Questions. And more questions. That's what you'll find in our New Riders TestPreps. They're great practice books when you reach the final stage of studying for the exam. We recommend them as supplements to our Training Guides.

What makes these study tools unique is that the questions are the primary focus of each book. All the text in these books support and explain the answers to the questions.

Scenario-based questions challenge your experience.

Multiple-choice questions prep you for the exam.

Fact-based questions test your product knowledge.

Exam strategies assist you in test preparation.

Complete yet concise explanations of answers make for better retention.

Two practice exams prepare you for the real thing.

Fast Facts offer you everything you need to review in the testing center parking lot.

MCSE TestPrep: Networking Essentials, Second Edition

0-7357-0010-9, $19.99, 11/98

MCSE TestPrep: Windows 95, Second Edition

0-7357-0011-7, $19.99, 11/98

MCSE TestPrep: Windows NT Server 4, Second Edition

0-7357-0012-5, $19.99, 12/98

MCSE TestPrep: Windows NT Server 4 Enterprise, Second Edition

0-7357-0009-5, $19.99, 1/98

MCSE TestPrep: Windows NT Workstation 4, Second Edition

0-7357-0008-7, $19.99, 11/98

MCSE TestPrep: TCP/IP, Second Edition

0-7357-0025-7, $19.99, 12/98

**MCSE Testprep:
Windows 98**

1-56205-922-X, $19.99, Q4/98

TESTPREP SERIES
FIRST EDITIONS

MCSE TestPrep: SQL Server 6.5
Administration, 0-7897-1597-X

MCSE TestPrep: SQL Server 6.5 Design
and Implementation, 1-56205-915-7

MCSE TestPrep: Windows 95 70-64
Exam, 0-7897-1609-7

MCSE TestPrep: Internet Explorer 4,
0-7897-1654-2

MCSE TestPrep: Exchange Server 5.5,
0-7897-1611-9

MCSE TestPrep: IIS 4.0, 0-7897-1610-0

New Riders | How to Contact Us

Visit Our Web Site

www.newriders.com

On our Web site you'll find information about our other books, authors, tables of contents, indexes, and book errata. You can also place orders for books through our Web site.

Email Us

Contact us at this address:
newriders@mcp.com

- If you have comments or questions about this book
- To report errors that you have found in this book
- If you have a book proposal to submit or are interested in writing for New Riders
- If you would like to have an author kit sent to you
- If you are an expert in a computer topic or technology and are interested in being a technical editor who reviews manuscripts for technical accuracy

international@mcp.com

- To find a distributor in your area, please contact our international department at the address above.

pr@mcp.com

- For instructors from educational institutions who wish to preview Macmillan Computer Publishing books for classroom use. Email should include your name, title, school, department, address, phone number, office days/hours, text in use, and enrollment in the body of your text along with your request for desk/examination copies and/or additional information.

Write to Us

New Riders Publishing
201 W. 103rd St.
Indianapolis, IN 46290-1097

Call Us

Toll-free (800) 571-5840 + 9 + 4557
If outside U.S. (317) 581-3500. Ask for New Riders.

Fax Us

(317) 581-4663

We Want to Know What You Think

To better serve you, we would like your opinion on the content and quality of this book. Please complete this card and mail it to us or fax it to 317-581-4663.

Name _____

Address_____

City _____State _____Zip _____

Phone _____

Email Address _____

Occupation _____

Operating System(s) that you use _____

What influenced your purchase of this book?
❑ Recommendation ❑ Cover Design
❑ Table of Contents ❑ Index
❑ Magazine Review ❑ Advertisement
❑ Reputation of New Riders ❑ Author Name

How would you rate the contents of this book?
❑ Excellent ❑ Very Good
❑ Good ❑ Fair
❑ Below Average ❑ Poor

How do you plan to use this book?
❑ Quick reference ❑ Self-training
❑ Classroom ❑ Other

What do you like most about this book?
Check all that apply.
❑ Content ❑ Writing Style
❑ Accuracy ❑ Examples
❑ Listings ❑ Design
❑ Index ❑ Page Count
❑ Price ❑ Illustrations

What do you like least about this book?
Check all that apply.
❑ Content ❑ Writing Style
❑ Accuracy ❑ Examples
❑ Listings ❑ Design
❑ Index ❑ Page Count
❑ Price ❑ Illustrations

What would be a useful follow-up book to this one for you? _____

Where did you purchase this book? _____

Can you name a similar book that you like better than this one, or one that is as good? Why? _____

_____

How many New Riders books do you own? _____

What are your favorite computer books? _____

_____

What other titles would you like to see us develop? _____

Any comments for us? _____

_____

Fold here and tape to mail

New Riders Publishing
201 W. 103rd St.
Indianapolis, IN 46290